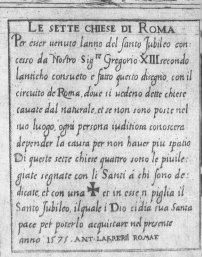

LE SETTE CHIESE DI ROMA

Per esser uenuto lanno del santo Iubileo con-
cesso da Nostro Sig.re Gregorio XIII secondo
lanticho consueto e fatto questo disegno, con il
circuito de Roma, doue si uedeno dette chiese
cauate dal naturale, et se non sono poste nel
suo luogo, ogni persona iuditiosa conoscera
depender la causa per non hauer piu spatio
Di queste sette chiese quattro sono le piuile-
giate segnate con li Santi á chi sono de-
dicate, et con una ✝ et in esse si piglia il
Santo Iubileo, ilquale i Dio ci dia sua Santa
pace per poterlo acquistare nel presente
anno 1575. ANT.LAFRERII ROMAE

# HOLY FACES, SECRET PLACES

Also by the same author

The Turin Shroud
Mind out of Time?
Jesus: The Evidence
The Exodus Enigma
Undiscovered
Worlds Beyond
The Evidence of the Shroud
The After Death Experience
Superself
Are these the Words of Jesus?

# HOLY FACES, SECRET PLACES

## An Amazing Quest for the Face of Jesus

Ian Wilson

Doubleday

New York    London    Toronto    Sydney    Auckland

PUBLISHED BY DOUBLEDAY
a division of Bantam Doubleday Dell Publishing Group, Inc.
666 Fifth Avenue, New York, New York 10103

DOUBLEDAY and the portrayal of an anchor with a dolphin
are trademarks of Doubleday, a division of
Bantam Doubleday Dell Publishing Group, Inc.

Originally published in Great Britain by Doubleday,
a division of Transworld Publishers Ltd.

Library of Congress Cataloging-in-Publication Data
Wilson, Ian, 1941–
Holy faces, secret places : an amazing quest for the face of Jesus
/ Ian Wilson. — 1st ed.
p.      cm.
Includes bibliographical references and index.
1. Jesus Christ—Face.   I. Title.
BT590.P45W54      1991

232.9—dc20                                          91-8643
                                                    CIP


ISBN 0-385-26105-5

To His Holiness Pope John Paul II
in the respectful hope
that a little more *glasnost*
may be allowed
within the Vatican's 'secret places'

# CONTENTS

vii

# ILLUSTRATIONS

## END-PAPERS

Sixteenth-century engraving of the 'Seven Churches' of Rome

## COLOUR PLATES

## BLACK AND WHITE PLATES

12    (above) Thomas Heaphy the Younger, self-portrait, National Portrait Gallery, London; (below left) Heaphy's 'copy' of the Sancta Sanctorum face, Print Room, British Museum; (below right) actual appearance of the Sancta Sanctorum face

13    (above) 'Holy face', Matilda chapel, Apostolic Palace, the Vatican; (left) Heaphy's 'copy' of the same, Print Room, British Museum

14    (above) 'Holy face', Church of St Bartholomew of the Armenians, Genoa, in frame; (right) Heaphy's 'copy' of the same, Print Room, British Museum

15    (above) Genoa 'holy face' with frame removed; (left) Heaphy's purported 'copy' of this same, Print Room, British Museum

16    (above) Matthew Paris, 'Veronica', British Library Arundel ms 157, f. 2; (below) Matthew Paris, 'Veronica', Corpus Christi College, Cambridge, ms 16, fol. 49v

17    (above) 'Veronica', Pierpont Morgan Library, New York, ms M 729, fol. 15r.; (left) 'Veronica', Gulbenkian Museum, Lisbon, ms. L.A. 139; (below left) 'Veronica', detail from British Library Yates Thompson ms. 27, fol. 44v

18    Master of St Veronica 'St Veronica', National Gallery, London

19    (left) Master of Flémalle, 'St Veronica', drawing, Fitzwilliam Museum, Cambridge; (above) Hans Memling, 'St Veronica', panel painting, Samuel H. Kress Collection, National Gallery of Art, Washington

20    (above) 'St Veronica', Bibliothèque Royale Albert I$^{er}$, ms. 11035–7, fol. 8v; (below left) Veronica, mosaic, detail from south entrance to St Vitus's Cathedral, Prague; (below right) Veronica, copy of 1621, Church of Gesù, Rome

21    (above) 'Holy face' of Genoa, photographed under X-ray; (left) the same, photographed using tomography

22–3  (above) Jacopo Grimaldi, Interior façade of old St Peter's, Bib. Vat. ms Barberino lat. 2733, fol. 120; (above right) Jacopo Grimaldi, Shrine of the Veronica, Bib. Naz. Florence, ms. II III 173, fol. 106; (below left) Pope John VII, mosaic, Vatican Grottoes; (below right) 'Healing of

the woman with the issue of blood', fresco, Catacomb of
SS Peter and Marcellinus, Rome

24     'Holy face' of Genoa, scenes from the Palaeologuan
frame

25     Early depictions of the 'holy face' of Edessa; (a) Bib. Vat.
Codex Rossianus 251, fol. 12v; (b) Menologion, Greek
Patriarchal Library, Alexandria; (c) Fresco, church of
Gradac, Serbia; (d) Fresco (now destroyed), church of
Spas Nereditsa, USSR; (e) Fresco, church at Sakli,
Cappadocia; (f) Detail from icon, St Catherine's Monas-
tery, Sinai; (g) Fresco, church of Panagia tou Arakou,
Lagoudera, Cyprus; (h) Fresco, church of the Archangel
Michael, Kato Lefkara, Cyprus; (i) Fresco, USSR, exact
location unspecified (reproduced from A. Grabar, 'La
Sainte Face', pl. III, 3)

26–7   Jacopo Grimaldi, *Umbella* of the Veronica, Bib. Naz.
Florence, ms II III 173, fol. 114

28     (above) Icon, 'Holy face of Edessa and King of Glory',
Collection of George R. Hann, Sewickley, Pennsylvania,
ref: Hann CI no. 73; (below left) Giovanni Pisano,
sculpted lectern, Staatliche Museen Preussischer Kulturbesitz, Berlin Dahlem; (below right) Epitaphios of
Milutin Uroš, Museum of the Serbian Orthodox Church,
Belgrade

29     (above) Detail from drawing of the Entombment of Jesus,
National Széchényi Library, Budapest, ms. MNY I, fol. 28;
(left) detail from eleventh-century Byzantine ivory 5 –
1872, Victoria & Albert Museum, London

30     (above) 'Acheropita' face of Christ. Mosaic, apse of the
basilica of St John Lateran, Rome; (below left) Christ
Pantocrator, mosaic, church at Daphni, Athens; (below
right) Christ Pantocrator, encaustic icon, monastery of St
Catherine, Sinai

31     (a) Detail from Spas Nereditsa fresco (see pl. 25d);
(b) Detail from Genoa 'holy face' X-ray (see pl. 21, top);
(c) Detail from Ponziano catacomb fresco (see col. pl.
VIII, below); (d) Detail from face on Turin shroud (see
pl. 1, above)

32     (above) Egyptologist Rosalie David about to examine
Manchester Museum Egyptian mummy no. 1770. Photo:

Manchester Museum; (below) Lindow Man, Photo: British Museum

## TEXT FIGURES

# AUTHOR'S PREFACE
# AND
# ACKNOWLEDGEMENTS

Books often have strange beginnings, and this one is no exception. Although I have long had an almost indefinable curiosity about supposed 'holy faces' on cloth, the idea partly came into being as a result of a heated discussion between myself and an Australian publisher-writer, Rex Morgan MBE, on the subject of the English artist Thomas Heaphy the Younger, who claimed to have gained direct access to, and actually sketched, the Veronica and other 'holy faces' back in the mid-nineteenth century. While Morgan accepted Heaphy at face value, I had long had serious doubts about him, and the only way of settling the difference seemed to be by retracing Heaphy's steps, and trying to gain the same access that he claimed to have gained. Others, notably including Episcopalian priest the Revd Kim Dreisbach of Atlanta, Georgia, encouraged the same idea, and with the enthusiastic backing of William Barry and Theresa D'Orsogna of my publishers Doubleday, the project was born.

In the event, the book became one of the most demanding I have ever undertaken, and would not have been possible without the generous assistance of individuals from many countries across the world. For direct help with background research I have been particularly grateful to the following: in Rome, Mario Fusco (expediting the obtaining of a microfilm of the Grimaldi manuscript); Professor Gino Zaninotto (correspondence on the Gregory and *Regula Sancti Spiritus* manuscripts); Professor

Heinrich Pfeiffer correspondence on his own research on the Veronica); Professa Emanuela Marinelli (general liaison in Italy); in Bologna, Professor Lamberto Coppini (invitation to a valuable iconographic congress in Bologna, at which the Genoa 'holy face' was shown); in Turin, Don Luigi Fossati (technical photographs of the Genoa 'holy face') in Paris, Père A. M. Dubarle, o.p. (correspondence on the Gregory and Pray manuscripts); in Valence, Roger Sartre (photographs of the Church of Gesù Veronica copy); in Vienna, Professor Hans Rohsmann (obtaining photo and background information on the Pietro Strozzi Veronica copy); in Spain, Dr Teresa Iglesias (obtaining photos and ancillary information on the Jaén and Alicante 'holy faces'); in Darmstadt, Professor Dr Werner Bulst (obtaining xerox of the long out-of-print Von Dobschütz *Christusbilder*); in Cyprus, Judith Stylianou (information on Byzantine frescoes of Cyprus); in Los Angeles, Isabel Piczek (direct eyewitness description of the Veronica); at the University of Southern Indiana, Professor Daniel Scavone (insights into Byzantine texts); at the University of Vermont, Professor Martha Caldwell (information on Marco Polo's asbestos): in Durham, North Carolina, Dr Alan and Mary Whanger (material relating to the polaroid overlay technique); in East Aurora, New York, Dorothy Piepke (a most valuable lead regarding the Pietro Strozzi Veronica copy); in England, Revd Maurus Green (introducing me to the Grimaldi manuscript), James Lees-Milne (correspondence on the Veronica pier), Anna Hulbert (information on medieval painting methods), Peter Jennings (advice on Vatican relations), Jean Glover (information on the St Bees fourteenth-century shroud burial) and Ian Dickinson (insights on shroud dimensions). To all of these, and any others inadvertently omitted, my grateful thanks; also to, from within the Vatican, papal private secretary Monsignor Stanislao Dziwisz and Secretariat of State assessor Monsignor C. Sepe.

Because research material has been spread over so many countries, not least of the book's difficulties has been a linguistic one. The Grimaldi manuscript, consisting of 130 double pages of Latin, posed a particularly daunting task, and I was greatly helped on key passages of this by now retired classics teacher, Bernard Slater, and by Matthew Heavens, of Pembroke College, Oxford. The translation from Italian of a key article by Professor Carlo Bertelli was kindly tackled by Maria Jepps of Shepton Mallet and typed by my father, and Maria, along with my near neighbour

Fausta Walsby, additionally helped with Italian correspondence.

With special regard to insights on carbon dating my thanks are due to Bill Meacham in Hong Kong, Professor Paul Damon of the University of Arizona, Dr Sheridan Bowman of the British Museum Research Laboratory, Professor Edward Hall and Professor Michael Tite of the Oxford Research Laboratory, and Dr Bob Otlet and Nick Hance of Harwell.

Among the institutions who have been particularly helpful are the Department of Prints and Drawings at the British Museum (the album of Thomas Heaphy's sketches); the National Portrait Gallery, London (portrait of Thomas Heaphy); the Royal Academy of Arts; the Biblioteca Nazionale, Florence (the Grimaldi manuscript); the Archivo di Stato, Rome (the *Regula Sancti Spiritus* manuscript); the Musée du Petit Palais, Avignon, the Musée Condé, Chantilly, the Fundaçao Calouste Gulbenkian Museum, Lisbon (the Gulbenkian Apocalypse – particular thanks to Maria Teresa Gomes Ferreira), the Sammlung für Plastik und Kunstgewerbe, Kunsthistorisches Museum, Vienna; also, as always, the British Library and the Central and University libraries of my home city of Bristol.

One man to whom rather unusual thanks are due is 'disc doctor' David Smith, who expertly retrieved weeks of research material (most particularly, my notes on the Grimaldi manuscript), stored on a non-backed-up word-processing disc that developed an unexpected electronic fault. Also, not least, special thanks to my wife Judith who checked each chapter, also Marianne Velmans, Sally Gaminara and Broo Doherty of Doubleday, London, who assiduously steered the editorial production within the UK.

One final note: it seems to have become a point of distinction between believers and unbelievers in the Turin shroud that the former, in writing of it, always use an upper-case 'S'. In the past I have preferred this capitalized form as the most expedient means of reference (just as one would write of the Great Wall of China). Here, however, in order to deflect criticisms of undue bias I have reverted to the lower case form. The distinction is scarcely likely to have bothered he whom the shroud may or may not have originally wrapped . . .

Ian Wilson
Bristol
Easter 1990

# INTRODUCTION

In the mythopoeic world of Mediterranean Christianity, both Latin and Greek, there has long been something primitive and arcane about the idea of 'holy faces' in secret places.

Dotted around the countries that border the Mediterranean are ancient churches and cathedrals that possess, under the closest guard, what they claim as a specially 'true' image of Jesus Christ. Belonging to western Christendom are examples in Rome, Genoa and Turin in Italy; in Laon in France, and in Jaén and Alicante in Spain. Eastern Christendom has others.

Rarely, if ever, will such an image be kept on regular public show. Instead it will be most assiduously secluded away, maybe inside the sacred building's treasury, or strong-room, maybe in the sacristy, maybe locked inside a shrine inside a chapel only to be entered by a privileged few.

Even within such a sanctum sanctorum, further tight security will prevent any too easy sight of the 'holy face'. There may be a locked grille guarding the innermost shrine, and inside this two or more similarly locked containers protecting the object itself. The keys that open the locks may be held by three or four illustrious persons, perhaps a canon, the local duke and archbishop, and the president of the treasury. Reminiscent of the modern safeguards against a nuclear Armageddon, the system will be such that no one of the keyholders will be able to gain entry without the keys of the others.

1

Some of the 'holy faces' that receive such protection are considered so holy that they are never shown to the public, as in the case of one that reposes in an aumbry, a sort of safe deposit box, inside the Pope's white marble private chapel within the Vatican Palace. Some may be exhibited just once a generation or so, to mark some special event, as has been the case with the so-called Turin shroud). Yet others may be exhibited on specially appointed feast days once or twice a year, but behind such thick plate glass, inside such a baroque confection of a frame, and from so high a balcony that the ordinary spectator is left little the wiser as to their appearance. For one, even in this, the twentieth century's closing decade, there exists no known photograph in the public domain, and sight is reserved exclusively for the ape and his closest attendants.

Of those whose appearance is known, the common denominator is usually a strangely disembodied face of Jesus set either directly onto a piece of cloth, or onto a panel to at least part of which a piece of cloth has been pasted or similarly affixed. The coloration will be extremely muted, usually little more than a sepia monochrome. The eyes may either be shown fully open, or partly open, as if suffering, or closed as if in death. Reflecting these variations of appearance, the traditions of the face's origins may be of it having been painted by St Luke or sketched by St Peter; may be of Jesus having wiped his face with it during the agony in the garden of Gethsemane, or when carrying his cross to Calvary; may be of it having become imprinted on Jesus's burial sheet as he lay dead in the tomb.

Still vividly recalled is my personal first sight of such an image, during early schooldays. On sale in a South London art shop was a cheap reproduction that, much later in life, I learned to be the *Jesus Christus*, an imaginative rendition of the Veronica of Rome by the late nineteenth-century Bohemian artist Gabriel Max, now in a private collection in Prague. While this was obviously just a painting, even then it strangely evoked both a curious power and a raw, underlying truth to the idea of a death or near-death image of Jesus once having been imprinted on a simple piece of cloth.

As a teenager I learned also, of course, of the Turin Shroud, the fourteen-foot length of linen purported to have enwrapped Jesus in death, and to have become imprinted with a double image, the back and front, of his entire figure [pl. 1, above, and 2, left]. From first sight in a magazine article, the famous 'negative' face from this

2

[pl. 1, left] struck me so forcibly as *not* by the hand of any artist that it impelled a decades-long hobby of enquiry into every aspect of the shroud's nature and origins, touching on medicine, archaeology, photography, Biblical studies, botany, physics, chemistry, microscopy, weaving, the history of art, and much more. On being accorded the exceptional privilege of examining the shroud at first hand in 1973, this served to convince me not only that no artist had produced such an image, but also that the shroud's face was the 'true' original from which all the other 'holy faces' had been copied by artists. This led to my writing a full book on this subject, published in 1978, a time of the shroud's first full public showing in forty-five years.

As has now become world-wide public knowledge, just ten years later, in October 1988, all the hitherto arguably impressive amalgam of knowledge suggestive of the shroud's authenticity was blown sky-high on release of the results of a radiocarbon test to scientifically determine the age of the shroud's linen. Under the universally respected supervision of the British Museum Research Laboratory, the radiocarbon laboratories of Tucson, Zurich and Oxford, produced closely compatible datings strongly indicative that the shroud had been manufactured sometime between 1260 and 1390. Particularly convincing was the fact that the finding readily corroborated historical documents in which a French bishop declared that the shroud had been 'cunningly painted' sometime around the middle of the fourteenth century. Effectively the shroud could be dismissed as just another of the many fraudulent 'relics' for which the Middle Ages was notorious.

But overlooked amidst all the enthusiasm for this apparent triumph of science over superstition has been one inescapable fact of history. Whatever the authenticity or otherwise of the shroud, and whatever the artistic or other origins of the 'holy faces', at least some of the 'faces' are quite irrefutably recorded substantially before the 1260 date that is the very earliest radiocarbon would ascribe to the shroud. So if the carbon dating genuinely obliges us now to discount the shroud as the source of inspiration for the 'faces' (and that will remain a qualified 'if'), from what *did* spring the strange idea of Jesus imprinting the likeness of his face on cloth?

To set this question in its proper perspective it is important to remind ourselves that in all history Jesus is not simply the only religious figure, but also the only individual of any kind with

3

whom the idea of an imprint on cloth is associated. The Moslems know nothing of the kind with Mohammed, nor the Buddhists with Buddha, nor the Jews with Moses or any other prophet.

Accordingly, although we will commence this book with the shroud, particularly in order to set it within this overall context, our intended task is nothing less than the most searching and wide-ranging enquiry into the 'holy faces' that is possible within the limitations of the elaborate security and secrecy which guards them. We will find times in which this security and secrecy can be in direct proportion to the interest value of the 'face' it protects. But although we must therefore expect that there will be instances in which the doors of holy places will stay firmly barred to us, nothing at all is learned by he who does not at least try to knock on them.

## Chapter One

# 'THE SHROUD IS MEDIEVAL'

*Someone just got a bit of linen,*
*faked it up and flogged it*

Professor Edward Hall, Oxford University

The 'secret place' of the Turin shroud is in the classic 'holy face' mould. For the visitor to Turin's cathedral of St John the Baptist who proceeds the length of the nave there is a mere glimpse through a window high above the main altar, where the apse would normally be, of the vague shape of something dark and glittering. This is the exalted private chapel of Italy's former royalty, the family of Savoy, built for the shroud by the architect Guarino Guarini between 1668 and 1694.[1]

Although the Savoys had their own exclusive entrance to this chapel from their adjoining palace, at times when the doors are not *chiuso*, there are also grandiose enough steps which lead up it from below. Yet as anyone who ascends these steep, curved steps soon notices, the architect cunningly omitted any direct light source, and also introduced certain architectural tricks to induce a feeling of disorientation.

On reaching the chapel, made entirely of black marble, the dark and glittering shape that was glimpsed from below becomes immediately recognized as a central black marble altar, in reality twin altars [col. pl. I, left]. Atop these, surmounted by a lavishly baroque sunburst, stands a second black marble structure, fronted by a locked iron grille. Behind this grille lies a second iron cage with triple locks. Inside this reposes a wooden case painted with a picture of the shroud. Inside this is an iron chest wrapped in asbestos. Only once this is opened can there be reached the silvered wooden casket, emblazoned with symbols of the passion,

5

inside which lies the shroud, covered in red silk and rolled around a velvet-covered staff.

What has now become described as the Turin shroud has been kept this way since 1694. In the early sixteenth century it was similarly kept in a silver casket inside a grilled recess within the altar wall of the Savoy family's Sainte Chapelle at Chambéry. When in 1532 a serious fire broke out in the chapel, the practice of keeping the four keys between three different individuals, not all of them reachable in time, very nearly caused its destruction.[2] It was only the prompt and heroic arrival of a blacksmith that enabled its rescue, although so leaving permanent scars from fire damage. Ever since, the occasions of the shroud being brought out for public display have become increasingly limited, the main ones this century having been 1931, 1933, 1973 (for television only) and 1978.

Thus when early in 1988 the decision was taken to allow the cutting from it of a sample for carbon dating, the secrecy habit was so deeply ingrained among the shroud's ecclesiastical and scientific custodians that they took the most elaborate precautions to ensure that the outside world would not know anything until after the event had taken place. Although rumour was carefully spread that the appointed day was to be 23 April, the actual day chosen was the 21st, when Italy's president was scheduled to visit Turin. Not only was it expected that press attention that day would be suitably distracted, but the more than usual *chiuso* notices in the cathedral would also be unlikely to raise any undue suspicion.

Furthermore, such was the 'thieves in the night' mentality that the hour set for the cathedral clergy to commence opening up the altar shrine was four in the morning, startling even the security guard, who appears not to have been informed. Carried from its 'home' chapel to the cathedral sacristy the shroud was carefully unrolled full-length onto a large table for a pre-requested viewing by the scientific representatives of the three laboratories chosen to perform the carbon dating. There it was that Professors Damon and Donahue of Tucson, Wölfli of Zurich, and Hall and Dr Hedges of Oxford all had their first opportunity to peruse the fourteen-foot length of linen, observing its very obvious patches and burns from the 1532 fire, and pondering its strange shadowy double imprint of a human figure, complete with bloodstains as from crucifixion.

Then with a video camera recording every move, Turin micro-analyst Professor Giovanni Riggi, long-standing friend of the cardinal-archbishop of Turin's chief scientific adviser, Professor Luigi Gonella, methodically snipped a seven-centimetre sliver from one of the shroud's corners. Under the supervision of the British Museum Research Laboratory's Dr Michael Tite, this was weighed, cut into portions suitable for carbon dating, the portions put into specially coded and sealed canisters, and finally handed over to the respective heads of the three carbon-dating laboratories, along with similarly-coded canisters containing portions from other cloths of already-known dates, supplied as controls.

A few hours later, silver-bearded, quiet-mannered Professor Paul Damon of the University of Arizona's Accelerator Facility for Radio-isotope Analysis, and his chief assistant Professor Douglas Donahue, were boarding a flight back to the United States carrying with them a tiny piece of cloth [pl. 2, below top] that, whatever its origins, had most certainly never known a journey so far west. One of Donahue's most prized recollections is the brief encounter with an American customs official on his arrival. Asked if he had anything to declare, he replied, 'Only a bottle of gin, some chocolate – and a piece of the Turin shroud.' He was waved through.[3]

Damon's and Donahue's radio-isotope laboratory is located at Tucson, amidst the tall saguaro cacti landscape of Arizona's Sonora desert. Together with the Oxford and Zurich laboratories, this laboratory owes its origins to the inventiveness of Professor Harry Gove of the University of Rochester's Nuclear Structure Research Laboratory, who during the late 1970s pioneered the development of the new accelerator-mass spectrometer method of radiocarbon dating that all three laboratories share. Through various political vicissitudes Gove had been baulked of being able to work on a shroud sample at his own laboratory, and so as a kindly gesture Damon invited Gove to travel the 2000 miles from Rochester to Tucson to be present when the shroud date would emerge on Arizona's computer, even though this was against the secrecy agreement that Damon had signed in Turin.

The central principle of carbon dating is that anything that has once lived, whether animal or vegetable, on death loses its natural radiocarbon content at a precisely determinable rate through time. First developed by Chicago's Willard F. Libby in the late 1940s, the early method of calculating the radiocarbon loss or 'decay' was by isolating the gas from combustion of the sample,

7

then measuring its proportion of carbon 14 to that of the stable carbon 12 with the aid of an advanced form of Geiger counter. The improvement pioneered by Gove was to convert the combustion to a pellet of pure carbon, or graphite, then with the aid of caesium, argon gas and a couple of million volts of electricity to so isolate the carbon 14 that it could be directly counted. One of the advantages of this latter method is that it needs substantially less sample than the earlier one, hence its choice for the shroud.

It is human nature that any not quite predictable event can stimulate the betting instinct, and even the dating of the shroud proved no exception. Although Damon, a Quaker, had no particularly preconceived ideas about the result that his laboratory would produce, Donahue, a Roman Catholic, at least hoped for a first century date, while the cynical Gove had already laid a bet with another nuclear physicist, Shirley Brignall of Brookhaven, that the shroud would be younger than AD 1,000. The two had agreed that whoever lost the bet would buy the other a pair of cowboy boots.[4]

In the event, when the Arizona laboratory's computer chattered out the result, it was Harry Gove's face that bore the broadest grin. According to the laboratory's instrument readings the shroud sample was only between six and seven hundred years old. The shroud itself had therefore to be medieval, and some thirteen hundred years younger than it would have to have been to have wrapped the body of Jesus. Although Damon, Donahue and Gove were the first to learn this news, and were obliged to keep it under wraps, later that summer their colleagues at the Oxford and Zurich laboratories independently produced similar datings, all supplied to the British Museum's Dr Michael Tite as central co-ordinator.

Despite some irritating prior 'leaks', it took until 13 October before these results were allowed to be officially disclosed to the world at large. In Turin early in the morning of that day the shroud's custodian, Cardinal Anastasio Ballestrero baldly stated the salient facts, and declared his acceptance of them on behalf of the Roman Catholic Church.[5] He would subsequently receive considerable vilification within Italy for this apparent capitulation.

The same afternoon Dr Michael Tite provided further details at a crowded press conference held at London's British Museum, accompanied on the platform by the Oxford laboratory's Professor

Hall and Dr Robert Hedges. To minimize the possibility of anyone getting the results wrong, Tite or someone else had scrawled on the blackboard in large numerals:

1260–1390!

According to Tite the three laboratories' datings were 'all within a hundred years of each other' and made it 95 per cent certain that the shroud had originated sometime between the years 1260 and 1390, and 99.9 per cent certain that it dated 'from about 1000 to 1500 AD'. The laboratories also exhibited a satisfying accuracy in their results from the control samples.

For the press it was a simple enough story, the essentially cliché'd one of an object of pious superstition having at last and deservedly been proved wanting under the remorseless scrutiny of science. That evening and throughout the subsequent few days numerous newspaper and television announcements across the world featured the familiar image of the shroud face, accompanied by the unequivocal declaration that it had been proved a fake. In typical disparaging vein Britain's *Independent* newspaper commented:

> The disappointment to believers in the shroud is unlikely to deter enthusiasts for the tens of thousands of relics, many of them the products of medieval tricksters, which repose in gilded cases and cushioned jewel-boxes in churches throughout Italy. In Rome one may view a feather from the Archangel Gabriel at the Church of Santa Croce in Gerusalemme. Other examples include vials containing the last breath of St Joseph, several heads of St John the Baptist, innumerable splinters from the True Cross, and two thorns from the crown.[6]

There followed in February 1989 a formal paper in the highly respected, international scientific journal *Nature*, carrying as its signatories the names of twenty-one of those most closely involved in the carbon dating. After carefully setting out all the procedures that had been followed to obtain the dating result, the paper commented:

9

These results therefore provide conclusive evidence
that the linen of the shroud of Turin is medieval.[7]

Inevitably there were a number of individuals, among them the
present author who, having conducted their own prior researches
on the shroud, felt that the word 'conclusive' for such a date
seemed overstrong, particularly given that carbon dating on its
own could certainly not yet offer any explanation for how
someone of the Middle Ages had produced an image of the
shroud's extraordinary subtlety and complexity.

Nonetheless, such was the seemingly overwhelming acceptance
with which the results were received that most objections of this
kind, if voiced at all, were tossed aside by the media. To the glee
of the British press, Oxford's Professor Hall derisively labelled
such protestors 'Flat-Earthers'.

Instead the most strident rebuttal that came to be raised,
predominantly taken up only by the Italian and French press,
was that of a French priest, Brother Bruno Bonnet-Eymard.
Representing a reactionary group calling itself 'The Catholic
Counter-Reformation in the Twentieth Century', Bonnet-Eymard
claimed nothing less than that it was the carbon dating itself
which had been faked.[8]

According to Bonnet-Eymard the villain of the exercise had
been the highly respected invigilator of the whole project,
the British Museum Research Laboratory's Dr Michael Tite.
Allegedly, shortly before going to Turin, Dr Tite had clandestinely
requested and obtained a sample of medieval linen, very similar
in appearance to the shroud, from a cope of the late thirteenth-
century French St Louis d'Anjou that is preserved in the church
of Saint-Maximin, Provence. This had been procured by fellow-
nuclear physicist Jacques Evin of the radiocarbon-dating laboratory of Lyon, France, and handed to Tite in Turin by Gabriel
Vial, a specialist from the Textile Museum of Lyon who had
been invited to be present at the taking of the shroud sample
in order to make a study of the cloth's weaving and sewing
characteristics.

When the sample for carbon dating had been cut from the
shroud and divided for the three laboratories, according to
Bonnet-Eymard there was a brief period during which Tite and
the Cardinal were alone in a side-room. This was the point at
which Tite was responsible for putting the shroud segments and

the control samples into the respective coded canisters for each laboratory. It was virtually the only part of the proceedings which was not videotaped and watched by others, and according to Bonnet-Eymard's allegations it provided Tite with just the opportunity he needed surreptitiously to dispose of the real shroud samples and replace them with ones from the medieval cope. The carbon dating was therefore rigged, Tite's less than impartial role being subsequently corroborated by his surprise appointment as Professor Hall's successor as Director of the Oxford radiocarbon laboratory.

Such sad, shabby allegations are given here simply because they have already gained an unjustifiably wide currency on the European continent, and need to be refuted with the swiftest possible despatch. For whatever the correctness or otherwise of the dating arrived at by the laboratories, there can be absolutely no serious justification for any such accusations. While Dr Tite genuinely did obtain material from the St Louis cope, this was as part of his totally legitimate search for control samples.

Not only is the St Louis cope's fabric one of plain-weave linen, quite different from the shroud's herringbone, the samples from it were supplied in the form of threads. Photographs taken by the laboratories of each of the 'shroud' samples before its submission to carbon dating clearly reveal the familiar Turin shroud weave, one sufficiently unusual that Tite was unable to find any exact parallel. Among other compelling evidence that the laboratories genuinely obtained samples from the true shroud is the fact that on a personal visit to the Oxford laboratory shortly after it had received the sample (and before it had begun to be processed), Professor Hall happened to remark to me on certain tiny blue-thread fragments he had found mixed up in the fabric. Knowing that similar threads had repeatedly been found during earlier micro-analytical work, I was able to explain these as from the shroud's relatively modern blue surround. This is quite aside from the slur that Bonnet-Eymard has cast on Dr Tite's honesty, a slur which even from my personal brief but amicable acquaintance with Dr Tite (now Professor of the Oxford Research Laboratory), carries not the slightest justification.

It is important, therefore, that setting all other considerations aside – and the various arguments for the shroud's authenticity have been amply argued elsewhere – the fact is squarely faced that the shroud has been fairly and competently dated to the

11

fourteenth century by individuals of unimpeachable integrity, using a well-respected scientific method.

Moreover, equally squarely to be faced is the fact that the fourteenth century was a time particularly notorious for the forgery of just such religious relics as the shroud. As Oxford's Professor Hall exaggeratedly but nonetheless justifiably told the British Museum press conference:

> There was a multi-million-pound business in making forgeries during the fourteenth century. Someone just got a bit of linen, faked it up and flogged it.[9]

Hall's assistant, Dr Hedges [pl. 2, below bottom], dismissing suggestions that the shroud's radiocarbon content might have been altered by a burst of radiation from Christ's resurrection,[10] added with some confidence that it was surely odd that this hypothetical burst should have been so precisely tuned to give a date of the fourteenth century, the earliest to which the shroud can be historically traced with any certainty.[11]

And most uncomfortable of all for anyone, like myself, still unable quite to accept the shroud as a human work of the fourteenth century, is the fact that precisely from this century there exist authoritative documents firmly attesting the shroud to have been 'cunningly painted' by an artist of this time, the main document being a forceful letter by the redoubtable fourteenth-century Bishop of Troyes, Pierre d'Arcis, to the anti-pope. While the existence of these documents has long been known and acknowledged, in recent years, with so much evidence suggestive of authenticity, they have somewhat too easily been set aside as inadequate to account for an image of the shroud's anatomic and photographic sophistication.

Now, in the light of the carbon dating and as a first base in our overall study of 'holy faces', they positively demand to be re-examined. As Arizona's Professor Paul Damon summed it up in a letter to me:

> Radio-carbon dating has simply confirmed the four-teenth-century investigation of Bishop Pierre d'Arcis . . . No one has questioned the integrity of the artist or his skill. The shroud is still an object worthy of contemplation and the identity of the unknown, brilliant

12

author is the greatest remaining mystery . . . Why don't
you address these problems?[12]

Even though, try as I might, I still could not understand the
shroud as a work of the century to which Damon and his
colleagues' laboratories had assigned it, it would have been less
than fair-minded not to acknowledge the considerable sound
wisdom in Damon's advice. To begin at the fourteenth century,
and at least to attempt to identify who might have made the
shroud at that time, and how he might have accomplished it,
seemed a reasonable enough point at which to start.

## Chapter Two

# INTO THE MIDDLE AGES

*. . . a certain cloth, cunningly painted . . .*

Pierre d'Arcis, Bishop of Troyes, 1389

If there is one document that more than any other seems to corroborate the carbon dating of the 'shroud', it is a six-hundred-year-old letter,[1] written in Latin, that reposes among the historical documents for the French department of Champagne preserved in the Bibliothèque Nationale, Paris. The time of the letter's writing was late in the year 1389, its author Pierre d'Arcis, Bishop of the city of Troyes which lies 100 miles south-east of Paris; and its intended recipient, His Holiness Clement VII, the man who for Frenchmen of the time was the rightful pope, ruling from Avignon in southern France, but who history has subsequently designated as an anti-pope. In Bishop d'Arcis's words:

> The case, Holy Father, stands thus. Some time since in this diocese of Troyes, the dean of a certain collegiate church, to wit that of Lirey, falsely and deceitfully, being consumed with the passion of avarice, and not from any motive of gain, procured for his church a certain cloth, cunningly painted, upon which by a clever sleight of hand was depicted the twofold image of one man, that is to say, the front and the back, he [the dean] falsely declaring and pretending that this was the actual shroud in which our Saviour Jesus Christ was enfolded in the tomb, and upon which the whole likeness of the Saviour had remained thus impressed, together with the wounds which He bore. This story was put about not only in

14

the kingdom of France, but, so to speak, throughout the world, so that from all parts people came together to view it. And further to attract the multitude so that money might cunningly be wrung from them, pretended miracles were worked, certain men being hired to represent themselves as healed at the moment of the exhibition of the shroud, which all believed to be the shroud of our Lord.[2]

For the Middle Ages, even more so than today, such accusations were highly serious, and d'Arcis went to considerable lengths to explain why he had brought them, and all that he knew of the background to the shroud's fraudulent creation. The matter had apparently arisen in the time of one of his predecessors, Henri of Poitiers, historically known to have been Bishop of Troyes between 1353 and 1370. According to d'Arcis, Henri had been alerted to suspicious happenings at Lirey, a tiny village some twelve miles from Troyes, and was

> . . . urged by many prudent persons to take action, as indeed was his duty in the exercise of his ordinary jurisdiction . . . Eventually, after diligent enquiry and examination, he discovered the fraud and how the said cloth had been cunningly painted, the truth being attested by the artist who had painted it, to wit, that it was a work of human skill, and not miraculously wrought or bestowed. Accordingly . . . he began to institute formal proceedings against the said dean and his accomplices in order to root out this false persuasion. They, seeing their wickedness discovered, hid away the said cloth so that the ordinary [i.e. the bishop] could not find it, and they kept it hidden afterwards for thirty-four years or thereabouts down to the present year.[3]

As d'Arcis went on, in this present year of 1389 the successor of the original Dean of Lirey had gone to his patron 'the Lord Geoffrey de Charny, Knight' and requested that the cloth be brought out again 'that by a renewal of the pilgrimage the church might be enriched with the offerings made by the faithful.' De Charny [fig. 1] (son of a previous Geoffrey de Charny of Bishop Henri's time, and therefore best referred to as Geoffrey II de Charny),

15

had then petitioned Clement VII's Apostolic Nuncio, Cardinal de Thury, for renewal of the expositions.

In this approach Geoffrey II apparently deliberately suppressed mention of any of the earlier controversy, representing the cloth he wanted to show merely as 'a picture or figure of the shroud, which many people came to visit out of devotion and which had previously been much venerated and resorted to in that church.' De Thury accordingly readily granted the appropriate permit, whereupon, in d'Arcis's words:

> . . . under cover of this written authority the cloth was openly exhibited and shown to the people in the church aforesaid on great holidays, and frequently on feasts and at other times, with the utmost solemnity, even more than when the Body of Christ our Lord is exposed; to

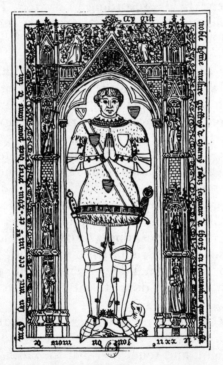

*Fig. 1. Geoffrey II de Charny, drawing made from the effigy on his tomb in the church of the Cistercian abbey at Froidmont, near Beauvais, destroyed in the First World War*

16

wit, by two priests vested in albs with stoles and maniples and using the greatest possible reverence, with lighted torches and upon a lofty platform constructed for this special purpose. And although it is not publicly stated to be the true shroud of Christ, nevertheless this is given out and noised abroad in private, and so it is believed by many, the more so, because, as stated above, it was on the previous occasion declared to be the true shroud of Christ.[4]

One minor weakness of d'Arcis's letter is that, of the two copies that survive, only one is complete, both are undated, and neither seems to be the original. Nonetheless there can be no question that a letter with at least something of this content was genuinely sent to Clement at Avignon. There have survived several other documents relating to the affair, notably a report by a Paris Parlement official who, at d'Arcis's instigation, had earlier tried unsuccessfully to seize the shroud at Lirey; also the response to d'Arcis that Clement sent in the form of several letters despatched from Avignon on 6 January 1390.[5] All these essentially corroborate that there was an exchange between d'Arcis and Clement at least something along the lines stated.

We know also that it was a difficult time for d'Arcis. His cathedral at Troyes had been under construction for nearly two centuries, in the most recent decades the work badly hampered by repeated English incursions into French territory as a result of the Hundred Years War. During the Christmas of 1389 much of the nave collapsed as a result of the fall of a clerestory window, followed shortly after by the fall of the great rose window of the north transept.[6] This can only have happened very shortly after his sending of the shroud letter, and certainly, at the time that Clement in Avignon was dictating his reply, d'Arcis in Troyes was heavily preoccupied recruiting a team of thirty workmen to clear the rubble from his aisles.

Nor can d'Arcis have been too pleased with Clement's reply when it arrived from Avignon.[7] Although this confirmed the original requirement that those in Lirey should make clear 'in loud and intelligible voice' that what they were showing was 'not the true shroud of Christ but a copy and representation', nonetheless it upheld the Lirey clergy's right to continue such expositions, and actually threatened d'Arcis himself with excommunication if he

17

attempted any further obstruction. Furthermore only five months later, on 1 June 1390, Clement two-facedly issued a bull granting special indulgences to those visiting the Lirey church, specifically stating that this was because 'the shroud with the imprint of Our Lord Jesus Christ is there preserved with veneration.'[8]

It is difficult not to suspect here a strong whiff of the corruption and nepotism with which all too much of the medieval papacy, both Avignon and Roman, was heavily tainted. Clement VII was the notorious Robert of Geneva who, fourteen years earlier, when leading a mercenary army trying to gain back the Papal States, had personally ordered the outright massacre of the citizens of Cesena, despite having previously, on his cardinal's hat, promised them clemency at a moment that they had him and his men cornered.[9] He had behaved with similar duplicity during the circumstances leading to his assumption of the Avignon papacy. From what may be the only known contemporary portrait of him, preserved on a sculpture at Avignon,[10] he looks a man not lightly to be crossed [pl. 3, left].

Cause for suspicion, shroud-wise, of his nepotism lies in the fact that he was nephew of Aymon of Geneva, the nobleman with lands in High Savoy who married Geoffrey I de Charny's young widow, Jeanne de Vergy, within two or three years of shroud-owning Geoffrey's death at Poitiers in 1356. At the time of this second marriage Jeanne de Vergy seems to have left Lirey to join Aymon at his Alpine domains of Anthon, Cruseilles, Rumilly and Mornex, all close to Annecy where Clement VII had been born and grew up.[11] And almost certainly Jeanne took the shroud with her when she joined Aymon. In High Savoy it would have been much safer than left in Lirey, where there was great danger from English marauders. This would go some way towards explaining the shroud's ready transfer from Margaret de Charny to the Savoy family during the next century; also d'Arcis's mention of its hiding 'for thirty-four years or thereabouts down to the present year'. Accordingly, Clement may even have been shown it during a visit to his uncle's home.

Furthermore, readily accounting for the new activity of 1389 in Lirey that so provoked Bishop d'Arcis is the fact that Aymon of Geneva had died only the year before,[12] seemingly resulting in Jeanne de Vergy returning to her former home in Lirey, bringing the shroud with her. If it was her intention to re-establish the former cult of the shroud in Lirey it would have been natural for her to seek Clement VII's support for this before her family link with him could grow cold, and not least before she herself died, as she must have been well into her sixties by that time. Her son Geoffrey II de Charny, a man well-respected within the French royal court, seems to have wholeheartedly supported her in this endeavour. It is evident from a remark in one of Clement's letters, that Geoffrey II had been in direct touch with Clement on the subject.[13] Similarly, Bishop d'Arcis remarked with some anger how Geoffrey had gone to the lengths of 'holding the cloth with his own hands . . . and showing it to the people' after he, d'Arcis, had expressly forbidden the Lirey clergy to do this.

But the real heart of the shroud mystery concerns the period of the cloth's first showings in Lirey at or about the time when Jeanne de Vergy was married to Geoffrey I de Charny. That is the time at which, according to d'Arcis, his predecessor Bishop Henri of Poitiers made his investigations, and when the artist who had purportedly painted the shroud made his confession. D'Arcis described these events as having happened 'thirty-four years or thereabouts' before the writing of his letter in 1389, which would set them at around 1355.

Ostensibly such a dating ought to make a lot of sense, as it would have been one year before the death of Geoffrey I de Charny on the field of Poitiers, and, as known from surviving documents, two years after Geoffrey had recommenced obtaining the necessary permissions and financial support to found the small collegiate church at Lirey where the shroud expositions would be held.

But there are serious discrepancies between what d'Arcis, from 1389, says happened back around 1355, and the acknowledgedly all too little that can be gleaned from the truly contemporary documents that have survived from that time. Thus d'Arcis described the never-named dean of Lirey procuring the shroud from an artist, setting up a cult of it, publicizing this 'not only in the kingdom of France, but, so to speak, throughout the world', and attracting pilgrims 'from all parts'. He then described Bishop Henri of Poitiers instituting a formal enquiry, discovering the shroud's fraudulence, and beginning 'formal proceedings against the said dean and his accomplices'.

Of the surviving documents, the first three comprise the act of the Lirey church's foundation on 20 June 1353; a bull and letter of Pope Innocent VI recognizing Lirey's canons and granting various indulgences, dated 30 January 1354; and a grant of additional indulgences given on 3 August 1354.[14] Strangely, although these documents list various relics associated with the church's foundation, they mention nothing corresponding to the description of the shroud.

The next main document is a letter from Henri of Poitiers to Geoffrey I de Charny, issued on 28 May 1356,[15] and therefore dating from theoretically during or after the period of Bishop Henri's investigations and confrontations with the Lirey clergy. Yet in this Henri goes out of his way to congratulate Geoffrey I on all he has done in founding the Lirey church, specifically using the words 'we praise, we ratify and we approve'. It seems impossible to believe that the controversy can have begun by this time, yet if it happened within the lifetime of Geoffrey I de Charny, as has consistently been supposed, there was scant time for it to do so. Less than four months later, on 19 September, Geoffrey I lay dead on the field of Poitiers.

Even the final surviving contemporary document,[16] issued from the papal court at Avignon on 5 June 1357 after Geoffrey's death), granting indulgences for those who visit the Lirey church on specified holy days, again contains no mention of the shroud.

Now in all this it might seem that Geoffrey I, at least, had nothing to do with the shroud. It is conceivable, and partly in accord with d'Arcis' statement, that it was perhaps procured by the anonymous rascally dean of Lirey during the period between Jeanne de Vergy's marriage to Geoffrey I de Charny and that to Aymon of Geneva.

Yet several sources, even though less than fully informative, seem to contradict d'Arcis by firmly ascribing the shroud's procuration to Geoffrey I. Clement VII's bull of 1390 mentions that it was 'the father of this Geoffrey [i.e. the present Geoffrey II], burning with the zeal of devotion' who had obtained the shroud for the church.[17] Margaret de Charny, Geoffrey I's granddaughter, asserted that the shroud had been 'conquis par feu' by her grandfather.[18] While there is some considerable uncertainty concerning what 'conquis par feu' means in this context: according to some interpretations, perhaps by the 'fire' of battle; according to others, as some form of feudal duel,[19] there is absolute consistency that it was Geoffrey I de Charny, not the dean, who was the first procurer.

Moreover, undeniable proof of a shroud cult at Lirey before

20

the time of Jeanne de Vergy's marriage to Aymon of Geneva, and firmly linked to Geoffrey I de Charny, is evident from a souvenir badge of the shroud, found in the mud of the Seine at the Pont-au-Change in Paris in 1855 [pl. 3, above].[20] During the Middle Ages jewellers, goldsmiths and money-changers had shops and stalls on the Pont-au-Change, and this badge most likely dropped from the hat of some pilgrim who had been to Lirey, had purchased the badge to wear on his hat (as was the 'fashion at that time – see [pl. 9, above]) and had then lost it while leaning over the bridge during a pause from his Paris shopping.

Whoever this unknown pilgrim was, the badge is of major importance because it is the first in all history to show the shroud as a double-imprint cloth, held out by two clergy. It must have been obtained during a visit to Lirey at the time of the mysterious first expositions of the shroud because it quite unmistakably bears the arms of Geoffrey I de Charny (three small shields on a larger one) and Jeanne de Vergy. Geoffrey II de Charny's arms are known to have had certain distinctive differences.

So we can only conclude either that Geoffrey I de Charny set up the shroud cult with Jeanne de Vergy during his lifetime, or that Jeanne de Vergy did so in their joint names after Geoffrey's death, but before she had married Aymon of Geneva. Similarly, whatever the part of the alleged rascally dean of Lirey, it can only be supposed from the use of the family arms on the souvenir, that both Geoffrey I and Jeanne, or at the very least Jeanne on her own, fully approved of, and supported the shroud showings.

None of this gets us very far, not least because, while we know very little of Jeanne, Geoffrey I was well-recorded historically, and virtually entirely favourably, as the very epitome of Chaucer's 'verray, parfit gentil knyght'. He wore on his epaulettes the motto 'honour conquers all'. He wrote deeply religious poetry, some of which has still survived.[21] He was chosen by France's king to carry into battle his country's most sacred banner, the Oriflamme of St Denis, an honour accorded only to the very worthiest of individuals. Not least, he died a hero, defending his king with his own body in the closing moments of the battle of Poitiers, and fourteen years after his death he was duly accorded a hero's tomb, at royal expense, in the Paris Church of the Celestines. It is extremely difficult to understand how such a man would have lent his name, still less the authority of his armorial shield, to the sort of fraud claimed by Pierre d'Arcis.

21

In such circumstances, even more obscure has to be the identity and background of the artist who supposedly 'cunningly painted' the shroud for either Geoffrey himself, or Geoffrey's wife. Bishop d'Arcis spoke of a 'cunning sleight of hand'. But if we ask what evidence for this we have from the present-day, we find that the overwhelming majority of American scientists who worked on the shroud in 1978 claimed that they had found no evidence for any paint having been used for the shroud's body and blood images.[22]

However there was one important exception to this view. From no less than seven years before the announcement of the carbon-dating result, Chicago micro-analyst Dr Walter McCrone, after having examined sticky-tape samples taken from the shroud's image, claimed that he had found clear evidence that these consisted of fine-grade iron-oxide particles suspended in a gelatinous binding medium, effectively a form of tempera.[23]

McCrone even offered historical evidence for precisely such a method of painting on cloth having been used during Geoffrey de Charny's time, at least in England and Germany. Perusing the first volume of the early nineteenth-century painter Sir Charles Eastlake's *Methods and Materials of Painting of the Great Schools and Masters*, McCrone found under the heading 'Practice of Painting Generally during the Fourteenth Century':

> Among other methods, common on this side of the Alps, may be mentioned the cloth-painting of the English and Germans, and their peculiar process in tempera . . . In the Treviso record, preserved by Guid' Antonio Zanetti, mention is made of a German mode of painting (in water colours) on cloth. This branch of art seems to have been practised on a large scale in England during the fourteenth century, so as to attract the notice of foreigners . . . after this linen is painted, its thinness is no more obscured than if it was not painted at all, as the colours have no body . . . As regards the English and German paintings on cloth, there can be little doubt that the thinness of execution for which they were remarkable . . . was adopted with a view to durability . . . The Anglo-German method appears, from the description, to have been in all respects like modern watercolour painting, except that fine cloth, duly prepared, served instead of paper.[24]

But intriguing as it is to speculate that the shroud might have been the work of a medieval English artist (and Geoffrey de Charny *was* in England, albeit as a prisoner of war, during the years 1350–51), McCrone has scant support for his hypothesis from at least one notable specialist in English medieval art, Anna Hulbert. Hulbert is a Courtauld-trained conservator who worked in Florence when many of the city's art treasures were damaged by floods, and who spends much of her daily life restoring and stabilizing medieval English works of art. But she confesses of the shroud:

> I cannot think of any known technique used in the Middle Ages that would have permitted an artist to get the image on the cloth without penetrating the linen fibres. An artist would undoubtedly have felt that the more it penetrated the cloth the more permanent the image would be . . . I have not seen the shroud under the microscope, but I have had the opportunity to make a close examination of the anonymous late medieval 'Buxton Achievement' painting in a Norwich (England) museum. It is the only medieval English canvas painting I can think of, and even on those parts which are too damaged to retain any image, there is plenty of evidence of painterly technique visible, even under low magnification.[25]

It is also worth noting that Eastlake spoke of the cloth being 'duly prepared', a preliminary which virtually any artist would have felt obliged to do before painting on a piece of linen. Yet Turin's shroud shows no evidence of any such preparation.

Even more difficult to understand of the Middle Ages, when artists were heavily reliant on outlines, and exhibited minimal interest in light and shade, is how anyone of that time could have produced on the shroud an image that, as is evident to anyone who studies both the shroud itself and negatives taken from it, not only consists *purely* of light and shade, but light and shade so exactly reversed that seen in negative it resembles a real photograph.

Just how singular this achievement should be regarded can be readily demonstrated from subsequent attempts by even the most competent artists to copy this effect from the shroud. Typical is a seventeenth-century water-colour copy,[26] painted on cloth, preserved in the church of Notre Dame at Chambéry, the town in which the shroud came so close to destruction in 1532 [pl. 4, above]. The face and body can be clearly seen to be rendered with a crude absence of relief reminiscent of the moulds used to make children's traditional gingerbread men. A similar effect is to be observed on a shroud copy of 1652 from the Monastery of Sts Joseph and Theresa, Naples.[27] Yet another example is a sixteenth-century aquatint, attributed to the Renaissance artist G. B. della Rovere, depicting the shroud and Jesus's deposition from the cross. While the deposition is depicted with typical Renaissance flair, the shroud figure is again reproduced as little better than a gingerbread man. It is quite clear that artists long after the Middle Ages simply did not understand the shroud's characteristics as a relief image.[28]

As a way of trying to understand how someone of the Middle Ages might have made an image of this kind, probably even without realizing its negative property, a University of Kentucky researcher, Joe Nickell, has produced what he argues to be good replications of the shroud by pressing a hot-water-soaked cloth over a bas-relief statue, then daubing on an iron-oxide pigment.[29] According to Nickell such replications conform to the very materials identified by McCrone on the shroud, they have the same sort of delicate sepia coloration, they appear not to have been created with visible brush strokes or paint, and they provide what Nickell claims is 'a true negative image' (although in the case of the latter it has to be a matter of individual opinion whether Nickell's negatives truly stand comparison with the subtlety of the face on the shroud).

But one further problem remaining for both Nickell's and McCrone's arguments is that on top of the creation of the negatively life-like body image we need to believe that the supposed artist-forger added the most complex set of blood-flows and other wound-marks that not only look extraordinarily lifelike and convincing to the ordinary layman, but have also been adjudged as such by medical specialists of international repute. The famous instance of the nail-wounds being located through the wrists is just one of numerous unique and near-unique physiological features that have been fully discussed elsewhere.

It is difficult to emphasize enough that despite plentiful medieval depictions of Christ's wounds, and wounds in general, those on the shroud are quite without parallel in their sheer naturalism, anatomical accuracy and subtlety. It took until the sixteenth century, and the publication of Andreas Vesalius's *De humani*

24

*corporis fabrica* ('On the structure of the human body'), before anyone began to produce seriously scientific medical illustration. Those of the Middle Ages were, in the words of British Library expert Peter Murray Jones [30] 'crude and childish', as is quite evident even from a fifteenth-century 'wound man' preserved in London's Wellcome Institute Library [pl. 4, below].

Furthermore, Professor James Malcolm Cameron of the London Hospital,[31] Dr Frederick Zugibe of Rockland County, New York,[32] and Dr Robert Bucklin of the County Coroner-Medical Examiner Office, Los Angeles,[33] are but three of a number of forensic pathologists and medical specialists of international repute who have adjudged the shroud wounds so convincingly those of a genuine crucifixion victim, that it is impossible to believe them to be the work of an artist.

As some way of avoiding the disquieting choice of either doubting these men's competence, or believing in a medieval artist-forger so brilliant that he still managed to fool them, one serious recent hypothesis, raised by British physician Dr Michael Straiton,[34] has been that some fourteenth-century crusader may have been captured by Saracens and crucified exactly as Jesus had been in deliberate mockery of the latter's death. According to Straiton, the body was then wrapped Middle Eastern style and the body image created by some process associated with strong sunshine. But of course this is in total contradiction of the charges levelled by Bishop d'Arcis.

While from this all might seem at a total impasse, the reality is: not quite. If, despite all we have seen, there was someone at Lirey who wanted to concoct a fake relic to bring prosperity to the new-founded church – and in contemporary terms, what Geoffrey de Charny had founded was a humble and under-funded wooden structure that would fall into disrepair in less than a century – there was one famous event, of precisely the mid-fourteenth century, that can scarcely have provided anything other than a powerful source of inspiration.

This was the showing at Rome, in the specially proclaimed 'Holy Year' of 1350, of the 'holy face' on cloth known as the Veronica, said to have been created when the sweat and blood was wiped from Jesus's face as he toiled towards Calvary. The pulling-power of this impression of Christ's face on cloth, linked with the liberal indulgences, or remissions from sins with which it was associated, was enormous. Rome, having been recently reduced to a near-ghost town through plague, internal strife and long papal absence, saw the city's prosperity turned round in this year. Many thousands of pilgrims flocked to it, all bringing offerings, and needing food and hotel accommodation. For the obvious souvenir market the local tradespeople produced under licence Veronica souvenir hat badges of precisely the same kind that we know Lirey to have produced less than a decade later in respect of the shroud [pl. 5, left].

If, despite all the difficulties discussed, this event really was the inspiration for someone faking the shroud, it is almost possible to reconstruct that individual's thought-processes. Why, if Jesus had left an imprint of his face as he toiled towards Calvary, might he not therefore have left a similar imprint of his whole body when he was wrapped in the shroud to be laid in the tomb? If such a shroud was not already known to exist, what a spectacular draw for pilgrims it would be if it could be specially created! All that was needed was some technical wizard to transform the idea into a reality . . .

Ironically, among the individuals who conceivably might have found themselves inspired by this idea, Geoffrey de Charny is probably the least likely. Throughout the Holy Year he most certainly did not go to Rome for he was a prisoner in England, not released (except for a brief remission to attend a wedding in Paris), until July 1351. But of course it is still possible that Lirey's dean made that pilgrimage. Alternatively it is also possible that the journey was made by some artist whose identity we cannot even begin to guess at.

Whatever, the very fact that in the Veronica there was a 'holy face' on cloth whose existence unquestionably stretched back well before the Lirey controversy now takes us firmly onto the main track of our enquiry: the origin of the whole idea of Jesus imprinting his likeness on cloth. In the search for the very holiest faces in the most secret places our quest first takes us to Rome.

*Chapter Three*

# OVER THE VERONICA
# STATUE

*Over the gigantic Veronica statue is a picture accounted
so holy that no layman may look upon it . . .*

Thomas Heaphy, 1861

It is a strange irony that the best-kept secret place can be one so familiar that few realize it contains any secret. This is certainly true of the 'secret place' of the holy face known as the Veronica. While every visitor to St Peter's in Rome sees the outside of it, ostensibly a simple dome-supporting pier or pillar, inside is a world so unknown and so closely guarded that it makes all that we have seen of the Turin shroud seem like a model of openness.

As, like any other tourist, you enter the portals of St Peter's, the guidebooks garrulously remind you that you are inside the largest church in all Christendom, 651 feet long, 435 feet wide, 452 feet high, with 395 statues, 44 altars, and 77 supporting columns. After you have strolled the length of the nave you may perhaps pause to look into the subterranean area, known as the Confession, that is believed to contain St Peter's tomb. Looking upwards, you will probably wonder at Bernini's magnificent ninety-five-foot-high baroque *baldacchino*, or canopy, suspended on four twisted bronze columns above this and the high altar. Looking yet further upwards, you may even gasp in admiration at the incomparable soaring dome which the great Michelangelo designed, but did not live to see to completion. Amidst all this you may scarcely notice around you the four great pentagonal piers or pillars that seemingly effortlessly bear the entire weight of Michelangelo's masterpiece.

The pier that we are interested in [col. pl. 1, above], is the furthest left as you face the Cattedra Petri, the baroque confection enshrining the ancient chair which St Peter supposedly sat on when he first arrived in Rome. As few visitors are told, the base of this pier, deep down below the present floor level, is the oldest part of the new St Peter's. It was here, at the bottom of a huge hole dug twenty-five feet below the floor level of the pre-Renaissance St Peter's, that crusty old Pope Julius II, who commissioned Michelangelo to paint the Sistine Chapel ceiling, laid the first foundation stone of the present building on 18 April 1506. Reportedly on this occasion such a large crowd of spectators gathered overhead that poor Julius, fearful that the excavation's walls might collapse and bury him alive, gabbled the words of the ceremony with inordinate haste.[1]

Initially, as conceived both by Bramante, Julius' chief architect for St Peter's, and by a successor, Antonio da Sangallo, the pier was not intended to be quite on its present-day scale. But when Michelangelo took over as chief architect in 1547, he made substantial alterations and improvements to his predecessors' designs. As recorded by the contemporary biographer Giorgio Vasari:

> Michelangelo found that the four principal piers, made by Bramante and retained by Antonio da Sangallo, were weak; so he partly filled them in, making on each side two spiral stairways up which the beasts of burden can climb with the materials, as can men on horseback, to the uppermost level of the arches.[2]

Even so it was not until early in the pontificate of Urban VIII (1623–44), some two generations after Michelangelo's death, that a specific function, over and above that of supporting, seems to have been decided for the inside of these piers. By this time St Peter's had come to possess in addition to the tomb of its name saint, three other major relics: the Veronica 'holy face'; the reputed skull of St Andrew; and the head of the lance said to have been thrust into Jesus' side. To these, in April 1629, Urban VIII added a large piece of the supposed True Cross, transferred from the Church of Santa Croce in Gerusalemme, prompting the Reverenda Fabbrica, the congregation who supervised all matters relating to St Peter's, to decide that each pier should be dedicated to one of the four relics.[3]

Externally, at the foot of each pier, there was to be hollowed out a niche for a statue of the particular saint most associated with the relic to which the pier was dedicated. High above this was to be set a suitably ornate balcony for display of the relic on special occasions. Behind this, inside the pier itself, some form of access was to be created together with (and here our information becomes vague), some suitable repository for the relic. The architect chosen by the congregation was the great Gian Lorenzo Bernini, whose talents were already obvious from his work on the *baldacchino*.

Now we know that Bernini had largely completed his task by 1641, and in respect of the Veronica pier the external features of this are there for all to see. On a suitably inscribed plinth at ground level stands a dramatic fourteen-foot-high marble statue of St Veronica [pl. 5, above] rushing forward in excitement, holding out a marble cloth etched with the likeness of Jesus's face. This was created by the sculptor Francesco Mochi. Above this is carved a dedicatory inscription telling us, in Latin, that Pope Urban VIII ordered the construction and decoration of this place as a suitably 'royal' home for the Veronica in the Holy Year of 1625. Above this inscription is suspended a balcony surmounted by wall decoration of twin twisted columns salvaged from the old St Peter's, with between these columns a sculpted relief of the Veronica carried aloft by angels, the work of N. Menghini. To the rear of the balcony can just be seen a bronze, grilled doorway that can only be presumed to lead to some room or stairway that is inside the pier. And it is with that doorway, and whatever lies behind it, that all the garrulouness of the guidebooks suddenly trails into silence.

For while there is no question that the pier is massive – at approximately sixty feet wide at its two fullest sides, twice as wide as the average domestic house, and about three times as high – no guidebooks carry either photographs or plans of its interior, nor is there any readily evident ground-level entrance. And although there is general agreement that the Veronica is kept *somewhere* within it, as confirmed not least by the already mentioned inscription, exactly how and where is much more obscure. Even the most erudite textbooks omit clear details of the work of Bernini's craftsmen inside the piers. And there can be serious discrepancies between one authority and another. For instance the *Blue Guide* to Rome reports that the Veronica, the lancehead of Longinus and the piece of the True Cross are all 'preserved in the podium of the pier of St Veronica'.[4] James Lees-Milne, author of one of the best general books on St Peter's, has contradictorily stated that each relic is kept separately, behind each balcony.[5] Yet Hungarian-born artist Isabel Piczek, one of the few living lay-people ever to have viewed the Veronica at close quarters, insists that it is kept in the sacristy – or certainly was supposed to when she was shown it privately during the 1950s (see p. 185).

Confronted by this apparent impasse, and knowing that Lees-Milne was a serving member of a small committee appointed by Pope Paul VI to investigate the already mentioned 'chair of St Peter', I wrote to him to ask whether he could explain the discrepancy, also whether he could offer any further elucidation as to how and where the Veronica might be kept. To my surprise, after apologizing that he no longer had the notes on which his book was based, he acknowledged:

> I doubt whether I ever knew for certain that the four relics were actually behind the balconies of the central piers. I took it for granted because *the authorities would never have allowed me to investigate* [italics mine].[6]

When one recognizes that this is from a man who is both an acknowledged authority on St Peter's and had actively helped the Vatican's officials in the investigation of one of their relics, some measure is gained of just how secret is the world in which the Veronica 'holy face' reposes.

Besides the élite among Vatican hierarchy, the only individuals known to move freely within the inner passages deep inside St Peter's are the *sampietrini*, the basilica's permanent maintenance staff of masons, carpenters, painters, glaziers and the like, whose jobs are handed down from generation to generation of the same families. Tracing their origins back to the year 1600, these are trained in their hereditary tasks almost from infancy. They have workshops hidden deep within the inner passageways and have long amazed visitors by their feats of getting to seemingly inaccessible parts of the basilica to light oil lanterns and to deploy huge rolls of damask as 'instant' trappings for special ceremonial occasions. As part of their 'family' codes, they jealously guard their own secrets. Yet even they, almost certainly, are not admitted to the Veronica's inner chamber.

In fact, at the commencement of this book the only report

known to me of anyone who had penetrated inside one of St Peter's piers and told his story was that of Aubrey Menen, a half-Irish, half-Indian resident of Rome who during the early 1970s was befriended by Monsignor Hugh O'Flaherty, a priest of the entourage of Pope Paul VI. Menen had happened to express an interest in viewing the pre-Michelangelo design model for St Peter's made by Antonio da Sangallo, and thanks to O'Flaherty's influence permission was 'very reluctantly' given for this. He has described having been conducted on a curious tour with considerable importance to our particular line of enquiry:

> An official took me into the basilica [i.e. St Peter's], opened a door, and led me up some steps. Soon I found myself in a winding corridor built inside the basilica's thick walls. The top was arched, the walls were white, and it was exactly as though I were walking in the narrow alleys of some Moroccan town. We walked a long way; then, going through a heavy wooden door with an antique lock, we came into a vast room. *We were inside one of the gigantic piers that support the dome of St Peter's* . . . [italics mine]. We passed to yet another room. It was in total darkness. We switched on flashlights, and there, filling the room, was Sangallo's model . . .[7]

Frustratingly, Menen offers no clue as to which of the four piers he was in. Indeed we may assume it was most likely not that of the Veronica. But he does make clear that the apparent way to gain access to any of them, presumably including the one containing the Veronica, seems not to have been through any doorway in the pier itself, but instead via passages in the basilica's walls. Furthermore his description leaves no doubt as to the scale of the unrecorded world inside both walls and piers alike. It is obvious that anyone who manages to penetrate into that world is very privileged indeed.

If then we begin by not even having any description, either verbal or visual, of the secret place where the Veronica 'holy face' is kept, scarcely less difficult to penetrate is the mystery surrounding the object itself.

As is well-known to the world's millions of Roman Catholics, the general idea of what the Veronica is supposed to be is straight-forward enough. Francesco Mochi's statue of St Veronica – work on which drove the sculptor to a nervous breakdown – clearly depicts it as an imprint of Christ's face on an excited young woman's veil. A sixteenth-century painting by the Master of the Pink of Baden [col. pl. II above], in the Musée des Beaux-Arts, Dijon depicts the apparent moment of its origin yet more graphically. Jesus is seen carrying his cross in the midst of crowds in Jerusalem, while to one side St Veronica holds up her veil to his face, thereupon finding the impression of his features left on this.

This dramatic scene became a particularly favourite part of the folklore of the Middle Ages. Actors recreated it for the education of the populace via the medium of 'miracle plays', the multi-compartmented tableaux performed on carts in public streets, that were the popular theatre of the time. Such productions aimed for maximum realism, and the German 'miracle play' of the Veronica story reportedly culminated in an anguished cry, 'O head full of blood and wounds!'. Even today visitors to Jerusalem are shown the spot where the original event is supposed to have occurred, marked by a chapel of the Little Sisters of Jesus, which has an eighteenth-century Veronica icon over its altar. And scarcely a Catholic church throughout the world does not have some picture or carving of this scene included generally as the sixth of the Stations of the Cross, the images designed to aid and inspire popular devotions during Lent and Eastertime.

Despite such apparent authority, however, it has long been recognized by scholars that it is an event that is not recorded in any canonical gospel, and derives ultimately from legend. As the story has become most familiarly known:

> Veronica was in her house when she heard the shout-ing and wailing from a crowd surrounding the soldiers who were leading Jesus to Calvary. She rose hurriedly, put her head to the door, looked over the heads of the crowd, and saw our Redeemer . . . Transported, beside herself, she seized her veil and threw herself into the street, oblivious to the insults and blows from the soldiers who pushed her back. Arriving in the presence of our Saviour, whose face was pouring with sweat and blood, she wiped [his face] with her veil . . . All honour to you, courageous woman . . . The Saviour granted you the most precious gift which he could make to a creature of this world, his portrait . . . imprinted on your veil.[8]

Pre-thirteenth-century versions curiously vary in certain salient details, although they stretch several centuries further back. Nor does St Veronica have any particularly bona-fide credentials as an historical saint, as was recognized by the ecclesiastical historian Cardinal Baronius as far back as the late sixteenth century. Baronius went so far as to drop Veronica from the *Roman Martyrology*, the Roman Catholic Church's official calendar of saints and martyrs.

Nonetheless there can be no doubt that there was, and seemingly still is, a real-life physical relic unhesitatingly linked with this story that attracted the most intense interest through several centuries, particularly during the Middle Ages. People from the most distant Christian countries, and from all walks of life, flocked to view it on the carefully restricted occasions on which it was shown, just as some three million of their modern counterparts queued to view Turin's shroud when the latter was brought out for the rare six-week exposition of 1978. Sometimes the crowds in Rome were so great that deaths and injuries occurred in the crush, in the manner of modern European soccer matches. If a crowned monarch visited the city, one of the greatest honours the pope could bestow was to allow the royal personage his or her own privileged, private showing of the Veronica. Some of the Christian world's greatest cathedrals clamoured to own copies specially sanctified by having been placed in direct contact with the original.

Accordingly perhaps the greatest surprise and enigma relating to the Veronica is that even up to this, the final decade of the twentieth century, whatever of it may still be preserved in the secret place inside the Veronica pier has been cocooned in such secrecy that there exists not even a photograph of it in the public domain. Nor is there any certainty that it has ever been photographed.

Of artists' copies that exist, most vary so much from one to another that trying to distinguish which may be the accurate ones is by no means easy. At the beginning of the sixteenth century, the great German draughtsman Albrecht Dürer produced some lively Veronica engravings [fig. 2a],[9] but they may well have derived more from imagination than observation.

These and similar examples were followed during the eighteenth and nineteenth centuries by further 'official' engraved copies that are sometimes still to be found hanging in dark corners of European churches [fig. 2b]. On these is to be seen a disembodied face, suffused with apparent blood and tears, and with eyes closed, accompanied by a seemingly reassuring inscription in Latin:

33

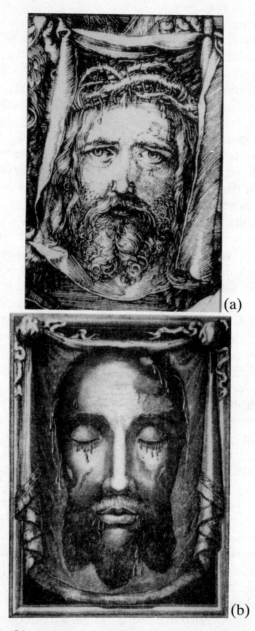

*Fig. 2. The Veronica: (a) early sixteenth-century engraving by Albrecht Dürer; (b) popular 'official' engraving of the nineteenth century. Such copies are of doubtful fidelity to the original.*

> The true likeness of the sacred face of Our Lord Jesus
> Christ, which in Rome at the most holy basilica of St
> Peter is devoutly preserved and venerated.[10]

At Tours in France in 1850 a special 'Confraternity of the
Holy Face' was founded specifically to disseminate engravings of
this kind. And around the same time at Rome they were highly
popular souvenir items among the city's tourists, particularly those
sold from the sacristy of St Peter's. But as the Abbé Barbier de
Montault, a nineteenth-century canon of the cathedral of Anagni,
remarked of the latter:

> They are printed on linen from a plate which seems
> to me to be a hundred and more years old, and are
> sealed with the seal and bear the signature of a canon,
> which seal and signature to me appear to signify only
> that the copy has touched the original, and that it has,
> in consequence, become an object of piety . . . [They]
> do not testify that the copy resembles at all the original.[11]

Further complicating the issue is that while there are other,
significantly older, 'holy faces' copies on cloth that are preserved
in a variety of shrines around Europe, not only is the exact
relationship of these to the Veronica unclear, several have also
been enshrouded in their own mesh of secrecy and highly restricted
viewing. Typical of these are the 'holy faces' of Genoa in Italy,
of Laon in France, and of Jaén and Alicante in Spain, all of them
of varying degrees of difficulty of access, and all of which will be
explored later in this book.

Perhaps most frustrating of all, amidst so many of the afore-
mentioned uncertainties, is the fact that there has not even been
general agreement that the original Veronica of Rome any longer
exists. The reasons for this are partly historical. When Rome was
mercilessly sacked by an army of leaderless Spaniards, Germans
and Italians in 1527, one contemporary Roman eyewitness, a
'messer Urbano' writing to the duchess of Urbino, spoke of the
relic at that time being passed from hand to hand in the taverns
of Rome, and its companion the 'holy lance' stuck mockingly on
the pike of a German *landsknecht*.[12]

In seeming contradiction of this there are later reliable reports
of what is certainly called the Veronica being exhibited in the years

1536, 1580 and 1600, to list merely the better-attested occasions within the century immediately following the sack of Rome. We have already seen how in the seventeenth century Pope Urban VIII went to elaborate lengths to house it and build a structure for its periodic display from the pier balcony (even though on such occasions any details of the cloth itself are essentially invisible to anyone looking from below). Some form of cloth kept inside the Veronica reliquary was certainly seen and examined during the nineteenth century, and whatever this was, it quite definitely survives to the present time, there having been a balcony showing during the Holy Year of 1950.

But the complication to the issue is that, according to some, the present-day cloth is not the same as the 'holy face' that drew so many admiring pilgrims to Rome during the Middle Ages. Those who hold this view refer particularly to the fact that the mere handful of published first-hand descriptions of the Veronica from within the last century and a half have reported that there is little or nothing of any image to be seen any longer on the cloth.

One such description was that of the already mentioned Abbé Barbier de Montault, who had the opportunity to see the Veronica at moderately close hand on 8 December 1854, when Pope Pius IX arranged a special showing of it and the other major relics of St Peter's after drawing hundreds of bishops to Rome for his proclamation of the doctrine of the Virgin Mary's Immaculate Conception. He reported:

> . . . one cannot see the face behind, hidden by a useless metal cover, and the place of the impression exhibits only a dark surface, giving no semblance of a human face.[13]

Another report, that of the last authoritatively known examination of the Veronica, which took place as long ago as 1907, derives from the eminent German Jesuit art scholar, Monsignor Joseph Wilpert. Uniquely privileged to be allowed to remove two plates of glass covering the Veronica, Wilpert described seeing only:

> . . . a square piece of light-coloured material, somewhat faded through age, which bore two faint rust-brown stains, connected one to the other.[14]

So had the original 'holy face' seen by medieval pilgrims simply faded or rubbed away into nothing as a result of the ravages of time? Had the original been lost without trace during the sack of Rome in 1527, after all? Or, as has been suggested by present-day German Jesuit scholar, Professor Heinrich Pfeiffer of Rome's Gregorian University, did the original survive the sack of Rome, only to disappear instead during all the confusion of the transition from the old St Peter's to the new one in the early years of the seventeenth century? Pfeiffer has argued[15] that the original may have been surreptitiously 'lifted' at that time and taken to Manoppello, near Pescara, where certainly a Veronica-type 'holy face' of uncertain origins has been preserved since the early seventeenth century.

All that can be said is that the Veronica that certainly *was* exhibited and preserved in St Peter's during the Middle Ages presents us with a 'holy face' on cloth dating from unquestionably earlier than the earliest date attributed to the shroud by carbon dating. Historically we know that, however uncertain its origins, it attracted virtually none of the forgery accusations that so dogged the Turin shroud. It raises fascinating questions concerning whether it still survives either in the 'secret place' in St Peter's, or at Manoppello. Among the many things we need to know about the St Peter's cloth are whether the still visible stains reported by Wilpert might be the vestiges of the original face; whether these might conceivably be enhanced by modern scientific techniques; not least, whether the fabric itself might or might not be of the same manufacture as the Turin shroud.

Perhaps one of the most fascinating features of all of the Veronica of St Peter's is that as an historical object it emerges from the obscurity surrounding its origins earlier than the twelfth century, and fades back into a similar obscurity not long after the end of the sixteenth century. Chronologically therefore there is a historical 'window', a period in which the Veronica enjoyed great fame, was seen by huge crowds, was copied by artists, and played a very visible, instead of a mostly invisible, part on the great stage of history.

On the well-tried principle, therefore, of commencing with what can be seen in the light before trying to explore that which lies in the darkness, that period of the 'window' seems the best at which to begin more detailed enquiries.

## Chapter Four

# A WELSHMAN AT
# OLD ST PETER'S

*. . . there is another image preserved at Rome, which
is called Veronica . . . held in such veneration that no
one sees it except through the curtains which hang in
front of it . . .*

Gerald of Wales, visitor to Rome, 1199–1203

I f we could somehow step back
in time to the late November of 1199, a year comfortably several
decades before the earliest ascribed by carbon dating to the Turin
shroud, we might be able to glimpse among the crowds of Rome
a somewhat short-tempered, middle-aged Welshman resolutely
making his way to St Peter's.

We know the Welshman's name to have been Gerald de Barri,
better known to historians as Giraldus Cambrensis, or Gerald of
Wales.[1] It was his first visit to Rome, and he had made the long and
difficult journey from his home country intent on gaining from the
vigorous and youthful new pope, Innocent III, proper recognition
of himself as bishop of the premier Welsh see of St David's.
Although his own countrymen had twice elected him to this see,
the England of Richard Coeur de Lion and his brother John had
persistently blocked his consecration, fearful that he might try to
make his national church independent of Canterbury.

The St Peter's that Gerald approached was, of course, a quite
different building to that with which we are familiar today. It was
already nearly nine hundred years old in Gerald's time, even then
the largest of all the world's churches, and a source of wonder to
every new visitor. For the most part it was the original basilica

that the Emperor Constantine had caused to be erected over St Peter's tomb when Christianity became the Roman Empire's official religion back in the early fourth century AD.

Ascending, not without difficulty, the thirty-five steps crowded with beggars and street-vendors, Gerald found himself first in a two-storeyed portico, littered with tombs. Although these were mostly of popes he might have been surprised to discover among them the last resting place of the English King Offa, builder of the famous dyke between England and Wales, and of Caedwalla, King of the West Saxons.[2]

Proceeding further, Gerald entered the vast, porticoed atrium known as the Paradise, so-called because it was sometimes decked with flowers. Here, although it was the cool of winter, he may well have refreshed himself at one of the two central fountains.

Now facing Gerald, and protected by yet another portico, lay a seeming choice of five entrances to the basilica proper. Yet the choice was actually narrower than it looked. To the far left was the Door of Judgement, reserved for the dead. Next to this came the Ravenniana door, reserved for those who lived in the Transtevere, the west bank of the Tiber. At the centre was the Romana door, to enter which you had to be either a Roman or a woman (accounts differ). It is possible that Gerald took the Argentea, or Silver door (so-called because it was once silver-plated), to the immediate right of this. But most likely he chose the Guidonea door, where there waited special multi-lingual guides to help first-time visitors such as he.

Once inside Gerald found himself in a vast, barn-like edifice, illuminated by innumerable wax candles, and segmented lengthwise by four rows of Corinthian columns, twenty-two columns per row, forming a nave and four aisles. Literally dozens of monuments and side-chapels littered these aisles, yet if Gerald had indeed chosen the Guidonea door the very first of these that he would have come to was none other than the 'secret place' of the Veronica as it existed in his time.

For the chapel that lay immediately inside this particular entrance way was a quaint, Byzantine-looking structure richly decorated with mosaics that had been commissioned by the Greek pope, John VII, in the years 705–7. It was actually dedicated to the Virgin Mary, Mother of God, but inside it stood a large shrine raised on columns that we know to have been the old St Peter's home of the Veronica. A Vatican library water-colour sketch of

39

the interior of old St Peter's,[3] made in the first decade of the seventeenth century [pls. 6–7], clearly shows this shrine at the beginning of the furthest right-hand aisle, together with the Latin inscription 'vultus sancti' ('holy face'). Shortly after the making of the water-colour the shrine was destroyed during the final phase of the destruction of the old St Peter's to make way for the new, and the Veronica moved to its so-secret home in the present-day Veronica pier.

Now although Gerald wrote a lively autobiography, one of the very few documents of this genre to survive from the Middle Ages, he disappointingly lacked the descriptive powers of a Samuel Pepys, and devoted most of his pages to the story of his relentless but ultimately unsuccessful struggle for recognition as bishop.

Nonetheless, in his *Mirror of the Church*, one of several additional surviving works from his pen, he shows that he took an interest not only in the Veronica, but also another 'holy face', or more accurately, 'holy portrait' that he found in Rome. Indeed this latter in his time at least seems to have taken precedence even over the Veronica, since he describes it first:

> Now the evangelist Luke was both a physician, very clever at looking after both body and soul, and an excellent painter. When, therefore, after the Ascension he made his home with the mother of Jesus, Mary said to him, 'Luke, why not paint my son?' And so, under her guidance, he first of all painted individual features of Jesus, and then, after many erasures and corrections, put them together into a single image. When he showed this to [Jesus's] mother, she studied the image closely and exclaimed, 'This is indeed my son!'
>
> He made two or three such images, one of which is kept at Rome in the Lateran, that is to say the Sancta Sanctorum. And when a certain pope took it upon himself to look at it closely, it is said that he was immediately blinded. After that it was completely covered with gold and silver, except for the right knee, from which there is a constant trickle of oil. Now this image is called the Uranica, that is to say, 'essential'. (Haec autem imago dicitur Uranica quae essentialis.)[4]

In fact this work has usually been referred to by other authors as

40

the Acheropita, or image 'made without hands'. But part of the interest arising from Gerald's mention of it is that with far more certainty than the Veronica it has survived even to this day. It can be seen by anyone visiting Rome's Scala Santa, or 'Holy Stairs', a flight of marble steps said to have been ascended and descended by Jesus on the day of his crucifixion. Reputedly brought from Pontius Pilate's palace in Jerusalem, these are located across the piazza from Rome's basilica of St John Lateran, and if you ascend them in the expected manner, on your knees, at the top you can look through a grille into the St Laurence, or 'Sancta Sanctorum' chapel that was once the popes' private chapel. It is one of the last remaining vestiges of the old Lateran palace where the popes lived before they moved to the Vatican.

Here the Acheropita stands on the altar [col.pl.III], with just visible a crudely painted face surrounded by a metallic gold halo, but otherwise still 'covered in gold and silver' just as it was in Gerald's day. A Latin inscription on this covering tells us that it was 'caused to be made by Pope Innocent III', the very same pope whom Gerald was visiting [pl. 8, right]. And although we may justifiably doubt Gerald's attribution of the underlying painting to St Luke, it was certainly already old even in Gerald's time. It is a work of considerable interest in its own right that we will be returning to investigate further in this book.

But meanwhile our prime interest, inevitably, concerns Gerald's description of the Veronica, which he specifically refers to as 'amongst the more precious relics of St Peter's' in his time. In his own words:

> But there is another image preserved at Rome, which is called Veronica, from a woman Veronica, who had so long prayed to see the Lord that at last she was granted her request. For once when she was going out of the Temple she met Our Lord, who said to her, 'Veronica, look now on the one you so wanted to see.' And as she looked at him, he took her cloak, put it to his face, and left on it the impression of his features. This image is also held in such veneration that no one sees it except through the curtains which hang in front of it. It is kept at St Peter's. We read that it was this same woman who touched the hem of Jesus's garment, and was healed of an issue of blood. It is also recorded that this same

41

woman, after Christ's passion, was ordered to travel from Jerusalem to Rome, bringing with her an image which she would have much preferred to have left behind. But as soon as she was brought into the presence of Tiberius Caesar he was healed of an incurable disease from which he had been suffering. And some maintain, playing upon the name, that Veronica is so called from *vera iconia*, that is to say, 'true image'.[5]

Now this positively confirms for us that the Veronica was even as early as Gerald's time, a real-life physical relic preserved in old St Peter's, and one that, like the Acheropita, seems to have been in Rome already for some while. Although Gerald does not himself state or describe its exact location within the basilica, we independently know this information from an English canon, Peter Mallius, writing fifty years before Gerald's time. In his *Description of the Vatican Basilica*[6] written about the year 1150 Mallius positively locates the Veronica 'in the oratory of the blessed Virgin Mary, Mother of God, which is called the Veronica', which immediately identifies it as the already mentioned chapel built by Pope John VII and lying immediately inside the Guidonea doorway.

Gerald also makes clear that although he may not have been privileged to see the Veronica directly for himself, hence his reference to the curtains kept in front of it, there was already well-established acceptance in his time that Jesus had imprinted his likeness upon it. Noteworthy in this context is his specific use of the words 'the impression of his features'.

Gerald also indicates the story's already well-established association with a woman 'called Veronica' on whose garment the imprint was created. Although he seems to know nothing of the idea of her rushing out on the road to Calvary, he nonetheless speaks of a similar though rather more casual encounter between her and Jesus, in the environs of the Temple, during which the image was created. He identifies Veronica as 'the same woman who touched the hem of Jesus's garment', an identification which as we will learn later, can certainly be traced back many centuries before Gerald's time.

However for us perhaps Gerald's most significant information is his insistence that in his time this image was 'held in such veneration that no one sees it except through the curtains which hang in front of it.' Gerald made his third and final visit to Pope Innocent III in Rome in 1203, and up to and including that date, although the Veronica's existence in St Peter's is mentioned, there is absolutely no record of it ever being shown to any crowd of ordinary people, nor of it being carried in public procession.

The only known exceptions to this rigid seclusion were certain special occasions in which the Veronica was brought out to impress particularly honoured visitors. There had been a recent example in 1191 when the youthful one-eyed French king, Philippe Auguste, paid a courtesy call on Innocent III's geriatric predecessor Celestine III *en route* back to France from taking part in the Third Crusade. According to a contemporary chronicle, Celestine

> . . . showed the king of France and his men the heads
> of the apostles Peter and Paul, and the Veronica, that is
> to say, the linen cloth which Jesus Christ pressed against
> his face, and on which even today that impression is so
> clear that Jesus Christ's face can be seen on it.[7]

But apart from this there is absolutely no evidence that in Gerald's time the ordinary public were ever shown the Veronica in such a manner. They had to be content instead with a once-a-year showing of the already mentioned Acheropita/Uranica from the Sancta Sanctorum chapel. Every Feast of the Assumption, the pope would first celebrate Mass at Rome's basilica of Santa Maria Maggiore, then return to his Sancta Sanctorum chapel within the Lateran palace, from which he would bring out the Acheropita image and carry it in procession across the Lateran field.[8] The Romans loved a procession, and an impresssive retinue of cardinals, deacons and ordinary clergy would follow the pope, all dressed in their best feast-day finery. The gathering would visit the churches of Santa Maria Novella and Sant' Adriano, at each of which the Acheropita would be set down and have its feet washed in water perfumed with the royal herb, basil. The Acheropita was unquestionably *the* 'holy face' for showing for Rome up to and including Gerald's last visit to Rome in 1203, while the Veronica continued to be kept in seclusion.

Furthermore, even when in 1204 King Peter of Aragon visited Innocent III to receive a formal coronation, although Peter is recorded to have prayed before the Veronica, there is no specific mention that he was actually shown it. He may have been

43

considered too minor or too flawed a monarch for such an honour. Or perhaps, unlike Philip Augustus, he was thought insufficiently worthy because he was not returning from a crusade. Whatever, the historical record leaves room for the possibility that, throughout King Peter's devotions, Innocent's canons kept the Veronica's screening curtains firmly closed.

But in 1207 Innocent seems to have introduced a new and most significant change of policy, one prompted, as it would seem, by a pressing and entirely worthy need for fund-raising.

The background circumstances were that after a mid-twelfth-century hey-day in which there had even been an English pope, the number of English pilgrims to Rome had declined substantially, one casualty of this being the extinction of the city's School of the English, which lay only a short distance from St Peter's, close to the banks of the Tiber.

Accordingly, early in his pontificate, Innocent III decided to use the redundant site to found a great new hospital, that of Santo Spirito in Sassia ('the Holy Ghost in the Saxon borough'), the building of which is still extant. Designed as a place of care where 'the hungry are fed, the poor are clothed, and the sick are supplied with all the necessaries', it was a project in which Innocent, deeply moved by the poverty and sickness he saw around him, took a genuinely pious personal interest. Despite being from a family who were not notable for their riches, he gave liberally from those personal funds he directly possessed or controlled, and adroitly encouraged others to the same end. Even our friend Gerald was persuaded to become 'a brother' of the hospital, as such having papal authorization to seek funds for it on his return to Wales.

But in order to give the project a boost of a particularly permanent kind, in 1207 Innocent instituted a yearly liturgical station[9] – a sort of combined papal visit and Mass – to be held at Santo Spirito on the first Sunday after the octave of Epiphany. A highlight of this was to be a procession along the third of a mile route from St Peter's to Santo Spirito, and so as to draw an especially large crowd Innocent arranged that the Veronica should be carried in this, just as we have seen had been traditional of the Acheropita on the Feast of the Assumption.[10] Borne by the canons of St Peter's who are still its traditional guardians, it was housed in a magnificent reliquary of gold and silver and precious jewels which, although it is not known to have survived, would more than likely have been made by the same craftsmen who created the gold and silver covering for the Acheropita.

Since the purpose of the event was predominantly to encourage others to give to the poor and needy, by way of demonstration of this Innocent ordered for this occasion the distribution of personal largesse to some 1,300 paupers, only 300 of these the inmates of the Santo Spirito hospital. Furthermore, since in his time the set gospel text for this first Sunday after Epiphany was that of Jesus's turning of water into wine at Cana, Innocent preached a sermon pointedly likening his acts of charity to this gospel miracle, with the presence of the Veronica representative of the presence of Christ himself.

But most dramatic of all, as the very high point of the whole proceedings, Innocent took personal hold of the Veronica and exhibited it openly to all present. Suddenly that which previously only the most exalted had been allowed to see was unveiled for the benefit of men and women from all walks of life. Given the awe in which the 'holy face' was regarded, almost inevitably the crowds would have reacted with considerable emotion, particularly when Innocent, in a specially composed prayer, reminded them that they were seeing the very face of He with whom they would be confronted on the dread Day of Judgement:

> Let us pray, O God, who in the image impressed on Veronica's veil wanted to leave your memorial for us who are sealed in the light of your face. We beg you to obtain for us through the merits of your passion and cross, that as we now on earth venerate and adore the very mystery of this likeness, so we may see it face to face unto salvation when the Judge comes.[11]

So as to reinforce yet further what he had done, Innocent granted special indulgences, or temporal remissions of their sins, to all those who were present at this Santo Spirito 'station'. Based on Christ's words to Peter, 'I will give you the keys of the kingdom of heaven . . . whatever you loose on earth shall be considered loosed in heaven', the idea of an indulgence was that it released the individual from so many days that he would otherwise spend in purgatory for the sins he or she had committed in life. Until not long before Innocent's time indulgences had been offered fairly sparingly, generally to those who had taken part in the Crusades, or were present at the dedication of a church. But now Innocent, with all the authority that had been conferred on him as a successor of St Peter, granted indulgences not only to those who were physically present at the Santo Spirito 'station', but also a ten-day indulgence to all those anywhere in the world who recited the special prayer to the Veronica that he had composed.

After Innocent's so dramatic and unprecedented exposure of the Veronica to common public gaze, accompanied by the granting of indulgences for praying before even copies of this likeness, it might be thought that there would be a sudden proliferation of such copies throughout Roman Christianity's world. But whether or not as an accident of history, there is little evidence of this. Instead a mystique, a pall of reserve seems to have continued to hang over the Veronica 'holy face' almost as if men and women still shrank from considering themselves worthy to view it directly, or to make copies from it.

As one indication of this, although a substantial number of religious illuminated manuscripts have survived from the thirteenth century, from all over Europe, it is well-nigh impossible to find in these any direct copies of the Veronica right up until the very last decade. Paradoxically the only seeming exceptions to this are some English manuscripts from around the middle of the century, notably the Westminster Psalter, the Lambeth Apocalypse, and the great *Chronica Majora* of Matthew Paris,[12] preserved at Corpus Christi College, Cambridge. These include illustrations [pl. 16] that are quite clearly supposed to be of the Veronica, for they are usually described as such and accompanied by a copy of Innocent III's prayer. In the *Chronica Majora* example, Paris specifically relates a story of the Veronica, while being carried by Innocent III in one of the annual Santo Spirito processions, having reversed itself 'in such a way that the forehead was below and the beard above'.[13] Furthermore a striking indication of the importance attached to these copies is the fact that they alone of all the illustrations in their manuscripts have been independently created on a separate piece of vellum.

But in a manner that has perplexed art historians, these 'Veronicas' depict Jesus with a neck and shoulders exactly as on the normal everyday 'Christ in Majesty' portrayals that decorated every church. They fail to show the disembodied face that subsequently became the very hallmark of everyone's understanding of the Veronica's true appearance.

46

(Above): *The 'secret place' of the Veronica 'holy face'? The massive south-western pier or pillar that is one of the four main supports of the dome of St Peter's. The Veronica is thought to be kept somewhere inside this pier, but there exists no public photograph or record of its exact location;* (left): *The 'secret place' of the Turin shroud: the elaborate late seventeenth-century altar-shrine that stands at the centre of the private chapel of Dukes of Savoy in Turin Cathedral*

I

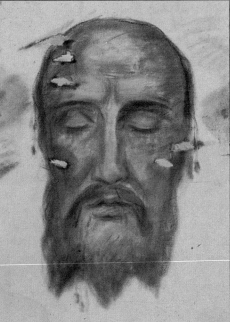

(Above): *Moment of creation of the Veronica? Jesus imprints his face on the veil of a Jerusalem housewife as he carries his cross towards Calvary. From an early sixteenth-century painting by the Master of the Pink of Baden (Thuring Meyerhofer?) in the Musée des Beaux-Arts, Dijon;* (right): *Actual appearance of the Veronica 'holy face'? A claimed facsimile by the nineteenth-century English portrait painter Thomas Heaphy the Younger. From Heaphy's original sketch as preserved in the Print Room of the British Museum*

*More ancient than the Veronica? The Acheropita 'holy face' that for at least twelve hundred years has been preserved in Rome's Sancta Sanctorum chapel, originally the popes' private chapel before papal residence shifted to the Vatican. The icon's cover is thirteenth-century, and its 'face' a crude over-painting, but beneath lies an intriguing though near totally-effaced original that dates at least as far back as AD 754*

**III**

(a): *The 'holy face' 'Santa Faz' or 'Santo Rostro' as preserved in the Cathedral of Jaén, southern Spain; (b): the 'holy face' preserved in the Convent of Santa Clara, near Alicante, southern Spain; (c): the 'holy face' preserved until 1870 in the Church of S Silvestro in Capite, Rome, and now in the Matilda chapel of the Vatican; (d): the 'holy face' preserved in the Church of St Bartholomew of the Armenians, Genoa*

IV

*Earliest-known depiction of the Veronica in its 'inner' frame. From the superbly illuminated mid-fourteenth-century manuscript,* Regula Sancti Spiritus, *in the Archivo di Stato, Rome. The pope shown holding the Veronica seems to be intended as a representation of Pope Innocent III, though it dates from more than a century after his time*

V

*The Veronica depicted as a naturalistic 'imprint' of Jesus's features:* (right): *detail from illumination of 'The Carrying of the Cross' by Jean Fouquet, Hours of Etienne Chevalier, Musée Condé, Chantilly;* (below): *St Veronica by the sixteenth-century mannerist painter Pontormo, from the second lunette of the Papal Chapel, Sta Maria Novella, Florence*

*Special facsimile copy of the Veronica as made in 1617 by Pietro Strozzi, secretary to Pope Paul V. This is preserved in the Schatzkammer of Sacred and Secular Treasures of the Hapsburg dynasty, the Hofburg Palace, Vienna*

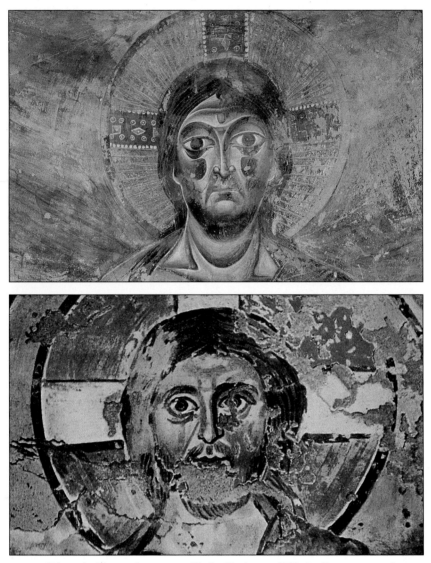

(Above): *Eleventh-century Christ Enthroned/Christ Pantocrator fresco from the apse of the Basilica of Sant' Angelo in Formis, near Capua, Italy, showing some of the so-called Vignon markings that have striking parallels to incidental blemishes on the Turin shroud;* (below): *Eighth-century portrait of Christ Pantocrator, exhibiting curious 'topless square' forehead marking identical in shape to a marking in the same location on the Turin shroud. From a fresco in the little-known catacomb of S Ponziano, on the outskirts of Rome*

VIII

Another apparent indication of this same reserve and restriction on direct copies derives from what we know of certain religious houses who became anxious to obtain copies of the Veronica holy face as an aid to their devotions. Curiously, in those examples we know of, we find them being given 'holy face' copies from the Byzantine east, which had its own independent tradition of Jesus imprinting his likeness on cloth.

One prime example of such a request for a 'holy face' was that around the year 1249 made by the Abbess Sibylle of the northern French Cistercian convent of Montreuil-des-Dames to her brother Jacques Pantaléon de Troyes, then working in Rome. Pantaléon sent her an impressive panel painting that has survived to this day as the 'holy face' of Laon [pl. 8, above]. He even specifically described this as a 'Veronica' in his accompanying letter, his chief concern its somewhat darkened appearance:

> Do not be surprised if you find his [Christ's] face black-ened and sunburnt, for those who dwell in temperate and cold climates and who live all the time in pleasant places, have fair, delicate skin, whereas those who are always in the fields have burnt, darkened skin. This is the case with the Holy Face, bronzed by the heat of the sun, as the Song of Songs has it. Our Lord has worked in the field of this world for our redemption.[14]

But as is quite evident from this painting's Slavonic-lettered inscription 'The Lord's Picture on the Cloth', and studies of it made by professional art historians, it is a Byzantine icon, the darkened appearance in Pantaléon's time almost certainly having been due to the eastern incense and candles that had been burnt before it. Making this all the more astonishing is the fact that at the time of this gift Pantaléon's work in Rome was as chaplain to Pope Innocent IV. So he more than anyone ought to have been able to obtain a direct copy of the Veronica, yet even he appears to have had to resort to a substitute.

Furthermore we find a similar instance in respect of a 'holy face' acquired at around this same time by a community of Poor Clare nuns at Palestrina in Italy. This particular community had been founded by Margherita Colonna of the formidable Colonna family who owned or controlled a major part of Rome, and also had a family seat at Palestrina. Although Margherita lived only to the age of twenty-five, she led a markedly saintly life, and had a particularly deep devotion to the Veronica, being specifically recorded to have made a special journey to Rome to view it,[15] presumably during one of the Santo Spirito processions that continued to be staged by Innocent III's successors.

Margherita is known to have been profoundly moved by the experience, and when after her death her community of nuns was moved to a more permanent home at Rome's church of S. Silvestro in Capite, it came to light that they had acquired, in undisclosed circumstances, their own special 'holy face'.[16] This one was so highly regarded that in 1870 this was moved to the pope's private chapel, where it survives to this day [col. pl. IVc]. And it too is unmistakably of eastern origin.

Even some three quarters of a century after Innocent III's initiative, this substantial mystique and reserve seems to have continued. Although the powerful Crusader Order of Knights Templar may have had their own privileged 'holy face' cult, they kept this closely to themselves, one of the few surviving clues being a panel painting found hidden at Templecombe in England.[17] Cardinal Bishop of Palestrina in Margherita Colonna's time had been the Franciscan Girolamo Masci, who in 1288 became Pope Nicholas IV. Yet it seems to have been only after achieving his high office that Nicholas felt empowered to commission a cope with a Veronica-type face as a gift for his home-town cathedral of Ascoli-Piceno.[18] And although there was a special facility for private showings of the Veronica on occasions other than the Santo Spirito procession – examples have survived of a special papal permit, a 'licence for showing the holy face' – throughout the thirteenth century at least this seems to have been very tightly controlled.

Nonetheless whether despite or because of the continued reserve, the Veronica's fame unquestionably spread extraordinarily during this century. Perhaps the greatest indication of this is a little-known passage in the famous *Travels* of the Venetian Marco Polo [fig. 3] which relates how in 1269, when Marco Polo himself was only fifteen, his father Niccolò and his uncle Matteo returned from a nine-year journey to the East, bringing with them what is thought to be the first piece of asbestos ever to reach the West. Referred to as 'salamander' by Marco, this was a gift from the great Mongol emperor Kublai Khan to the pope as a special protection for the Veronica. In Marco Polo's own words:

*Fig. 3. The thirteenth-century Venetian traveller Marco Polo. His father and uncle brought the first known asbestos back from the East – as a special protection for the Veronica*

There is one of these cloths in Rome. Niccolò and Matteo Polo took it as a gift from the Great Khan *to wrap around Christ's sweatcloth* [i.e. the Veronica]. On this cloth was written in gold: Tu es Petrus et super hanc petram edificabo ecclesiam meam (You are Peter and on this rock I will build my church).[19]

There is even some reason to believe that this most historic piece of asbestos may survive to the present day, for according to Maurice Collis, author of an authoritative book on Marco Polo:

Henri Cordier, one of Polo's editors, states that he had enquiries made at the Vatican and was informed that . . .

49

such an asbestos towel (or part of one) was preserved there.[20]

If this information is correct – Cordier disquietingly remarks that there seems to have been a cataloguing confusion by which the Vatican authorities thought it had come from a Roman tomb – then this piece of asbestos alone has to be of profound historical and technological interest in its own right. Yet, at the time of writing, this has remained another of the items long locked in that seemingly impenetrable world behind the Veronica pier.

In summary then, it is quite clear that by the end of the thirteenth century, when the individuals associated with the 'shroud' controversy at Lirey were still yet to be born, the fame of Rome's Veronica 'holy face' had already spread world-wide. In his *Vita Nuova*, written about the year 1291, the great Italian poet Dante Alighieri spoke of a pilgrimage 'seemingly from a distant land' going to Rome to view and venerate the Veronica, presumably for the occasion of the annual Santo Spirito procession that was still their only normal opportunity.

But to anyone with a more commercial bent than Innocent III, this once-a-year event had to be an under-exploited resource. Sooner or later someone was bound to think of the extra offerings to Rome's shrines and the extra trade for Rome's citizens that could accrue if the Veronica could be exhibited on a much more regular basis, perhaps continually over a period of a year. Of course, it would have to be a very special year. But in the centenary of 1300, and the pontificate of Boniface VIII, thought and pope met head-on.

## Chapter Five

# LAUNCHING OF THE HOLY YEARS

*Like one that comes, perhaps from Croatia, to see our
Veronica, and . . . who says within himself, as long as
it is shown 'My Lord Jesus Christ, very God, was this
then your true semblance?'*

Dante Alighieri, 'Paradiso', *circa* 1300

**A**s the story runs it was on the
second Sunday of the Epiphany, in the year 1300, when Pope
Boniface VIII was just about to take part in the annual Veronica
procession from St Peter's to Santo Spirito, that he happened to
come across a clearly very old man from Savoy being carried into
St Peter's by his sons. Informed that the old man was no less than
one hundred and seven years old, Boniface asked him why he had
made such a long journey – from even the nearest part of Savoy
to Rome was well over two hundred miles – at so great an age.
The old man replied:

> I remember that at the beginning of the last century
> [i.e. 1200] my father, who was a labourer, came to
> Rome and lived here as long as his money lasted out, in
> order to gain the indulgence. He told me not to forget
> to come at the beginning of the next century [i.e. 1300],
> if I should live so long, which he did not think I
> should do.[1]

When Boniface asked what indulgence he hoped to gain by this,
the old man responded:

51

A hundred days indulgence [i.e. remission of a hundred days that might otherwise be spent in purgatory] every day of the year.

As even Boniface himself acknowledged at the time, there was absolutely no documentary evidence that any such indulgence had ever been granted back in the year 1200 (which was, of course, the pontificate of Innocent III). Nonetheless, arguing that if this was what people expected, something of the kind should be given to them, on 22 February 1300, Boniface proclaimed the year a Holy Year. The highlights were to be the most liberal indulgences for all those who visited Rome's shrines of St Peter's and its sister basilica, St Paul-outside-the-walls. And there were to be weekly showings of the Veronica. So historic was the event that even in the seventeenth century a marble inscription with the text of the proclamation was carefully built into the portico of the present-day St Peter's. This can still be seen between two of the doors. And whatever the doubtful nature of its origins, the idea of a Holy Year has gone on to become a now regular and expected part of the Roman Catholic calendar.

One inevitable irony is that, of all popes, it should have been Boniface VIII who began so ostensibly holy an institution as a Holy Year. On any scale of holiness Boniface was nearer to an Attila the Hun than to a Francis of Assisi.[2] Upon Nicholas IV's death in 1294 the conclave of cardinals, unable to agree on a successor from among their own number, had rashly chosen an eighty-six-year-old unworldly recluse to become the new pope, Celestine V. Boniface, at that time Cardinal Benedict Gaetani, used every conceivable ruse to coax Celestine into resignation, then, on assuming office himself, had the old man hunted down, imprisoned, and quietly smothered to ensure he could not possibly make a come-back. As pope his overriding preoccupation seems to have been the accumulation of power and riches. When the Colonna family, among others, took exception to his greed and land-snatching, he gave orders for the wholesale slaughter of every man, woman and child in their stronghold of Palestrina, and for the whole town to be razed to the ground. However much allowance must be made for hostile biographers, there can be no mistaking the boast of his bull of 12 June 1299:

We ploughed the earth of Palestrina with salt, so that

52

nothing, neither man nor beast, be called by that name Palestrina.

Yet this was the man who by a similar bull seven months later made Innocent III's ten-day indulgence look positively paltry with the offer 'not only the most full and copious, but the fullest possible pardon of all their sins' to all those who 'with appropriate piety' made the journey to visit Rome's St Peter's and St Paul-outside-the-walls during what was left of the year 1300. With typical accountancy mentality he set a tariff of thirty days of such visits for Roman citizens, and fifteen days for all foreigners, shrewdly ensuring that there would be priests day and night at each basilica's altar to receive the offerings that expressed the 'appropriate piety'. He specified that Holy Years should take place only once a century. And although in the bull proper Boniface did not specifically mention the showing of the Veronica or any other relic, the contemporary chronicler Giovanni Villani recorded that during this same year 'for easing the soul of Christian pilgrims' it was ordered that the Veronica should be exhibited in St Peter's every Friday and on all solemn feast days.[3]

Whatever his faults, and these were many, Boniface had a good eye for a crowd-pulling success, and this, as the first-ever Holy Year, was certainly no exception. Although, given its somewhat belated proclamation, and the limitations of medieval communications, the event of 1300 might have been thought to draw comparatively few participants, this was by no means the case. As described by Villani:

> It was a wonderful spectacle. There were continually upwards of 100,000 pilgrims in the city, without counting those that each day came and went, and yet all were cared for and abundantly supplied with provisions, both men and horses, and all this in the best order, without disturbance or conflict.[4]

According to William Ventura, a pilgrim from Asti,[5] who left Rome at the end of the year, the total number of visitors had reached two million by this time. Even if this number was most likely an exaggeration it at least gives some measure of the event's impact on the European imagination.

Thus preserved in both Villani's and other contemporary

accounts are colourful descriptions of the appearance and behaviour of the pilgrims. Only a few were royalty, most notably Charles Martel of the House of Anjou, and Charles de Valois, brother of the king of France. The poet Dante Alighieri was there, mingling with the crowds on the Ponte Sant' Angelo, and made the event the starting date of his *Divine Comedy*. The famous artist Giotto was there, apparently specially invited by Boniface VIII, and soon after he decorated the outside loggia of Rome's true cathedral church, the St John Lateran Basilica, with a fresco of Boniface proclaiming the Jubilee. This has survived to this day, and can now be seen on one of the piers of St John Lateran's nave.

Of the ordinary people who attended, some wore pilgrim garb, others their national dress. Some were up to a hundred years old, led by their children. Youths carried mother or father on their shoulder. They came on foot, on horseback and in wagons, loaded with their baggage, and carrying those who were exhausted and sick. Reportedly at their first sight of Rome's distant towers they would break into joyous shouts of 'Roma, Roma', and throw themselves on their knees. Because they all needed food and lodging, and had come in a spirit of piety, they inevitably represented good business both for Rome's traders and for its churches. According to Villani 'from the offerings made by the pilgrims much treasure was accumulated.' Ventura described two clergy at St Paul-outside-the-walls working day and night to gather in such offerings with rakes.[6]

Furthermore there is more than enough evidence that the viewing of the Veronica was a major high point, if not the absolute peak experience, of all these people's journeys. In the 'Paradiso' of his *Divine Comedy* Dante wrote:

> Like one that comes, perhaps from Croatia
> To see our Veronica
> And whose old hunger is never satisfied
> But who says within himself, as long as it is shown
> 'My Lord Jesus Christ, very God,
> Was this then your true semblance?'[7]

Although in general the huge influx of pilgrims seems to have been managed very well (in his 'Inferno' Dante even mentioned a rule of the road over the bridges leading into Rome), such was the interest in the Veronica that it was specifically of moments when it was shown that tramplings and injuries were recorded. Despite very few English having been allowed to attend (Edward I was operating a ban on any money being taken overseas), a casualty of one such incident was an English Benedictine monk, William of Derby, who was among a party of four from St Mary's Abbey, York. As the Veronica was held up, the crowd surged forward, trapping William at his vantage point, and severely crushing his leg. He was so badly injured that he did not live to return home.[8]

Earlier we noted how during the thirteenth century there appeared to be substantial restrictions on the making of copies of the Veronica. But with Boniface such restraints seem to have begun markedly to lessen. Among the street-sellers' booths that had long lined the approaches to St Peter's, selling everything from figs to tooth-extractions, there now sprang up officially registered 'Pictores Veronicarum' or 'Artists of Veronicas'.[9] These seem to have been a recognized guild[10] who made and sold all manner of Veronica souvenir images, from hand-painted copies on vellum, to lead and tin hat-badges. For the Veronica at least, the age of Lourdes-style commercialism had begun.

Such was Boniface's nature that, having instituted the Holy Year and ensured its efficient administration, he took little interest in its devotional aspects. At the Eastertime his main preoccupation was the knighting of his nephew Roffred, whose horsemen friends scandalized pilgrims with unseemly antics on the steps of St Peter's. Authoritarian, grasping and ill-tempered, ultimately Boniface's high-handedness met its deserts. One night in September 1303 the Colonnas managed to surprise and capture him while he was staying at his family retreat of Anagni. Although Anagni's citizens subsequently succeeded in rescuing him, the shock and rough handling broke his pride and he was dead within a month.

It had been the aid of the nationalist-minded king of France, Philippe the Fair, that lay behind the Colonnas' attempted coup, and when Frenchman Bertrand de Got was elected as Clement V two years after Boniface's death, there began a succession of French-born popes whose first loyalty lay to the French crown. Unsafe in Rome, where they were ever likely to be assassinated by one or other of the Italian factions, these French popes took up residence at Avignon in southern France, thus beginning the period of the so-called 'Babylonian Captivity' of the papacy.

For Rome a highly serious effect of this was the loss of its whole ethos as the seat of the spiritual leader of western Christendom, accompanied by a palpable decline in its material prosperity. Without the presence of a pope and his court there rapidly diminished the number of visiting delegations that brought regular trade to Rome's citizens. Without a pope there was no one with the will to implement the necessary maintenance and refurbishment of the city's great ecclesiastical buildings. Many of the great ceremonies that gave the city colour and life disappeared, among them the annual Veronica procession to Santo Spirito. Without a pope to hold the Veronica up before the crowd, the whole event was cancelled.

When the despised Louis of Bavaria walked into the city at the head of an army in 1328, the canons of St Peter's are reported to have dutifully hidden the Veronica for safety, but there was no one to oppose the intruder. Rome was more and more left to the mercy of thieves, kidnappers and murderers. Grass and weeds grew in the streets. The water ducts became blocked. Churches were left derelict and their more precious materials looted or vandalized. Those who could remember actually began to look back with affection to the good old days of Boniface VIII.

So it was that in 1342 a delegation representing eighteen members of Rome's most influential families made their way to Avignon to request a crucial audience with the latest French pope, Clement VI.[11] After admiring the expensive new improvements that Clement was making to his already fortress-like palace, they made him an impassioned double plea. First, despite the obvious dangers, they wanted him to return to Rome as his only rightful seat as a successor to St Peter. Second they wanted him to proclaim a Holy Year, just as Boniface had done. But pointing out the shortness of human life and how very few people of the present time were likely to be alive by the end of the century, they urged Clement to set this for the year 1350. As the poet Petrarch, thought to have been a member of this delegation, expressed it:

Wherefore more quickly bring that season round
Which washes clean the world's iniquity.[12]

Although Clement listened respectfully to the Romans' plea, he enjoyed too agreeable and well-protected a life at Avignon to be prepared to risk his neck on any too precipitate return to Rome. Nevertheless he did agree to declaring the year 1350 as the second ever Holy Year of Jubilee. And he even issued the proclamation bull for this as early as 1343, thus giving the event no less than seven years' notice:

> Considering . . . the prayers of our people of Rome who by special and solemn embassies humbly supplicate us . . . We, wishing that as many souls as possible should participate in this indulgence and recognizing that from the brevity of human life but few survive until the century . . .have decided that the term of the said concession shall be reduced to fifty years.[13]

In all this time the Veronica had by no means been forgotten, even at Avignon. There was a great deal of theological interest at this period in the whole concept of the divine face as seen at the Last Judgement, and Clement V's successor John XXII (1316–34), even though he never stepped foot in Rome throughout his long pontificate, had composed a highly popular hymn in the Veronica's honour:

> Save, Holy Face of Our Saviour
> In which gleams the image of divine splendour
> Imprinted on a snowy cloth of brilliant whiteness
> Given to Veronica as a token of love.[14]

This same John XXII also granted an indulgence of no less than ten thousand years 'to all truly contrite penitents making a devout prayer in supplication before the face of the Saviour.'[15]

As for Clement VI, besides his bull proclaiming the Holy Year, either he or someone pretending to act in his name seems to have issued a second one guaranteeing extra-special indulgences specifically to pilgrims venerating Rome's 'holy face'.[16]

One of the two 'holy faces' this mentioned was a highly revered Christ-face in mosaic that had long decorated the apse of the St John Lateran Basilica, [pl. 30, above]. This face was said to have appeared miraculously when it was first consecrated back in the early fourth century. And because Clement, even from Avignon, wanted to help this ancient basilica – if he ever did return to Rome, it was his true cathedral church, and had been badly damaged by fire in 1308 – he seems to have specified veneration of this image, and added the basilica itself to the list of those which pilgrims were expected to visit.

57

But inevitably it was the Veronica that was the other of the two 'holy faces' mentioned, and took pride of place. According to the bull, its veneration was to be regarded as the supreme moment of the Holy Year pilgrim's visit to Rome, and the blessing accompanying its exposition one of the necessary conditions for gaining the indulgence.

While all this was promised for the year 1350, even Clement, when he remarked on 'the brevity of human life' in his proclamation, can have had little idea how many would not live to enjoy the new Holy Year's benefits. For in 1348 all Europe became swept by the Black Death, wiping out an estimated one-third of the entire population. At papal Avignon the death-toll was 400 a day, a single graveyard receiving 11,000 corpses in six weeks. The disease was a loathsome one, accompanied by particularly repulsive smells, and scarcely a family throughout Europe was not affected.

As for Rome, this was but one of a succession of disasters. First there were floods in 1345, then a revolution in 1347, then the Black Death. Not least, a devastating earthquake struck in September 1349, causing severe damage to all three of the basilicas that Clement VI had specified pilgrims were to visit commencing just three months later. As Petrarch melodramatically described the city even in the autumn of the Holy Year:

> The houses are overthrown, the walls come to the ground, the temples fall, the sanctuaries perish, the laws are trodden underfoot. The holy dwellings of Sts Peter and Paul totter, and what was lately the temple of the Apostles is a shapeless heap of ruins to excite pity in hearts of stone.[17]

Nonetheless, horrified though many were by the ruin they saw to the Queen of Cities, the very need for spiritual solace in the wake of the Black Death horrors seems to have caused pilgrims to pour into Rome seemingly in even greater numbers than they had in 1300. In the words of Matteo Villani, successor of the chronicler of the 1300 Holy Year:

> On the Feast of the Nativity 1349 the Holy Indulgence commenced for all those who went on pilgrimage to Rome, visiting, as ordered by Holy Church, the basilicas

of St Peter, St John Lateran, and St Paul-outside-the-walls, to which pardon men and women of all sorts ran in great and incredible numbers . . . And they made the pilgrimage with great devotion and humility, bearing with much patience bodily discomforts of all kinds, arising from extreme cold, frost, snow, inundations, rough and broken roads and insufficient shelter. Germans and Hungarians in multitudes passed the night in the open air herding together and making great fires to lessen the cold. The hosts at the inns were too busy – not, indeed, to provide bread, wine, etc., but to take the money that was offered for them. To number the crowds was impossible, but it was estimated that from Christmas to Easter there were constantly at Rome from ten to twelve hundred thousand people, and at Ascension and Pentecost eight hundred thousand . . . The visits to the three churches, when we take into account the going and returning to the place where each person lodged, involved on the average a journey of eleven miles. The roads were so crowded that all the pilgrims, whether they travelled on foot or on horseback, went very slowly.[18]

Once again, whether or not the bull specifying veneration of the Veronica had been of true papal authorship, it was quite unmistakably the regular expositions of this that formed the high point of many of these individuals' Holy Year experiences. Petrarch beautifully expressed this in a contemporary sonnet:

The old man goes away, hoary and white
From the sweet country where he spent his years
And all the little family despairs
Seeing its loving father vanish quite
Then dragging slowly on his ancient load
Through the very last days of his life's span
He uses his goodwill, helps as he can,
Broken by time, and weary of the road:
And come to Rome, following his desire
To behold here the image and the form
Of him whom in the sky he hopes to find.[19]

59

For the Veronica's greater visibility and protection during the showings three Venetians, Nicolo Valentini, Bantino de' Garzonibus and Franceschino in Glostro donated for it a magnificent glass case, ornamented with silver crowns.[20] This has survived to this day, and unusually for items associated with the Veronica, was put on display – empty – at a Rome exhibition in 1984.[21] Such were the numbers who pressed forward to see the Veronica that this housed during the medieval showings that again we hear of suffocations and tramplings underfoot. Indeed this very real danger seems to have prompted a renewed brisk trade in specially authorized private viewings.

A curiosity of these is that even now they were subject to considerable bureaucracy before they could be granted. Although Clement VI had given his Legate in Rome, Cardinal Annibaldo Ceccano, essentially full powers for the most far-reaching arrangements relating to the Holy Year, it seems that for these private showings nothing less than the pope's personal permission would do. This is quite evident from the fact that there flowed across the 400 miles from Avignon a constant stream of such permits:[22] for 'the Countess "Insulen" coming to Rome with great devotion'; for 'Bishop Stephen Elven and those of his family making pilgrimage to Rome'; for 'Philibert de Spinassia, Gerard de Bourbon and William de Bourbon, soldiers making pilgrimage to Rome', and many more.

Again symptomatic of the Veronica's heady profile in the Holy Year experience is the fact that, far more than after the 1300 Holy Year, depictions of it in a variety of forms became increasingly common after 1350. From 1353 there occurs in a French manuscript, the Hours of Yolande of Flanders, the first-known depiction of the woman St Veronica holding up her cloth in the form that subsequently became so familiar.[23] By the 1370s Prague sported a depiction of it in mosaic at the south entrance to St Vitus's Cathedral,[24] while in Spain a particularly holy copy, the 'Santo Rostro', most likely Sienese workmanship, was acquired by Bishop Nicolas de Biedma for the cathedral of Jaén [col. pl. IVa].

Not least, among ordinary people the sporting of a Veronica souvenir badge, most often worn on the hat, became the very hallmark of the well-travelled pilgrim during the second half of the fourteenth century. Thus in England around 1360 the author of the English alliterative poem 'The Vision concerning Piers Plowman' wrote of a character wearing:

many a crouche [cross] on his cloke and keys of Rome
and the Vernicle [Veronica] before.[25]

In Florence a few years later, when the artist Andrea da Firenze
(also known as Andrea di Bonaiuto) painted his magnificent
fresco 'The Church Militants' for the Spanish chapel in the
church of Santa Maria Novella, he included the figure of an
elderly pilgrim wearing a conical hat,[26] at the apex of which can
be seen a painted Veronica badge [pl. 9, above], one of the very
few surviving depictions of the hand-painted Veronicas sold by
Rome's guild of 'Pictores Veronicarum'.[27] In the late 1380s, when
Geoffrey Chaucer is thought to have composed his world-famous
*Canterbury Tales* he included in his Prologue description of the
unsavoury Pardoner:

A Vernicle [Veronica] hadde he sowed upon his cappe.

Furthermore in Paris's Musée de Cluny can be seen actual examples of the lead versions of these badges [pl. 9, left]. And there
they rub shoulders with an already mentioned badge with which
they are contemporary, that of the 'shroud' of Lirey . . .
   Which serves to remind us that it was at this very point in time,
in the wake of the 1350 Holy Year, that the cloth we now know
as the shroud of Turin made its first known début on the stage
of European history. As we have already seen, the Veronica had
already been around for at least two hundred years by this time.
   Accordingly if the shroud really is a work of the fourteenth
century, as carbon dating and the d'Arcis memorandum seem
to indicate, it is difficult to believe other than that the Veronica
expositions of 1350, and the wide fame these achieved, must have
served as its inspiration. Geoffrey de Charny, Jeanne de Vergy,
and the canons of Lirey were all alive at this time, and it is inconceivable that they would not have heard of the Veronica showings
in Rome. Which makes it all the more ironic that if indeed one of
these Lirey people surreptitiously employed an artist to make the
shroud as a rival to this latter, that unknown artist should have
succeeded in hoodwinking so many of the twentieth century, yet
have so lamentably failed to convince those of his own time.
   In this regard it is also worth noting a certain as yet
unremarked significance to the years 1389 and 1390, when there
began the so-controversial renewed expositions of the shroud

at Lirey. Apart from a short-lived attempt in 1367, Rome had stayed popeless until 1377 when the still French Pope Gregory XI gave in to the popular pressure for a return from Avignon. Although Gregory died soon after, the subsequent extremely fraught conclave elected an Italian, Urban VI, setting off the famous Great Schism. In this, Urban stayed on as the 'legitimate' pope in Rome, whilst our familiar friend Robert of Geneva set himself up at the so-conveniently just vacated Avignon palace as anti-pope Clement VII.

Here it is interesting to note that in 1389 Urban in Rome decided that 1400 was still too long to wait for the next Holy Year, and called one for 1390, with intervals of thirty-three years thereafter. Politically it was a shrewd move, for by being seen displaying the Veronica and giving dispensation to the usual huge crowds of pilgrims, Urban could effectively demonstrate to the world the legitimacy of his claim over that of his rival at Avignon. In the event he did not live to do so.

But well worth pondering in this same context is that had anti-pope Clement VII been truly inspired by the Lirey 'shroud' he might have seized upon this to set up as a powerful anti-cult to that of the Veronica. After all, size-wise it was a far more impressive piece of cloth to hold up before huge crowds. Yet in the event it does not even seem to have occurred to him to do so.

The huge irony is that while in Clement's time the shroud wallowed seemingly helplessly besmirched by forgery accusations, nothing of this kind sullied the Veronica, and this despite the intense rivalries and factions with which the fourteenth century was otherwise riven. As a new century dawned, one that Urban's calendar-juggling had denied Holy Year status, the Veronica was about to enjoy yet new heights of popular esteem and enthusiasm. But it was also to be a time of the greatest threats to its very survival.

## Chapter Six

# FROM OVER-INDULGENCE TO OBSCURITY

*The holy relics have been scattered. The Veronica was
stolen. It was passed from hand to hand in all the taverns
of Rome . . .*

Messer Urbano, Rome, May, 1527

**I**t is difficult to think of a period
when there was more confusion over who was rightful pope than
during the first quarter of the fifteenth century. At a time of
intense national rivalries, there were often three rival claimants,
each feverishly wheeler-dealing to secure a better power base than
the rest.

Some measure of the dangers to the Veronica during these
years can be gained from the time in 1409 when the theoretically
legitimate pope Gregory XII had effectively sold Rome to King
Ladislas of Naples, whose army became unwelcome guests in the
city. One of the clerics of St Peter's, Antonio Petrus, who was
keeping a diary at this time, recorded how on 3 October 1409, the
sacristan and canons took the Veronica out of its normal shrine
and took it for safety to the house of one Giovanni d'Oleo.[1] Later
it was taken to the great Roman fortress of Castel Sant'Angelo,
which stands at the approach to St Peter's.

Although the following January the canons deemed Roman life
sufficiently settled for the Veronica to be returned to St Peter's,
their optimism proved premature. In the September one of the
anti-popes, the former corsair John XXIII, heading a mercenary
army provided for him by Angevin Louis II of Sicily, swept
Gregory and the Neapolitans out of Rome and ordered a private

showing of the Veronica for himself and his military patron within the papal palace.[2] The next year, clearly in an effort to persuade the populace of his legitimacy, this same anti-pope arranged for a traditional public exposition of the Veronica.[3] But John's mercenaries turned against him, and despite attempts at double-dealing and treble-dealing, he in his turn was ousted, and the canons of St Peter's, amidst all the confusion and uncertainty, once again temporarily returned the Veronica to Castel Sant'Angelo for its safety.

Between 1414 and 1418 the Council of Constance tried to sort out the whole sorry mess by forcing Gregory XII to resign, disgracing John XXIII, ignoring the Avignon contender (who had moved to Spain), and electing a guileless Colonna, Oddo, as Pope Martin V. In 1423 Martin actually managed to hold a somewhat lack-lustre Holy Year, following Urban VI's thirty-three-year formula. But it took until 1443 before a Venetian pope, Eugenius IV, who had had to spend ten years exiled in Florence, was able to return to Rome to begin a period with at least a semblance of greater stability. One of his very first actions was to stage a special exposition of the Veronica as part of his thanksgiving ceremony in St Peter's.[4] When he died three years later his fifty-year-old successor, Nicholas V, swiftly decided to abandon Urban VI's thirty-three-year cycle for Holy Years, and called one for the year 1450.

After all the earlier troubles this proved a surprising success, certainly in terms of the numbers who attended. One eyewitness likened the bands of pilgrims who made their way to Rome to flights of starlings, or armies of ants. As vividly described by the contemporary Roman chronicler Paolo di Benedetto di Cola dello Mastro:

> I recollect that even in the beginning of the Christmas month a great many people came to Rome for the Jubilee. The pilgrims had to visit the four principal churches – the Romans for a whole month, the Italians for fourteen days, and the foreigners for eight. Such a crowd of pilgrims came all at once to Rome that the mills and bakeries were quite insufficient to provide bread for them. And the number of pilgrims daily increased, wherefore the pope ordered the cloth of St Veronica to be exposed every Sunday, and the heads of the Apostles Saints Peter and Paul every Saturday; the other relics

in all the Roman churches were always exposed. The pope solemnly gave his benediction at St Peter's every Sunday . . .[5]

This food supply problem in fact became so acute that in order to minimize the time any one pilgrim was expected to stay in Rome, Nicholas scaled the number of days of required visits down to three. But even so, after just a brief respite at the end of January, the volume of pilgrims took on yet further vigour. As reported by Paolo dello Mastro:

In the middle of Lent, such a great multitude of pilgrims again appeared, that in the fine weather all the vineyards were filled with them, and they could not find sleeping-place elsewhere. In Holy Week the throngs coming from St Peter's, or going there, were so enormous that they were crossing the bridge over the Tiber until the second or third hour of the night. The crowd was here so great that the soldiers of Sant' Angelo, together with other young men – I was often there myself – had often to hasten to the spot and clear a passage through the throng in order to prevent serious accidents. At night many of the poor pilgrims were to be seen sleeping beneath the porticoes, while others wandered about in search of missing fathers, sons, or companions, so that it was pitiful to see them.[6]

But this was by no means the worst of the problems that were to beset Rome's 1450 Holy Year. With the onset of summer a severe outbreak of plague struck both pilgrims and citizens alike. Although this subsided with the colder weather, the overcrowding of Rome with huge numbers of pilgrims did not, and there were fatalities from both cold and starvation.

Particularly traumatic, however, was a major disaster yet again associated with the exceptional crowds who thronged to view the Veronica whenever it was shown. On 19 December a crowd even larger than normal had assembled to venerate this at St Peter's and to receive the expected accompanying papal blessing, when at about four o'clock in the afternoon Nicholas V, apparently indisposed, sent word that he would be unable to come to St Peter's that day.

The crowd dutifully poured out of the basilica, the richer of them mounting their horses, others their mules, and made their way *en masse* towards the Ponte Sant' Angelo, the narrow bridge over the river Tiber. But in the crush some of the horses and mules took fright whereupon there ensued a traffic jam of such proportions that many dozens of those on foot were pushed down, trampled underfoot, or fell into the Tiber. Although the commanding officer of the Castel Sant' Angelo did his best by shutting the bridge's gates to prevent any more trying to cross, the crush lasted for an hour, at the end of which many were found to be dead. These were carried into the Church of San Celso. In the words of Paolo dello Mastro:

> I myself carried twelve dead bodies, and it was pitiful to see there 172 corpses; the weeping and lamenting of those who found fathers, mothers, sons and brothers among the dead resounded in the streets right into the middle of the night. Truly it was misery to see the poor people, with candles in their hands looking through the rows of dead who lay there.[7]

Yet despite such adverse occurrences, nothing seems to have diminished the Veronica's popularity, and not least as an artistic theme it reached its height during the next few decades. Among the Holy Year crowds had been the great Flemish artist Rogier van der Weyden, who subsequently produced a dramatic panel depicting St Veronica holding the relic as the right-hand wing of a crucifixion triptych.[8] Another artist who seems to have extended a trip to Rome so as not to miss the Holy Year was the highly talented French miniaturist, Jean Fouquet. In the Book of Hours he subsequently produced for the French treasurer Étienne Chevalier, Fouquet included a vivid illumination of the moment of the Veronica's creation as Jesus carries his cross towards Calvary, together with an exquisitely detailed frontal image of St Veronica holding the cloth towards the spectator.[9] Hans Memling [pl. 19, above] and Martin Schongauer were among many other artists who also portrayed the Veronica theme at around this same time. It is quite apparent that the concept of how the image was created had reached the form in which it has subsequently become popularly understood right up to the present day.

It is equally evident that the Veronica had by now long

supplanted the Acheropita of the Sancta Sanctorum chapel as the image which was invoked and carried in procession in times of trouble. When Constantinople fell to the Turks In 1453 yet another source of anxiety was added to that engendered by the wars raging across Europe, resulting in the Venetian Pope Paul II in 1470 carrying the Veronica barefoot in a solemn procession calling for divine protection, just as Pope Stephen II had carried the Acheropita, calling for help against the Lombards, seven centuries before. Paul also made the final and most lasting change to the timing of Holy Years, decreeing that they should be held once every quarter century, commencing with 1475.

Paul II did not live to see the 1475 Holy Year, and this was not one of the best attended, largely due to the serious dangers to travellers from the wars which were raging in France, Burgundy, Germany, Hungary, Poland, Spain and elsewhere. Nonetheless

*Fig. 4. The Veronica and Veronica exposition, Mirabilia*
Romae *woodcut of 1475*

the printing press was beginning to appear in the more major European cities, and one of its first and most popular products was a guidebook to Rome, the *Mirabilia Romae*, published in several languages,[10] which although it had only a few woodcut illustrations, included no less than two of the Veronica [fig. 4].

The first of these woodcuts, as reproduced on the previous page, gives us our closest glimpse of what an exposition of the Veronica actually looked like at this time. In this we see three tonsured churchmen, almost certainly canons of St Peter's, standing on a high platform, two with lighted torches, and one holding up the Veronica in its frame, while below stands a large crowd of pilgrims, several also carrying candles. A further edition of this guidebook produced by Stephen Planck[11] in 1489 provides a slightly more developed and updated version of this scene [fig. 5, opposite], notably showing the exposition platform or balcony now to be furnished with elaborate candle-holders.

Alongside these historically unique visual images, there has also survived from this same time important verbal descriptions from the diarist John Burchard. Burchard was master of ceremonies to the Genoan pope Innocent VIII (1484–92), and had a meticulous eye for detail. According to his entry for Easter 1486:

> The pope . . . was carried in procession to the place of public Benediction, along the furthest left aisle of the church, that is, the aisle of the Holy Face, which was then exposed in the place aforesaid. The pope gave a solemn public benediction, as the custom is, and then a plenary indulgence, which was pronounced by the cardinal-deacons de Savelli in Latin, and Colonna in the vulgar tongue.[12]

We find similar for the Easter of the year 1490:

> After the elevation of the Host by the pontiff, by command of His Holiness, the Veronica was shown to the people . . . The mass ended, the pope retaining his cloak, saw the Veronica, and went up in procession to the Place of Public Benediction and gave plenary indulgences, which were announced by the Lord Deacon-cardinals of St George in Latin, and of Colonna in the vulgar tongue.[13]

Clear from these and entries for other years is that the Veronica was now not being exhibited solely in Holy Years or times of special urgency, or thanksgiving, but annually. In line with its now firm association with Jesus's passion, Easter was the time chosen for these showings, rather than Epiphany, as had been begun by

*Fig. 5. Exposition of the Veronica, from the* Mirabilia Romae *edition of 1489*

Innocent III. We also learn something of the location where the showings were held, notably that these were within St Peter's and seemingly from some sort of platform or balcony either connected to, or in the immediate vicinity of the Veronica chapel. This same location seems to have been used for the pope's special indulgence blessing. Given the confined space, even within a basilica as large as the old St Peter's, it is scarcely surprising that there occurred crushings. Also evident is that, whereas Innocent III and his immediate successors had personally held the Veronica up to the people, this task was now delegated to others. The *Mirabilia Romae* wood-engravings seem to show it being secured by a strap around the neck of the canon holding it, presumably as a safety-measure in the event of him dropping it.

After Innocent VIII's death in 1492, there succeeded the notorious Spanish-born Borgia pope Alexander VI, father of ten children by no less than four mistresses. Yet, corrupt though Alexander undoubtedly was, even he, in a manner not uncommon among ecclesiastical villains, seems to have had a healthy respect for the Veronica. Thus when in 1494 Charles VIII of France marched into Rome *en route* to lay claim to the kingdom of Naples, the terrified Alexander took the Veronica with him as he fled along the passageway he had had specially built between the Vatican and the fortified Castel Sant'Angelo.

Similarly Alexander took a strong interest in the arrangements for the Holy Year of 1500, even if, as we learn from John Burchard, there occurred a somewhat amusing example of the confusion and discontinuity that could arise due to the long gaps between one Holy Year and the next.

As earlier mentioned, the St John Lateran Basilica had as its own 'made without hands' 'holy face', [pl. 30, above] a large mosaic that reputedly had wafted of its own accord through the basilica's furthest right-hand door, the one that was the exact equivalent of St Peter's Porta Guidonea. This door had therefore been designated a Holy Door, to be kept specially sealed and only opened in Holy Years.

Now as it happened, in St Peter's as part of the Veronica chapel there was what appeared to be a false door set against the inside of the basilica's entrance wall, very close to the Guidonea door. And somehow or other the idea seems to have developed during the fifteenth century that this, rather than the one in the Lateran, was the door that had to be specially opened up by the pope at the beginning of each centennial year. As Burchard related of the visit on Wednesday 18 December 1499 made by Alexander VI to the Veronica chapel to discuss the detailed arrangements for the commencement of the Holy Year:

> Then I [i.e. Burchard] took the opportunity to show his Holiness the place in the chapel of St Veronica which the canons of the basilica declare to be the so-called golden door which was wont to be opened by the sovereign pontiffs each hundredth year, an arrangement which I had frequently heard mentioned and insisted upon in ordinary conversation. His Holiness was of the opinion that it ought to be opened in the same way at the inauguration of the Jubilee, and he gave directions to have blocks of marble arranged and cut for the adorning of the said door to such height and width as the outline of the door indicated on the inside, giving orders that the walls in front and at the side of the said chapel should be entirely removed, that the people might pass through more freely.[14]

Unfortunately for Burchard's idea of what had been customary, when a master mason set about creating a doorway that the pope could easily break through for the opening ceremony:

> . . . it was discovered that there had never been any door at all in this place, but that the wall was solid and even, built into the other part of the wall on either side. There had only been an altar in that place which we thought was a doorway. But since the populace had this idea, I was unwilling to disturb them.[15]

In the event, this element of the 1500 Holy Year ceremony, a piece of play-acting in which the pope knocked through a specially thin layer of walling to open up the door for all the pilgrims, proved such a success that it thereafter became the opening highlight of all subsequent Holy Years. Pope Paul VI performed exactly the same ceremony in the most recent one of 1975.

Nor did this cause any waning of interest in the Veronica. As *the* guidebook of the time, the *Mirabilia Romae* promised enormous indulgences for those attending a showing of the

Veronica: three thousand years if they were Romans, six thousand years if they were from other parts of Italy, and twelve thousand years if they had come from further afield, with remissions in three kinds for all sinners. In France there flourished a special confraternity of the Veronica which had among its members Anne of Brittany, beloved wife of King Louis XII of France. At Anne's death In 1514 the brothers of this confraternity conducted a special burial ceremony for her heart in her home town of Nantes, carrying torches 'decorated by a Veronica and the face of Christ . . .'[16] The Veronica theme continued to be a favourite one among great artists, among these the German Albrecht Dürer, and the Florentine mannerist Jacopo Pontormo, who painted St Veronica with her cloth in one of the lunettes in the Papal Chapel at Santa Maria Novella, Florence.[17]

But when in 1506 Pope Julius II laid at the base of the present Veronica pier the first foundation stone of the enormous undertaking of building a new St Peter's, it was inevitable that the financial costs were going to be huge. Given the already rife corruption of the time, it was equally inevitable that the indulgences system [fig. 6] would be stretched to absurdity to try to meet these costs, and that it would not be long before someone, somewhere, would begin to question the whole charade. As is now well-known, that history-changing moment came on All Saints' Day 1517 when the German monk Martin Luther nailed up his ninety-five theses on the door of the castle church at Wittenburg, thus setting in train the whole Protestant revolution. Now everything popish lay in danger, particularly the indulgences system, and therefore, not least because of its close association with it, even the Veronica itself.

By one of those ironies of history the pope in whose time this danger reached its greatest height was Clement VII, recognized as the legitimate holder of that name by contrast to the notorious Robert of Geneva of a century and a half before. Clement made the not uncommon mistake of arousing the enmity of the Colonna family, who had the backing of the Holy Roman Emperor Charles V, and on 6 May 1527 he faced a full-blooded attack on Rome by mixed-nationality troops of Charles V, many of them Lutherans schooled to a hatred of the iniquity into which they believed Rome to have fallen.[18]

When the attack came, Clement VII and his court managed temporarily to hold out in the Castel Sant'Angelo, but for most

*Fig. 6. The sale of indulgences, from an early sixteenth-century engraving*

Romans unable to reach this before its portcullis slammed down there were unspeakable iniquities. Many thousands were killed, women raped, and churches and houses looted and ransacked [fig. 7]. The papal Swiss Guard was wiped out to a man. Patients of Innocent III's Santo Spirito Hospital, all too vulnerable because of the hospital's close proximity to Castel Sant'Angelo, were thrown into the Tiber. Nuns were reportedly offered for sale on the streets. In St Peter's the tomb of Julius II was ripped open and desecrated. And somewhere in all this confusion – and this question is one most central to this book – the Veronica may or may not have been seized and destroyed.

One of the main reasons for believing the former consists of the explicit testimony of two immediately contemporary letters, both highly emotionally charged, from the traumatic scenes so recently witnessed, written on 14 and 21 May, respectively only a week and a fortnight after the main sack according to the first of these sent by one Messer Urbano to the Duchess of Urbino:

The holy relics have been scattered. The Veronica

73

*Fig. 7. The Sack of Rome, May 1527. Troops of the emperor make mockery of a papal procession. From a sixteenth-century engraving*

was stolen. It was passed from hand to hand in all the taverns of Rome without a word of protest. A German stuck onto a pike the lance that pierced Jesus' side, and ran mockingly [with this] through the Borgo.[19]

According to the second, sent by Cardinal Salviati to Baldassare Castiglione, the papal envoy in Madrid:

Burned is the great chapel of St Peter and of Sixtus: burned is the Holy Face of St Veronica . . . the heads of the Apostles are stolen . . . the Sacrament thrown into the mud . . . reliquaries trampled under foot . . . I shudder to contemplate this for Christians are doing what even the Turks never did.[20]

Given the earlier remarked information that there does not appear to be any image on the cloth preserved as the Veronica

74

at the present day, several notable scholars have accepted these reports that the Veronica really was stolen and destroyed at this time. Among those who have taken this view has been the German art scholar Monsignor Joseph Wilpert,[21] the English Benedictine scholar Fr Maurus Green,[22] and others.

But historical evidence is rarely totally straightforward, and also to be taken into account is other contemporary evidence which suggests that both 'Messer Urbano' and Cardinal Salviati may have relied too much on emotional hearsay, and that the Veronica survived unscathed. Thus according to a German booklet written by one of the Lutheran lansquenet soldiers who took part in the sack, and published in the same year:

> They looked for papal bulls, letters and accounts in the monasteries and convents so as to burn them and tear them. Their shreds replaced straw in houses and stables for the donkeys and horses. In all the churches – St Peter's, St Paul's, S Lorenzo's, and even the little ones, chalices, chausables [sic], monstrances and ornaments were taken; *not finding the Veronica* [italics mine], the looters took other relics.[23]

Similarly, according to the Roman citizen Marcello Alberini, who was another direct witness of the sack, and who later in life wrote an account of this in his *I Ricordi*:

> The Veronica, the head of St Andrew at St Peter's, those of the apostles Peter and Paul at St John Lateran, and the miraculous effigy of the Saviour in the Sancta Sanctorum . . . could not have been desecrated by those infamous hands.[24]

Furthermore there are several references to expositions of the Veronica in the years immediately following. A showing in the Holy Week of 1533 is mentioned in the Journal of Biagio de Cesena.[25] Three years later, on the Easter Sunday of 1536, both the Veronica and the Holy Lance were recorded to have been shown when Charles V, whose men had so abused Clement VII, was welcomed to Rome by Clement's successor Paul III.[26] It is similarly recorded to have been shown for six days during the Holy Year of 1550.[27] Since on all these occasions there would inevitably have been individuals who had seen it pre-1527, it is difficult to believe that no one would have remarked on any significant change of appearance of what had been shown previously.

We also learn that in 1575 Rome was once again able to stage a Holy Year with all the old fervour, including expositions of the Veronica. A superb contemporary engraving [pl. 10] preserved in the Print Room of the British Museum shows a huge crowd – independently estimated at 300,000 – in St Peter's Square for the ceremony of the opening of the Holy Door, with Michelangelo's not yet completed dome beginning to rise triumphantly over the old basilica. It also seems that the Veronica was again being shown at times other than Holy Years, for the French essayist Michel de Montaigne reported of a showing witnessed by him on Holy Thursday 1580:

> No relic has such veneration paid to it. The people throw themselves on their faces on the ground, most of them with tears in their eyes and with lamentations and cries of compassion.[28]

Montaigne went on to describe the holding of such expositions several times a day:

> . . . with such an infinite concourse of people that to a great distance from the church, at every point from which the eye could catch a glimpse of the platform from which the relics [the Veronica and the Holy Lance] were shown, there was nothing but a dense crowd of men and women.

But if we might feel reassured that the Veronica genuinely did survive the sack of 1527, the image of Michelangelo's half-completed dome in the British Museum engraving of 1575 alerts us to another impending event with a quite different element of danger for the Veronica. This was the planned demolition of the still standing part of old St Peter's – that which included the old Veronica shrine – in order to make way for the rest of the new construction. Although we might not expect this to offer any hazard to the Veronica, some idea of how little of antiquity was respected by those who worked on the new St Peter's can be gained from an event in 1588. Needing a water container, they simply opened up the tomb of Pope Urban VI, emptied out his bones and used his sarcophagus as a water tank for the next quarter century.

Michelangelo's dome was finally completed in 1593, and during the Holy Year of 1600 what we may presume to be still the original Veronica was yet again shown in the traditional way in the old basilica. But in 1606 the Veronica was removed from its old shrine in order for the latter to be broken up, along with many other of the old St Peter's monuments. And according to one present-day scholar, Professor Heinrich Pfeiffer of Rome's Gregorian University,[29] at this point there may have occurred a surreptitious switch or theft of the original Veronica while it lay temporarily in the Vatican archives awaiting transfer to the new basilica.

Supporting Pfeiffer's opinion is a chronicle written about 1640 by the Capuchin monk Donato da Bomba[30] which describes 'the holy face' (which may or may not refer to the Veronica), being stolen by one Pancrazio Petrucci in 1608. In 1618 this was apparently sold by Pancrazio Petrucci's wife to a Dr Antonio de Fabritijs, who then gave it to the Capuchin order. And at around this same time a Veronica-type image of Jesus began to be recorded at the church of Manoppello, near Pescara. Extant to this day, and readily accessible, it is a striking image of Jesus's face with open eyes, painted on cloth with a very transparent paint [pl. 11, left]. Pfeiffer believes that this could be the original Veronica.

Certainly one most curious and undeniable fact is that despite Pope Urban VIII's elaborate efforts during the 1630s to make a new, permanent home in the pier of St Peter's for what was supposed to be still the original Veronica, the relic sank into a very strange obscurity thereafter. Effectively the window that had opened on it during the pontificate of Innocent III now slammed shut. For reasons that are by no means clear, Pope Urban VIII even banned the making of any further artistic direct copies.

Paradoxically, almost from the very time that the Veronica lapsed in this way the shroud, which in 1453 had been acquired by the Savoy family, and from 1578 had arrived at its now permanent home in Turin, began to attract much of the public attention that the Veronica lost. From the late sixteenth and early seventeenth centuries, during which there appears not a single engraving of a Veronica exposition, there begin to appear many showing the shroud being exhibited to huge crowds from a balcony of the Savoy family's Royal Palace [pl. 11, above].

77

Accordingly this makes all the more mysterious the nature of the cloth, purported to be the original Veronica, that still lies somewhere within or in the vicinity of the Veronica pier of St Peter's. Is it really still the same cloth that pilgrims were trampling each other to see before 1527? Could Heinrich Pfeiffer be right that the original was stolen in the early 1600s? While a direct examination of the present-day cloth, or even the sight of a photograph of it, remain beyond reach, all we can do is look to whatever other visual and verbally descriptive information may be available to us. In this regard, nothing at first sight looks more encouraging than the claim of an English artist to have actually both viewed and sketched the Veronica sometime during the mid-nineteenth century.

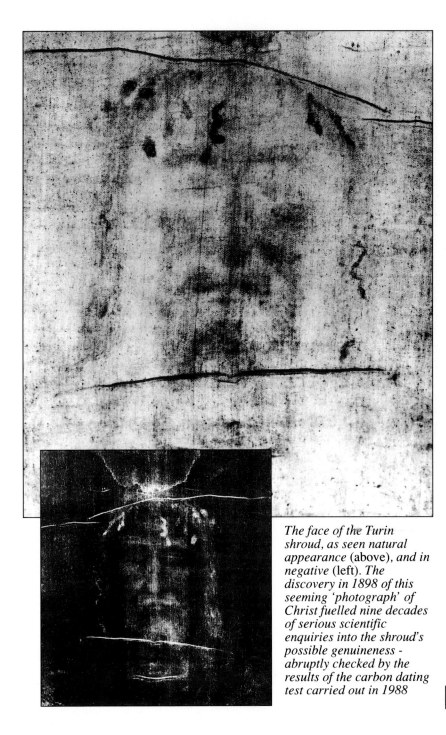

*The face of the Turin shroud, as seen natural appearance* (above), *and in negative* (left). *The discovery in 1898 of this seeming 'photograph' of Christ fuelled nine decades of serious scientific enquiries into the shroud's possible genuineness - abruptly checked by the results of the carbon dating test carried out in 1988*

*(Right): The complete, fourteen-foot-long shroud, natural appearance. Imprints and bloodstains seemingly from the naked body of a crucified man can be seen framed by scorches and patches from a fire historically recorded in 1532; (below top): Shroud sample as allotted to the Arizona radio carbon dating laboratory. This and its companion pieces handed over to the Oxford and Zurich laboratories were reduced to graphite during the carbon dating process; (below bottom): Dr Robert Hedges of the Oxford radio carbon dating laboratory with some of the equipment used for the work on the shroud*

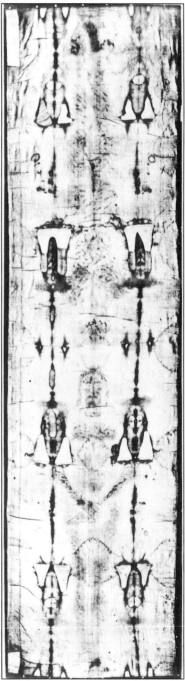

(Above): *Pilgrim's souvenir badge of an exposition of the shroud at Lirey,* circa *1350. The badge, created in lead, and most likely worn on a hat (see pl.9 above), was found during the last century in the mud of the Seine near the Pont-au-Change, Paris. The only surviving example of its kind, it is today displayed in the Musée de Cluny, Paris;* (left): *Anti-pope Clement VII, the former Robert of Geneva, who upheld the shroud expositions despite the Bishop of Troyes' allegations. Sculpture, Musée du Petit Palais, Avignon*

(Above): *Typical 'gingerbread man' type artist's copy of the shroud, sixteenth/seventeeth century, from the Church of Notre-Dame, Chambéry, illustrating the minimal understanding of the shroud's subtle 'negative' properties, even by competent artists of the Renaissance and after; (below): Fifteenth-century medical illustration of wounds, showing how unconvincingly these were depicted, even more than a century after the time of the hypothetical 'forgery' of the Turin shroud. From the collection of the Wellcome Institute for the History of Medicine, London*

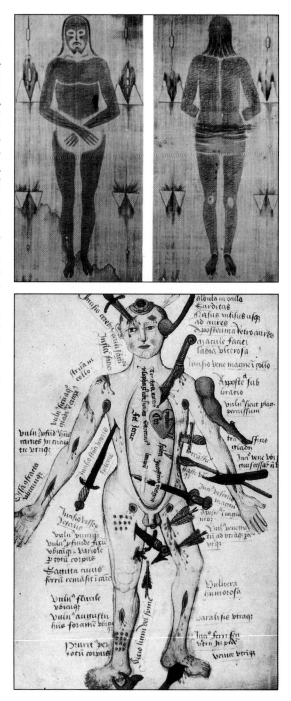

(Above): *The larger than life-size statue of St Veronica, by the seventeenth-century sculptor Francesco Mochi, which stands at the foot of the Veronica pier of present-day St Peter's;* (left): *Fourteenth/fifteenth-century lead souvenir badge commemorating a pilgrimage to Rome to view an exposition of the Veronica. Like the Lirey example (pl.3,* above)*, this was found during the last century in the mud of the Seine, and is today displayed in the Musée de Cluny, Paris*

*Pen and wash sketch of the interior of old St Peter's,
early seventeenth-century, shortly before the
building and its shrines were demolished to make
way for the present-day edifice. The shrine of the
Veronica can be seen in the furthest right-hand
corner, accompanied by the inscription* vultus sancti

à Paulo V. Pont. Max. noui gratia Templi
tectorum artificiosa coronatione.

(holy face). In actuality the shrine was inside a
special chapel built by Pope John VII (705-7), but
the walls of this are either deliberately not indicated
in this sketch, or had already been removed at the
time it was made

(Above): *The 'holy face' of Laon. In the mid-thirteenth-century, French-born papal chaplain Jacques Pantaléon de Troyes (later Pope Urban IV) sent this painting to his abbess sister Sibylle, specifically as a copy of the Veronica of Rome. In reality, it is a twelfth-century Byzantine icon depicting a different 'holy face' known to have been preserved in Constantinople between AD 944 and 1204. The icon, measuring 44 x 40 cm, is today preserved in the Cathedral of Laon;* (right): *Pope Innocent III from a contemporary mosaic. Innocent broke with tradition by exhibiting the Veronica publicly in 1207 for the purpose of raising funds for the Santo Spirito hospital which he had founded*

*Chapter Seven*

# A DECEPTIVE VICTORIAN ARTIST

*Of all these things . . . before I had done, I had made
such copies as I wanted*

Artist Thomas Heaphy the Younger, 1861

With no available photograph of
the present-day Veronica, it ought to be a most welcome discovery that there was one Victorian artist who, according to his own
account, broke through all ecclesiastical barriers and made a
colour sketch directly from the Veronica. Since nineteenth-
century artists' copies of subsequently destroyed ancient Egyptian
monuments can often be most helpful to present-day Egyptologists,
a nineteenth-century professional copy of the Veronica should be
similarly valuable to our own study.

The artist-copyist in question was Thomas Heaphy the Younger
[pl. 12, above], who was born into an artistic London family in
1813 and became a professional painter whose work ranged from
fashionable romantic themes to portraits of the famous among the
British gentry.[1] A fellow of the Royal Society of British Artists,
and a member of the highly respected English Royal Academy,
Heaphy had a string of important contacts, from the celebrated
art critic John Ruskin to the Archbishop of Canterbury.[2] Unusual
therefore though it might seem for a Protestant Englishman to
have managed to penetrate into the most jealously guarded of
Catholic sacred precincts, Heaphy certainly had both the charm
and a potentially helpful circle of friends.

According to his own account, Heaphy had developed a
fascination for the Veronica-type 'holy face' from almost as long
as he could remember:

79

When quite a child I had possessed myself of an old copy of an antique portrait of our Lord, on which, with perhaps childish partiality and enthusiasm, I set an extraordinary value. It was represented as depicted on the folds of a cloth, which was supposed to be suspended to the top corners of the picture, and an inscription below described it as being the true effigy of Our Lord, miraculously imprinted on the cloth as he lay in the sepulchre . . . As a work of art it was such as the criticism of the schools would reject, but never have I elsewhere met with any picture in which was so perfectly represented the calm mystery of death so thinly veiling the divine life behind.[3]

Heaphy's father, Thomas Heaphy the Elder, had amassed a substantial fortune by painting portraits of the Duke of Wellington's officers during the Peninsular War against Napoleon. He subsequently wisely invested this money in property developments in the St John's Wood area of London. And when in 1831 he invited his now seventeen year-old son to accompany him on an extended sketching trip to Italy, the young Thomas was more than enthusiastic, acknowledging:

> . . . the prospect of seeing the original of my picture, which I learnt from some writing at the back, existed in the sacristy of St Peter's, formed no small part of my anticipations.[4]

But consistent with our remarks that the Veronica, if it still existed, had already at that time been shut away from human gaze, the seventeen-year-old Heaphy's anticipations soon suffered a set-back:

> Arrived at Rome, my first visit was to St Peter's. I will not stay to describe my impressions on entering. I looked round for my picture, but it was not there; numberless others were there certainly, capital pictures most of them, many magnificent, but the likenesses, in all of them, to my thinking, were but lifeless copies of mine. Again and again did I search through every chapel and every corner; it was not to be found. I

80

appealed to an official, but he knew nothing of it. While arguing with him that he must be mistaken, an ecclesiastic in violet (I presume he was a bishop) mildly asked me what I wanted. Having explained myself, he said that it would be impossible to comply with my request to see the picture; it was there certainly, but kept with other sacred relics in the sacristy, over the large statue of St Veronica, on whose handkerchief the miraculous picture was imprinted; but its sanctity was such that no one was allowed to inspect it, excepting the Holy Father and two of the sacred conclave, and they only on one day of the year (Palm Sunday) after absolution and communion. In my ignorance I tried the effect of a dollar on the bishop, but, smiling, he put my hand aside, saying, 'My dear boy, I am sorry, but I can do nothing for you.'[5]

But on taking up a full artistic career the young Heaphy refused to be dampened in his enthusiasm for the 'holy face', merely widening his interest to encompass the whole mystery of the origins of the traditional likeness of Christ that has come down to us in art. He made several journeys to Italy, including one to paint an altar-piece that had been commissioned for a Protestant church in Malta, and he seems to have used these excursions to pursue his 'holy face' researches, although not without encountering serious obstacles even in the case of other images less sacred than the Veronica. In his own words:

The difficulties in the way of obtaining permission to sketch from a few even of the most inaccessible objects seemed absolutely insurmountable. Some of the mosaics in the churches seemed to be regarded with peculiar jealousy. Permission to draw in the catacombs could only be obtained from the cardinal vicar; but it was of no use applying, it had been granted on one occasion, but never would be again. Certain ancient pictures in the churches were not only too sacred to be copied, but might not even be looked at: others might certainly be seen on one day of the year, but then only for a very short time. To certain officials in the Vatican the bare suggestion of making a sketch from any of the

81

contents of the cases was enough to make them stand aghast at my audacity; whilst the very existence of some things that I knew to be there was strenuously and vociferously denied.[6]

Despite such difficulties, in 1861 Heaphy wrote a series of articles, 'An Examination into the Antiquity of the Likeness of Our Blessed Lord', in which he set out all that he had learned in the course of his researches. The articles were published in the prestigious *Art-Journal*, and in the very first of these Heaphy outrightly claimed to have gained access to all the objects of his quest, including the Veronica. In his own words:

> . . . of all these things, even of the last, before I had done I had made such copies as I wanted.[7]

With particular regard to the Veronica, although Heaphy was able only to publish an uncoloured woodcut of this[8] in the *Art-Journal*, he let it be known that he had made a full-colour sketch from the original. After his sudden death in 1873 this was used for one of twelve hand-coloured engravings included in a special posthumous book, *The Likeness of Christ*, based largely on what he had written for the *Art-Journal*. As he described the Veronica in this:

> In the sacristy of St Peter's, over the gigantic statue of St Veronica, is a picture accounted so holy that no layman's eyes may look upon it – and I am informed, no church-man's, save the pope's and his necessary attendants; and even the Holy Father himself only inspects it on one day of the year, and immediately after confession and communion . . . Like most others of the same class, it is much obscured, and, in many parts, nearly obliterated by the decay of the cloth on which it is executed. But the very rags and stains, by dimming its execution, and taking away the appearance of the hand of man, seem to add to its singular impressiveness. The wet, matted hair, the tears, the blood-drops from the crown of thorns, so expressive of the stern reality of death, while the calm, nearly closed eyes, the gently parted lips, speak not of corruption, but of the spirit at that moment in Paradise,

and of the shortly to be accomplished Resurrection. So replete is this image with concentrated thought and feeling that it almost forces on us the conviction that unless he that produced it was in the fullest sense of the term inspired, he saw that which he depicted. Like others of the greatest triumphs of art, this effort has been accomplished with the meanest of instruments; a piece of cloth, without anything in the shape of preparation, the pigment transparent and, apparently, nothing more than a mere stain, and all aid from colour entirely discarded. Nevertheless this dimly figured head, on a tattered rag – for its inspiration, its conception and its power of execution – is certainly unsurpassed, perhaps hardly equalled, in the whole range of art.[9]

The original of Heaphy's accompanying Veronica sketch [col. pl. II, right] can be examined as part of a complete album of his copies of early likenesses preserved in the Print Room of the British Museum.[10] And at face value it is a most striking and impressive piece of work, executed on a carefully frayed and tattered piece of cloth in apparent exact imitation of the original. There are holes and stains deliberately made in places as if in replication of wear and other damage. The face with half-closed eyes has been very lightly conveyed in a convincing-looking transparent brown monochrome. If it could be accepted as what it purports to be, a like-for-like facsimile of the true Veronica, then it would rank among the most valuable visual images in this entire study.

What first arouses a certain suspicion is Heaphy's unmistakable reticence in disclosing anything of the exact circumstances, or even the year in which he managed to gain such privileged access to the Veronica. Also we may recall that in 1854 the Abbé Barbier de Montault reported seeing 'only a dark surface, giving no semblance of a human face'[11] when he was shown the Veronica at the time of the declaration of the Immaculate Conception. We may also remember that Barbier de Montault's description was reinforced by the German scholar Wilpert's examination in 1907. Yet Heaphy clearly both described and sketched explicit facial features on the Veronica that he claimed to have seen.

Despite these problems there has to remain the possibility that Heaphy might genuinely have gained some very special access, and that perhaps his artistic eye was able to detect features that eluded others. One individual who conceivably could have granted such access was Gregory XVI, pope when Heaphy and his father made their 1831 trip to Rome. A despotic but cultured man who founded the Vatican's Egyptian and Etruscan museums, Gregory was a generous patron of artists. He undoubtedly had some interest in the Veronica, because the most recent known frame in which it has been enclosed has been reliably reported to bear his coat of arms.[12]

A somewhat stronger possibility, at least on the basis of Heaphy's own writings, is that the necessary permission might have come from Cardinal Leonardo Antonelli, the right-hand man of Pope Pius IX, whose long pontificate stretched from 1846 to beyond Heaphy's lifetime. Heaphy specifically recorded gaining a crucial interview with this Antonelli ('He was despotic in Rome; he could do anything') after hand-delivering a last-resort plea to him at the Vatican Palace. Told by an official to call back in three days, to Heaphy's surprise Antonelli reportedly not only gave him an audience on this occasion, but expressed an interest in Heaphy's field of study. In Heaphy's own words:

> Emboldened by the reception these requests had met with, I ventured upon the most daring of all: 'Would His Eminence obtain for me permission for the penetralia of the Vatican?' This seemed almost too much for His Eminence but I should certainly hear from him in three days . . . I retired delighted. Nor was I disappointed; on the second day came the much-coveted permission (that for the Vatican included), signed by the respective officials . . . .[13]

All this might be just sufficient to sustain some credibility in Heaphy were it not for the fact that besides the Veronica he made copies of certain other 'holy faces' that are now at least a little more accessible, at least via photography, than they were in his own time.

One of these is the already familiar Sancta Sanctorum 'Acheropita' that we first came across when this was described back in the thirteenth century by our old friend Gerald of Wales. As in the case of the Veronica, Heaphy included an uncoloured woodcut of this[14] in his *Art-Journal* article, backed up by a coloured sketch [pl. 12, below left] in his master album. And just like Gerald of Wales, he reported it attributed to the hand of St Luke.

But one curiosity is that both in the *Art-Journal* and in his album notes Heaphy described this image as 'now preserved in the Bibliotheca [i.e. the library] of the Vatican.' This is somewhat puzzling because, from the very first record of this image in AD 754, through to Gerald of Wales's time, and right up to the present day, there is no known reported occurrence of this image being kept anywhere other than in the Sancta Sanctorum Chapel of the old papal palace of the Lateran. And this latter is easily a brisk half-hour's walk from the present-day Vatican Palace.

Furthermore, even if we allow for some possible obscurely recorded temporary removal of the image to the Vatican Library at the time of Heaphy's visit to Rome, a more serious problem arises from the fact that Heaphy's sketch exhibits several major inaccuracies when compared with a modern photograph of the original [pl. 12, below right and col. pl. III]. For instance, with regard to the overall outlines Heaphy indicated the image's gold nimbus cover as terminating at the base in two points, whereas in reality the base is but a simple straight line. His placing of the jewels and relief on this nimbus is by no means precise.

And particularly disturbing is his rendition of the face as realistically proportioned, with expressive eyes, delicately-shaped nose and lips, and naturalistic light and shade. For quite obvious from photographs of the original is that in reality this is a particularly crude piece of painting, the shape of the face nearly circular, the eyes over-large and staring, the nose extending in a most unnatural straight line to a seemingly non-existent upper lip, and the whole palpably lacking in any naturalistic light and shade. Heaphy's copy also omits a historically interesting and early-attested damage mark below the left-hand eye. Accordingly at best it looks as if Heaphy injected rather too much of his own artistic fancy. At worst the possibility is raised that he never even saw the original, but worked from someone else's highly inaccurate copy.

And if this gives rise to a certain concern about the accuracy of Heaphy's Veronica copy, this concern deepens when we study two other 'holy face' images of which he made apparent facsimiles on tattered pieces of cloth every bit as detailed as that of the Veronica.

The first of these [pl. 13, left] consists of a sketch pasted into his album against which has been scrawled:

> Picture in S. Silvestro, Rome, rigidly excluded from the
> public. Not to be published.

This immediately identifies the sketch as at least purporting to
be from the same 'holy face' known to have been owned by the
community of Poor Clares founded at Palestrina in the thirteenth
century by Margherita Colonna. We know that this community
was moved to Rome's church of S. Silvestro in Capite, and that
its 'holy face' was kept, as correctly reported by Heaphy, 'rigidly
excluded from the public' until 1870, when it was transferred to
the Matilda chapel, the pope's private chapel, within the Vatican.

But although this 'holy face' thus remains largely inaccessible,
nonetheless there does exist a definitive modern photograph made
by Dante Vacchi *circa* 1971 [col. pl. IVc]. And when this is compared with Heaphy's sketch, confidence in Heaphy hardly begins
to be restored. The Heaphy sketch is of another impressionistic
face on a tattered piece of cloth, with surrounding the top half
of the head the vague indication of a halo in the form of the
Christian Chi-Rho monogram. The photograph, on the other
hand, shows a face surrounded by a metallic cover that sharply
frames the outlines of the hair and beard, and thus completely
conceals possible background details such as the Chi-Rho monogram. So was Heaphy privileged not only to see this closely
guarded 'holy face', but even to see it removed from its normal
frame? Unfortunately, because this particular 'holy face' has
never been photographed with its cover entirely removed, we
have to at least allow him this possibility.

However it is in respect of the second highly detailed cloth sketch
by Heaphy, one purporting to represent yet another otherwise
inaccessible 'holy face', that any remaining shreds of Heaphy's
credibility finally evaporate. Probably since the late fourteenth
century there has been kept at the church of St Bartholomew of
the Armenians in Genoa, northern Italy, an elaborately framed
'holy face' icon claimed to be a cloth portrait which Jesus
sent from Jerusalem to a King Abgar of Edessa back in the
first century AD. This is generally thought to have been given
to the Genoese doge Leonardo Montaldo by the Byzantine
emperor John V Palaeologus, and Montaldo, when he died in 1384,
bequeathed it to the church in his will.

Unquestionably access to this 'holy face' has always been
difficult. In his first *Art-Journal* article Heaphy described how,

on arriving in Genoa in 1831 during his visit with his father, he was told that access was:

> impossible, excepting on one day of the year, and then only after confession, and other religious observances impossible to a Protestant.[15]

Writing in 1904 the erudite German scholar Ernst von Dobschütz remarked that it is kept:

> in a shrine which cannot be opened except with eight keys in possession of eight different magistrates and noble families.[16]

Nonetheless Heaphy produced no less than two purported copies of this. The first, reproduced both as a wood-engraving in the *Art-Journal*[17] and as a surprisingly rough sketch in his album, shows the face encased in a clearly Byzantine-looking frame [pl. 14, right]. According to Heaphy's accompanying handwritten note in his album:

> This picture is now in the sacristy of the church of St Bartolomeo in Genoa . . . being accounted miraculous, it is excluded from public gaze and great difficulty was experienced in obtaining access to it.

But then onto the next page of his album[18] Heaphy pasted his second copy [pl. 15, left], a particularly elaborate and detailed cloth 'facsimile' entitled in his own handwriting:

> Larger copy of the foregoing picture in the Church of San Bartolomeo at Genoa *without the frame in position* [italics mine].

It is quite obvious that by contrast to the first drawing this one has been created with all the apparent loving attention to the replication of wear-holes and other damage that we earlier noted of the Veronica copy. There can be seen a long, irregular shaped 'fray' hole cut into the cloth above the crown of the head, and a smaller, triangular-shaped one to the right-hand side of the head. The face, hair and beard have been vanishingly conveyed in a semitransparent burnt umber monochrome, and impressive-looking 'stains' added in raw sienna. Vestiges of two bars of the cross of a Chi-Rho monogram are vaguely discernible in the top left-hand corner. Along with all else this sketch and the just-quoted words in his own handwriting, effectively constitute a blatant statement by Heaphy that he indeed examined and copied the Genoa 'holy face' with its Byzantine frame removed, just as we have conceded he *might* have done in the case of the S. Silvestro image.

But in truth, did he? Unfortunately for Heaphy, the Genoa 'holy face' is unusual insofar as it is by far the best documented of all of this genre, having been definitively photographed and studied in recent years, complete with the fullest removal of the Byzantine frame. It is one I was even privileged to examine for myself when it was made a surprise exhibit at an iconographic conference held in Bologna in May 1989.

As straight comparison with the original [pl. 14, above, and col. pl. IVd] immediately reveals, even Heaphy's sketch with the frame in position exhibits disquieting anomalies. Not least he drew the base outlines of the hair and beard, arguably the most fundamental elements of the whole composition, pointing to the right instead of, as in actuality, to the left. Such an error, inconceivable if Heaphy had genuinely been copying from the original, strongly suggests his true source was some rather poor local engraving whose creator had not even bothered to make the necessary mirror-reverse correction to his image.

But even more telling are the results of a full-scale specialist examination of the icon headed by the well-respected Italian art specialist Colette Dufour Bozzo in 1969.[19] In this year Ms Bozzo and a few accompanying specialists were allowed to completely remove the several pieces comprising the Byzantine silver-gilt frame, and to photograph and document in entirety all that lay beneath. Among various surprises there came to light a piece of Byzantine embroidery decorated with the motif of a horse, used as a backing to the frame. It was also found that the icon had been painted partly on a piece of cloth that had been pasted onto some two-thirds of the wood-panel backing.

But although the icon was stripped down to its barest essentials, and even X-rayed, it revealed nothing remotely resembling the holed and stained piece of cloth sketched by Heaphy [pl. 15, above]. In the light of this, Heaphy's so elaborate 'copies', inevitably including his one of the Veronica, can only be construed as pieces of pure fiction. It would seem that in reality Heaphy never ever gained the privileged access he claimed. For reasons we can only guess at, he seems merely to have liked to pretend that he had.

In fact there was at least one percipient individual who suspected as much even in Heaphy's own lifetime. In the wake of Heaphy's *Art-Journal* articles an anonymous contributor to the scholarly *Quarterly Review* remarked of Heaphy's wood-engraving of the Genoa icon within its frame:

> as this is taken from a copy sold in Genoa, we cannot be certain that it truly represents the original.[20]

Clearly struck on a raw nerve, Heaphy hit back with a vigorous response in the journal *Athenaeum*:

> Italy contains many portraits of Our Lord of undoubted antiquity but . . . unfortunately for the student they are generally accounted miraculous, on which account they are rigidly excluded from the public gaze. In three instances, more especially, it is supposed to be impossible for the layman to obtain access to the pictures. In the work I published, however, I gave copies of these portraits without stating the means by which I had been enabled to do so. I had obvious reasons for this reticence, but it is certainly a notable example of the *argumentum per saltum* for the Quarterly Reviewer to assume that because the pictures are not accessible to the public, I therefore got my illustrations from prints sold in the streets.[21]

In support of his claim that he had directly studied the Genoa image Heaphy volunteered, 'I shall be happy to show my two transcripts from that picture to anyone who may wish to see them.' Of course he could do this with confidence, because he knew that there was no one in England with the necessary inside knowledge to prove these to be false. And to show that he genuinely had gained access to at least some other 'holy faces' he imparted that he had examined the one of S. Prassede (a crude sketch purported to have been made by St Peter) in the company of 'amongst others, Mr Statham of

60 Wimpole Street, and the late Mr Gattley the sculptor, both of whom were permitted to take the picture in their hands.'

Now quite possibly Heaphy genuinely did examine this so-called S. Prassede image. It is a totally uninspiring work that has never been in the same genre or league as the others.[22] But there can be no doubt that in the case of the key 'holy faces' on cloth, the Veronica and those of Genoa and S. Silvestro, Heaphy lied both in word and in paintbrush.

It speaks volumes for the secrecy still surrounding the 'holy faces' that his lie could and did last for more than a hundred years. In 1881, after some sharp-witted bargaining, Heaphy's widow Eliza sold the album of his sketches to the British Museum Print Room for the then not inconsiderable sum of £130. There still survives the correspondence of her negotiations,[23] in which she name-dropped shamelessly: 'PS The Archbishop of Canterbury takes a great interest in the proposal to place them [the sketches] in the BM.' In 1904 the art critic Lionel Cust reproduced Heaphy's Genoa sketch in the prestigious *Burlington Magazine*, remarking in ignorance: 'Heaphy's drawing . . . is of special interest, as it shows the portrait free from the ornamental frame super-imposed.'[24] The following year Heaphy's friend Sir Wyke Bayliss, then President of the Royal Society of British Artists, lavished praise on Heaphy's 'exquisite facsimile drawings' and reproduced several in his popular book, *Rex Regum*.[25] Even as recently as 1982 the Genoa and S. Silvestro sketches were uncritically reproduced by the present-day University of Washington art expert Professor Joanne Snow-Smith as part of her specialist monograph on the *Salvator Mundi* of Leonardo da Vinci.[26]

For us there can be little satisfaction that a cheat, albeit one from over a century ago, has at last been exposed. Rather, a note of sadness that one who might have been a valuable guide to our quest has proved instead a time-wasting deceiver.

Nonetheless this set-back should in no way blunt our quest. For as we noted in our earlier chapters on the Veronica's history, there were many artists who made apparent copies of the Veronica from before the still so controversial time when it may or may not have been destroyed in the Sack of Rome of 1527. Albeit rare, there also occur certain literary descriptions from this same pre-1527 time. So it is to these that we will now turn.

## Chapter Eight

# GETTING PRE-1527 COPIES TO SPEAK . . .

*It made me to think of the Holy Veronica of Rome
. . . Of the brownness and blackness, the ruefulness and
leanness of this image . . . how might this image be so
discolouring and so far from fair?*

Julian of Norwich *circa* 1373

Despite there being many copies of the Veronica that have survived from before 1527, unquestionably many others have been lost to us as a result of the vicissitudes of history.

For instance, in England alone thousands of portable works of art and illuminated manuscripts, inevitably including Veronica copies, were destroyed at the time of the dissolution of the monasteries. More disappeared in 1547, when English curates were ordered to take down from their churches all images which attracted pilgrims or offerings. Yet more would have been swept away as Lutheran-inspired iconoclasm spread over most of northern Europe. And even in the Catholic south, Veronica copies were specifically the target of a destruction order given by Pope Urban VIII in 1629.[1]

Yet a substantial number escaped, only to present us with a quite different problem, their variations in appearance. Often they differ so substantially one from the other that it is quite evident that while some of the artists may have been trying to create true copies, albeit often at second hand, others must blithely have used their imaginations. The difficult question raised is: which ones are which?

Indeed, this problem surfaces from the very first historically known appearance of Veronica copies in western Europe, an appearance that followed not long after Pope Innocent III's pioneering introduction of the Santo Spirito Veronica procession in 1207. As earlier remarked, in general very few copies seem to have been made during the rest of the thirteenth century, the curiosity being those that have come down to us, insofar as they can be adjudged copies at all, derive predominantly from England.

The two best-known of these are the work of Matthew Paris, a monk of St Albans who was prolific during the mid-thirteenth century both as a chronicler and as a gifted illustrator. The first [pl. 16, above]consists of a drawing inserted as a later addition into a psalter that is now in the British Library.[2] Dating from about 1240, this is thought to be the earliest known representation of the Veronica in Western art.[3] The second [pl. 16, below], from perhaps a decade later, forms a pasted-in insert[4] into the *Chronica Majora*, a lively world-history which Paris both co-authored and illustrated, and which is preserved today in the library of Corpus Christi College, Cambridge. The special importance of both drawings seems indicated by their unusual nature as inserts. They seem quite definitely intended to be the Veronica because in each case they are accompanied by the words of Pope Innocent III's Veronica prayer, and the *Chronica Majora*'s associated text describes Innocent's procession to Santo Spirito. Experts are also confident that both are by the hand of Paris himself.[5]

But the confusing feature of these and similar surviving English examples from around this time is that besides not showing Jesus' face on a suspended cloth, in the manner we have subsequently come to expect of Veronica copies, they curiously depict him with neck and shoulders, instead of the traditional 'disembodied' appearance. Almost certainly the reason for this is that Paris and his fellow-artists in far-away England had never seen the Veronica for themselves, and therefore simply followed the likeness of Jesus with which they were familiar in churches. Paris may also have been influenced by the twelfth century English chronicler Gervase of Tilbury who, writing from the time the Veronica was kept permanently screened, spoke of it with affected knowledgeability as 'the true picture of the Lord in the flesh, representing his likeness from the chest upwards.'[6]

It was also an English artist, the illustrator of a little-known late-thirteenth-century *Apocalypse*, now in the Gulbenkian Museum at Lisbon, Portugal,[7] from whom has survived the first–known depiction of the Veronica as a suspended cloth [pl. 17, left]. The artist's continued ignorance of the true appearance of the Veronica at this time, however, seems evident from the fact that he followed his earlier fellow-countrymen in depicting Jesus' neck.

Also from about the end of the thirteenth century there occurs a Veronica-type 'holy face' in a Franciscan manuscript, the *Supplicationes Variae*, preserved in the Laurentian Library, Florence, though this is not specifically identified as a Veronica.[8] Not lacking in such identification, however, is a particularly fine 'holy face' miniature [pl. 17, above] which a French illuminator of the same period included in the Psalter and Book of Hours[9] he created for Yolande de Soissons, a wife and mother of the northern French nobility. This manuscript is now in the Pierpont Morgan Library, New York, and study of the miniature immediately reveals it quite definitely to have been intended as a Veronica, for it is again accompanied by Innocent III's prayer and mention of the indulgences he promised for the recitation of this.[10] Yet although on both this and in the aforementioned Franciscan one the face is represented as disembodied, neither show a suspended cloth, and again it can only be presumed that both artists worked more from imagination than any real knowledge.

Perhaps not unexpectedly, therefore, it was only in the wake of Boniface VIII's Holy Year proclamation of 1300, and more markedly, following Clement VI's particularly popular Holy Year of 1350, that artistic renditions of the Veronica began to become more prevalent, and to assume what we might expect, at least, to be some greater accuracy as copies. For instance, from 1353, in the Book of Hours of another Yolande, Yolande of Flanders, there has survived as a mere margin illustration[11] the first-known depiction of St Veronica holding up the cloth [pl. 17, below left]. On this, despite the small scale, and water-damage to the whole manuscript, the Christ face can be clearly seen as disembodied in the subsequently 'traditional' manner. And thereafter this type of image in a variety of permutations enjoyed the sort of wildfire popularity that we have already seen of the whole Veronica cult.

The difficulty arises when we try to sift from this plethora of Veronica cloth-images which ones might or might not be the most accurate depictions of the Veronica's true appearance at the time they were made.

Thus because some are by first-rate artists, it is rather easy to

93

be beguiled by these into believing that they must be the truest copies. In London's National Gallery, for instance, can be seen a superb panel painting [pl. 18], created about 1420, the sole theme of which is St Veronica holding up the cloth before the spectator.[12] It is attributed to an unknown artist usually referred to as the Master of St Veronica, and despite a large circular halo it looks sufficiently naturalistic and authoritative that we might not unreasonably expect it to be a particularly definitive copy.

Quite similar, though more lifelike, not least because of its lack of a halo and more free-flowing hair, is a drawing [pl. 19, left] that has been attributed to the Master of Flémalle, thought to have been Robert Campin, who flourished in the early 1400s. This drawing, one of the finest draughtsmanship, is now in the Fitzwilliam Museum, Cambridge.[13] Of very similar appearance (apart from a cruciform ray halo) is the St Veronica panel which Flemish artist Roger van der Weyden created around 1450 as one wing of a triptych now in the Kunsthistorisches Museum, Vienna.[14] And again seemingly of the same family is Bruges artist Hans Memling's little panel painting of the Veronica [pl. 19, above], created around the time of the 1475 Holy Year, which now hangs in the Samuel Kress collection in the National Gallery of Art, Washington.[15] If one compares these highly competent images one with the other, reviews their spread over several decades, and takes into account the technical excellence of their creators, they could very readily be adjudged as providing us with our best authority for the Veronica's appearance at the time of its end-of-Middle Ages hey-day.

By contrast, altogether less appealing and convincing might seem a tiny illumination in the Prayer Book of Philippe le Hardi, Duke of Burgundy, preserved in the Bibliothèque Royale, Brussels, and dating from the early 1400s [pl. 20, above].[16] This shows a disproportionately large Veronica cloth being held up by a most fashionably dressed young St Veronica, and as in many other copies we should ignore the disparity of scale as mere artistic licence. One indication of this illumination's importance is that in common with Matthew Paris's Veronica illustrations, it was created separately from the main manuscript (in this instance, painted on a piece of leather), and then carefully fastened into the manuscript.

But the particularly significant and striking feature is the seemingly 'cut-out' look of the face, the outlines of the hair sharply and unnaturally delineated, and the beard terminating in a harsh,

94

geometric triangle. There is also a very primitive quality to the rendition of the facial likeness. As is quite obvious from the same artist's perfectly pleasing and naturalistic portrayal of St Veronica, the characteristics cannot be due either to artistic incompetence or to any eccentricities of style. The question raised, therefore, is whether they are based instead on an attempt to convey at least something of the true appearance of the original, i.e. the Veronica itself?

First, it is apparent that the Philippe le Hardi Prayer Book illumination is not alone in its 'cut-out' mode of portrayal of the Veronica. Another,[17] closely contemporary, is to be found in a Book of Hours, the so-called *Très Belle Heures*, owned by Philippe le Hardi's brother and fellow-enthusiast as a collector of illuminated manuscripts, Jean, Duke of Berry. Another occurs in a French manuscript of *circa* 1440.[18] Further afield, a similar Veronica is to be found as part of a wall-painting in the parish church at Mariapfarr, Salzburg, Austria, dating *circa* 1430.[19] And dating from as early as 1370 is a mosaic Veronica of the same type [pl. 20, below left] which forms part of the scene of the Last Judgement at the south entrance of St Vitus's Cathedral, Prague, Czechoslovakia.[20]

But why the 'cut-out' appearance? And why should this be considered more authentic than the visually far more appealing copies made by Roger van der Weyden and Memling?

The first clue derives from that historically highly important wood-engraving of a Veronica exposition in the age of printing's first guidebook to Rome, the *Mirabilia Romae* [fig. 5 and 8a overleaf].

If we re-examine this we can see that the Veronica has been drawn being shown to the pilgrims in what appears to be a double frame. The outer section of this may well be the glass case recorded to have been donated by three Venetians in 1350. This frame [fig. 8b overleaf] is the only item closely associated with the Veronica that has been put on proper public display in recent years. It was included in an exhibition in Rome in 1984. The fourteenth-century glass has become cracked at some time, but the rectangular wooden surround readily corresponds with that seen in the *Mirabilia Romae* engraving.

But it is the inner section as seen in the *Mirabilia Romae* which interests us. Even allowing for the limitations of an early wood-engraving, it conveys the impression of the face appearing

95

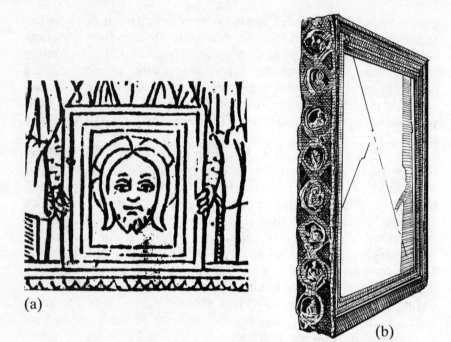

(a)

(b)

*Fig. 8. (a) The Veronica in its frame, late fifteenth century. Detail from the* Mirabilia Romae *engraving; (b) The Veronica frame as made by Venetians for the Holy Year of 1350, present-day appearance*

as if from behind some form of mount sharply cut out in the exact shape of the hair and beard – a mount inevitably reminiscent of those covering the Genoa and S. Silvestro 'holy faces' purportedly studied by Heaphy.

Now if we only had the *Mirabilia Romae* to rely on, it would be easy to dismiss this as mere imagination. But in the event it is supported by a highly important manuscript illustration, more than a century older, that we are able to publish here for the first time. The manuscript in question is the *Regula Sancti Spiritus* in the Archivo di Stato, Rome, and it comprises a superbly illuminated new Rule made sometime around the middle of the fourteenth century for the Santo Spirito Hospital founded by Pope Innocent III.

Due to the effects of age the manuscript is now in an extremely friable condition,[21] but of great interest is folio XIV, the first page of the text proper. At the base of this can be seen an exquisitely

96

coloured illumination [col. pl. V] showing a seated pope, with a lion at his feet, holding up a 'holy face' that, given the content of Santo Spirito, can only be the Veronica. This appears set on a black cloth emblazoned with a double barred cross, the *crux gemina* that was the Santo Spirito hospital's corporate symbol.

The crucial feature here is that this illumination seems to provide us with a unique depiction of the Veronica *in the form that it was exhibited* in the mid-fourteenth century; the exact equivalent of the *Miribilia Romae* engraving for the fifteenth. First we see surrounding it an azure-blue circle with a slim, seemingly pearl-studded frame. Possibly this was the jewelled reliquary in which it was recorded to have been carried during the Santo Spirito procession. Inside this we see a single rectangular frame. This serves to further corroborate for us that the outer one, as seen in the *Mirabilia Romae* engraving, was most likely the one later added by the Venetians.

But it is the appearance of this inner frame that is all-important. Its colour is gold, and it seems to take the form of a 'cut-out' mask that covers all but the face itself. Just as we anticipated, it exactly resembles the metallic covers of the Genoa and S. Silvestro 'holy faces'. Now the sharply 'cut-out' appearance of the Philippe le Hardi and related Veronica copies makes total sense. Paradoxically it is the ones with this rather crude feature, rather than the naturalistic but over-polished works by Memling, Roger van der Weyden, and others, that may be adjudged the truer copies.

Now having managed one important advance in our understanding of the Veronica's appearance before 1527, can we go on to achieve any others? If we turn once more to the generality of Veronica copies there is another feature of apparent confusion and discontinuity that we can scarcely avoid noticing: the way so many differ from each other in terms of Jesus's apparent physical and mental state at the time the image was theoretically created.

Some of these differences are quite fundamental. The earliest Veronicas, for instance, almost invariably show Jesus with wide-open eyes and apparent radiant health. From no later than 1370 there begin to appear examples showing him crowned with thorns, as in the case of one of that date which forms part of an altar-piece in the Wallraf-Richartz Museum, Cologne.[22] Nonetheless 'healthy' examples (the Roger van der Weyden and Memling versions among them), continue to flourish side-by-side with these right up to and including the first quarter of the sixteenth century.

But whether with or without a crown of thorns, from at least as early as the fifteenth century there begin to appear examples which show Jesus as visibly suffering, bleeding and tear-stained, his eyes half-closed. A typical example is the companion to the National Gallery's Master of St Veronica panel painting, today in the collection of the Pinacotheca, Munich.[23] We should not necessarily be too surprised at this, for in an earlier chapter we noted how there was a shift in the general understanding of how the Veronica was created. While in the thirteenth century Gerald of Wales and others thought of Veronica meeting Jesus sometime before his arrest, the idea had become 'established' by the fifteenth century of her rushing forward to wipe his face as he toiled towards Calvary. It can be argued that art merely followed the evolution of the legend.

Nonetheless, given the fact that there was a real-life and regularly exhibited piece of cloth inextricably linked to this legend, such a change in understanding could scarcely have been possible unless the image's facial features were sufficiently vague or ill-defined to allow this to come about. So to what extent do we have any evidence of this?

In this regard, given the intense interest that the Veronica aroused, and the huge numbers who flocked to Rome to see it, one of the greatest frustrations of the subject is just how few of these eyewitnesses, even ones who wrote down blow-by-blow descriptions of all else that happened at the time, paused to set down for posterity exactly what it looked like. We cannot blame them, for even the gospel writers did no better of the human appearance of Jesus.

Thus one typically inadequate description of the Veronica is that recording its showing to King Philippe Auguste of France in 1191:

> '. . . the Veronica, that is to say, the linen cloth which Jesus Christ pressed against his face and on which even today that impression is so clear that Jesus Christ's face can be seen on it.'

Exactly what was so clear about the impression?[24] What was its colour? Were the eyes open or closed? Were there any unusual stains, and if so where? If this was the Face that people of the Middle Ages believed they would come face to face with at the

Last Judgement, writer after writer of the time omitted to tell us a jot of what it actually looked like.

Regrettably therefore what may actually be the best available description derives from no better than a very mystically-minded fourteenth-century English nun, Julian of Norwich, who although almost certainly she never saw the Veronica for herself, at least seems to have heard something of its appearance from others who had. On 8 May 1373, Julian claimed to have received a series of visions which a few years later she wrote down as her *Revelations of Divine Love*. And of one of these – 'a figure and likeness of our foul deeds' shame' – she remarked:

> It made me to think of the Holy Vernacle [Veronica] of Rome: which he hath portrayed with his own blessed face when he was in his hard Passion, wilfully going to his death, and often changing of colour. Of the brownness and blackness, the ruefulness and leanness of this Image many marvel how it might be so, since he portrayed it with his blessed face who is the fairness of heaven . . . Then how might this image be so discolouring and so far from fair?[25]

At least therefore we learn from Julian that the face on the Veronica most likely had a somewhat dark and mottled appearance. It is not exactly much, but it does help us to understand how the facial image might have been so difficult to distinguish that it was subject to a variety of different interpretations.

In this regard, given that the tradition of the Veronica's creation was of it having been created of sweat and blood from Christ's countenance, we might expect the face on the cloth to have at least something of this watery, impressionistic quality. So to what extent did any artists' copies reflect this? The straight answer is, not a lot. With the age of impressionism centuries in the future, most artists before 1527 seem to have followed one another in simply setting down a meaningfully lifelike interpretation of the face on the cloth, regardless of the subtleties or otherwise of the stains they actually saw. In the light of this it might be easy to suppose that the Veronica face was itself in similar vein, and not the sort of shadowy negative-type impression with which we have become familiar from the 'shroud' of Turin.

But fortunately two artists from before 1527 do seem to

have been sufficiently independent-minded to depart from their colleagues' mainstream and to set down at least something more along the lines of what may actually have been visible on the cloth.

The first of these was the brilliant fifteenth-century French miniaturist, Jean Fouquet, already mentioned for the exquisite Veronica scene he included in the Book of Hours he illuminated for the French Treasurer, Étienne Chevalier.[26] Particularly notable about Fouquet is that he was a master of detail. Despite many of his miniatures being no bigger than a man's hand, they often include highly accurate depictions of the buildings of Paris as they existed in his time. He had also quite definitely visited Rome, because he is known to have painted there the portrait of Pope Eugenius IV shortly after the latter's return from his exile in Florence. And since the Veronica was exhibited on Eugenius' return (see page 64), and Fouquet is in any case thought to have stayed on until the Holy Year of 1450, he certainly had the opportunities to see the Veronica for himself, and by his very nature would inevitably have tried to convey as accurate as possible a rendition of it.

Of considerable interest therefore is that below Fouquet's Book of Hours miniature of Veronica wiping Jesus's face during the Carrying of the Cross he set into the initial letter 'D' an inset panel showing Veronica holding out the cloth towards the spectator [col. pl. VI, right]. Although minuscule in scale, and showing the cloth freely suspended, rather than in its frame (as Fouquet would almost inevitably have seen it), the significant feature is that the face has been rendered with a convincing impressionism.

A yet more striking example, however, comes from the work of the powerful Mannerist artist, Pontormo, who in 1515 was given the task of creating frescoes in the papal chapel in the church of Sta Maria Novella, Florence. In the second lunette of this chapel Pontormo painted a highly individual fresco of St Veronica holding up the cloth [col. pl. VI, below], and on this we see an extraordinarily faint and watery impression of a face. The image is highly impressionistic, totally without outlines, and so subtle in its blotches that it is virtually impossible to tell whether it conveys a face alive or dead, suffering or non-suffering, with eyes open or closed. So does this gives us our truest indication yet of the face on the Veronica?

Unfortunately we have no certain information that Pontormo actually saw the Veronica for himself. And whatever, just twelve

100

years after his creation of the fresco Rome suffered its fateful sack in which the Veronica may or may not have been destroyed.

But having thus managed to establish at least something of the appearance of the frame in which the Veronica was kept before 1527, also something of the likely blotchy, impressionistic image of the face as it appeared on the cloth, is this all we are able to reconstruct? Given the bewildering plethora of other Veronica-type 'holy faces', so far, from the copies made pre-1527, we have noted nothing absolutely individual or unique to the Veronica's appearance by which to recognize it with any certainty in anything appearing post-1527.

Prime in this regard has to be the incidence or otherwise of any signatory damage blemishes. For instance, late sixteenth- and seventeenth-century paintings and engravings of the Turin shroud consistently feature the highly distinctive patches and burn marks from the fire damage which this cloth suffered in 1532. Sight of these marks in any copy therefore instantly identifies the particular shroud as that of Turin and none other. In like vein, if the damage marks which Heaphy included on his purported 'copy' of the Genoa 'holy face' had checked out with the actual image beneath the cover, then we could have been confident that he had genuinely seen this with the cover removed. The fact that they did not check out definitively established Heaphy's fraudulence.

So the question arises, might there be any Veronica copy made before 1527 which shows scars that the original may have suffered before that time, and which may help to identify it in any subsequent copies?

Yet again we find that the vast majority of copies are singularly unhelpful. Just as most of the artists omitted to try to reproduce the impressionistic character of the stains representing the face, so they also omitted any other blemishes that may or may not have been there.

But yet again there does seem to have been at least one curious exception. At the Convent of Sta Clara near Alicante in southern Spain, surrounded by all the now familiar 'secret place' mystique, is kept what the Spanish of the region regard as their Veronica or *Santa Faz*, a highly revered 'holy face' that is fortunately known to us from modern photographs [col. pl, IVb].

Both from the appearance of this, and from what is historically recorded of it, this one is not in the 'truly ancient' league of 'holy faces'. It seems to have been acquired for Alicante around the year 1484 by its local bishop, Mosén Pedro Mena.[27] During the pontificate of Pope Sixtus IV, Venice had been struck by a severe plague, which killed thousands, and this 'holy face' was apparently sent from Rome to the stricken city as a token of divine succour. After the abatement of the plague the cardinal who brought it back to Rome had apparently then died soon after, making it easy for Mena, then the cardinal's chaplain, to acquire it for a grateful Alicante.

Stylistically the 'holy face' is odd, almost amateur. But it is certainly neither Byzantine nor Gothic, and it seems reasonable therefore that it was a Veronica copy made at about the very time we first hear of it historically, the beginning of the last quarter of the fifteenth century. Corroborating our signalling of the importance of those Veronica copies with the 'cut-out' appearance, it is immediately obvious that this one, too, is of just such variety. And we would indeed expect nothing less than a very close and special copy of the Veronica to be sent to Venice, in order for its intended purpose, the relief of the city from plague, to have the maximum chance of effectiveness.

What is therefore fascinating is that this copy does feature certain curious blemishes, ones that clearly appear to have been deliberately painted on, rather than to have been suffered by the copy itself. The most obvious of these is what looks like a large droplet on the left cheek; a feature that as the *lagrima*, the tear-drop, has its own special place in Alicantean legend. Also evident is another mark over the left eye, and what looks like a long, horizontal hole in the top right-hand corner of the forehead.

So could whoever created the Alicante copy have included these marks as faithful renditions of what he saw on what he was copying, i.e. the original Veronica itself? Since that copyist was working no later than the last quarter of the fifteenth century, are these therefore the tell-tale 'signatory' markings which we have been seeking, the ones by which the true Veronica of the Middle Ages may or may not be recognized in any copies (or original), from *after* 1527? Fortuitously, in order to help us answer these very questions, a very conscientious seventeenth-century Roman archivist is about to come to our aid.

*Chapter Nine*

# BREAKTHROUGH – THANKS TO A CONSCIENTIOUS NOTARY

*His Holiness's private secretary . . . so meticulously captured the sacred likeness . . . the whole appearance, that certainly nothing better or more pleasing could have been provided*

Jacopo Grimaldi, notary of St Peter's, 1620

When in the summer of 1505 Pope Julius II set in motion the herculean task of building the present-day St Peter's, the broad plan was to work on half the basilica at a time, commencing with the western, or high-altar end, over which was to be built the dome. Contemptuous of anything but the classical past, Julius allowed his architect Donato Bramante the freest rein for his 2,500 workmen to demolish and clear this half, sparing only the area of St Peter's tomb, which had to be protected with a temporary cover. Of the rest, all the historic tombs, statues, mosaics, candelabra and other items were simply broken up and thrown out as useless garbage, earning Bramante the not undeserved title, '*il ruinante*'. Particularly unforgivably for a supposedly civilized time, there was not even the slightest attempt to make any record of what was destroyed.

Exactly a century later, with the finished dome now soaring resplendently over the western end, it was obvious that the time had come to demolish the remaining half – the part that included the old Veronica chapel – in order to make way for a correspondingly magnificent new nave and façade. By now the demolition decision was virtually unavoidable, not least because of a very visible lean

103

to the old walls, and occasional falls of overhead masonry. Even so there were strong objections, particularly from the ecclesiastical historian and Vatican Librarian, Cardinal Cesare Baronius.

Accordingly, concerned that his architect Carlo Maderno should not become another '*ruinante*', the newly elected Sienese pope Paul V gave orders for the preservation wherever possible of the more historic items from the old basilica. In the case of tombs, two canons were deputed to superintend the opening of these, and the translation of their remains to the Grotte Vecchi, the vast crypt that had been created by the elevation of the floor of the new basilica eleven feet higher than that of the old. The more interesting items of old sculpture, mosaics, inscriptions and the like were also to be kept in the same location, pending possible reuse. Particularly importantly, the basilica's official clerk or notary, Jacopo Grimaldi, was appointed to make a careful record of all those items whose destruction was unavoidable.

Although Grimaldi is virtually unknown outside historical circles, he was one of those patient, albeit unremarkable archivists to whom subsequent historians tend to be more indebted than they usually acknowledge. Several of his manuscripts survive to this day, and from these we learn that he was still a boy in 1581, so he would have been perhaps in his late thirties when he took up his work on recording what was about to be destroyed of old St Peter's. Quite evident is that he was conscientious in his tackling of this, and besides a good command of Latin he had a more than passable artistic ability.

Thus one of the tombs scheduled for destruction was a superb Gothic one created for the initiator of the Holy Years, Boniface VIII, and Grimaldi not only made a careful drawing of this,[1] he stayed to watch as Boniface's close-sealed coffin was prised open. Via his pen we learn that the three-hundred-year-old body of the pope was found to be almost perfectly preserved, wearing a great oval sapphire ring, sandals decorated with a golden rose on the feet, and an alb beautifully embroidered with scenes from the life of the Virgin, which Grimaldi sketched. Grimaldi similarly recorded the openings of several other papal tombs, among these those of Sixtus IV, Innocent VIII and Marcellus II.

However, for us Grimaldi's most uniquely valuable contribution is his assemblage of a most comprehensive 131-page archive specially devoted to the Veronica. Written in Latin under the title 'A brief account of the most holy Veronica sweatcloth of our

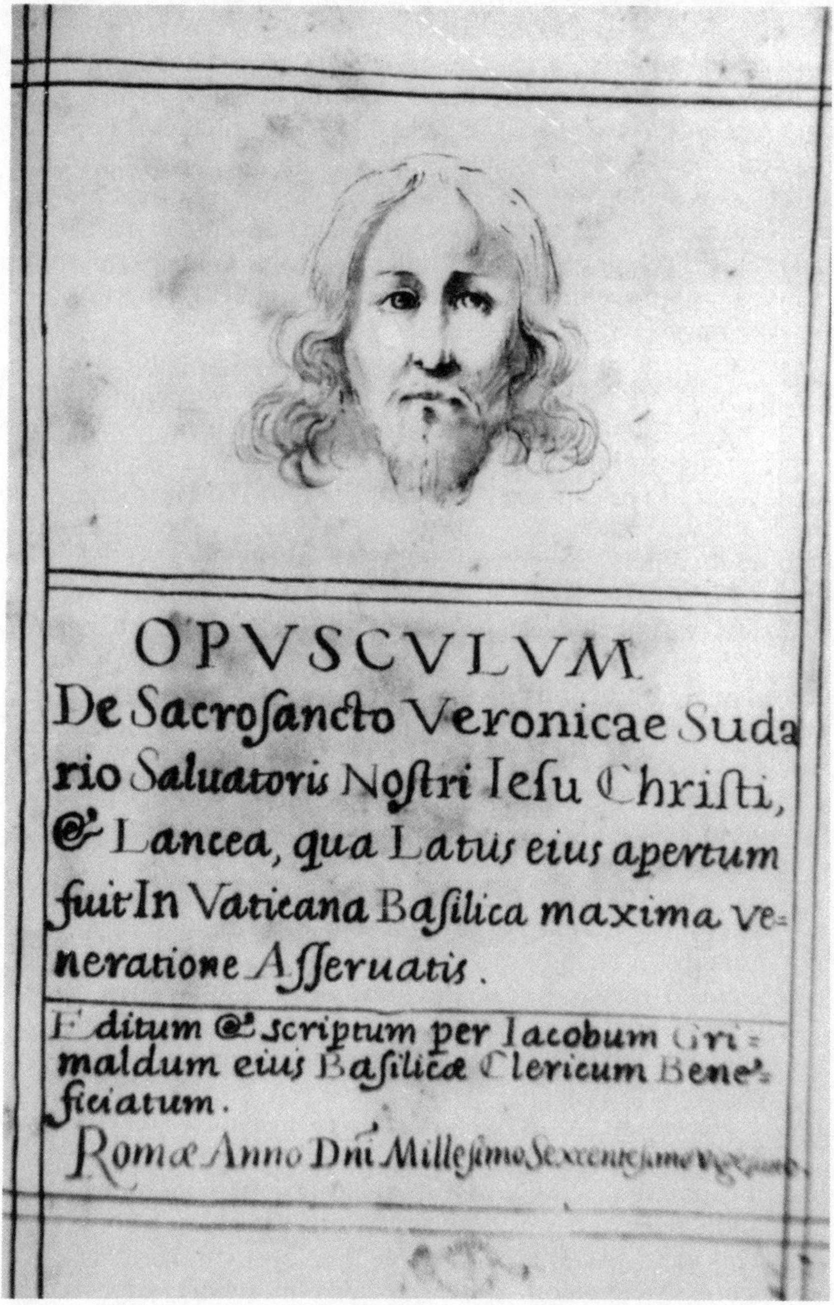

# OPVSCVLVM

De Sacrosancto Veronicae Suda
rio Saluatoris Nostri Iesu Christi,
& Lancea, qua Latus eius apertum
fuit In Vaticana Basilica maxima ve=
neratione Asseruatis.

Editum & scriptum per Iacobum Gri=
maldum eius Basilicæ Clericum Bene=
ficiatum.

Romæ Anno Dni Millesimo Sexcentesimo vigesimo.

Fig. 9. The title page of notary Jacopo Grimaldi's
archive document on the Veronica. From a manuscript
of 1620 preserved in the Biblioteca, Nazionale, Florence

105

Saviour Jesus Christ . . . as preserved with the greatest veneration in the Vatican Basilica', this was completed in 1620 and survives in copies preserved in Rome, Florence [fig. 9], Milan and Paris.[2] It incorporates description and sketches of the old Veronica chapel and its mosaic decorations, the appearance of the shrine in which the Veronica was kept, and chronologically ordered extracts from old archives relating to the Veronica's history. Some of this latter material will prove invaluable to us when we begin to try to probe the Veronica's earlier history.

Of most immediate interest, however, is Grimaldi's careful recording of the major data and circumstances relating to the Veronica at the time he served as notary. A typical gem are his remarks concerning the condition of the glass frame that had been made by the Venetians in 1350. Noting that this was no longer with the Veronica, but kept separately in the 'archive' of St Peter's, he described it as 'cracked into two parts through carelessness on the part of the sacristans – at least as would seem most likely.'[3] This observation enables us to date the already noted crack in the glass [see fig. 8b, page 96] to at least as early as the first years of the seventeenth century, suggesting, despite Grimaldi, that the damage might perhaps have been sustained during the Sack of Rome.

But much more pertinent to us is Grimaldi's description of the making of a very special Veronica copy in 1616. According to his entry for that year:

> The most serene Constance of Austria, Queen of Poland, motivated by the intense devotion to the sacred sweatcloth [i.e. the Veronica], sent a letter of supplication to our Most Holy Lord, Pope Paul V, begging him . . . to send her an exact copy [verum exemplar] of [this] . . .
>
> His Holiness, kindly consenting to the pious entreaties of so famous and charitable a Catholic queen, entrusted the painting of this to Pietro Strozzi, the Florentine nobleman who was His Holiness's private secretary. This man, who was a most able theologian and classical scholar, and who had honours also in architecture and painting, so meticulously captured the sacred likeness – the features, the bloodstains (insofar as these became imprinted), the forehead, the eyes, in short, the whole

appearance – that certainly nothing better or more pleasing could have been provided in response to her [majesty's] request . . .

Created with the greatest care possible as a copy of the holy face imprinted on the Veronica veil, this was enclosed in a silver frame worked in the shape of the most ancient and original frame and entrusted to Master Damian Fonsecca of the Friars Preachers [the Dominican Order], as he was setting out for Poland in pursuit of his religious calling . . . In Poland it was given to Bishop Francesco, Papal Nuncio at the court of Sigismund III, King of Poland who handed the sacred likeness to Queen Constance. When the queen saw the image, she knelt before it in prayer, venerating it in the humblest fashion, her eyes filled with tears, as the Nuncio proclaimed: 'Behold he who was fairest of all mankind, as he became in his most dread passion, revealing [to us] his sad, discoloured face at the very brink of death.'[4]

First worthy of note here is that the Queen Constance who requested the Veronica copy was the second wife of the religiously tolerant Polish king, Sigismund III. She had been born into the Styrian, or Austrian branch of the Hapsburg dynasty, and was such a devout Catholic that her marriage to Sigismund in 1605 had been deeply unpopular among the powerful Protestant minority still within Poland at that time. With tension between Catholic and Protestant at its height throughout Europe – 1616 was just two years before the outbreak of the religion-dominated Thirty Years' War – Constance would have represented to Paul V a major bulwark of Catholicism. He would therefore have felt considerably obliged to help her with anything supportive of her deep faith.

But equally fascinating, and indicative of the very ethos of the 'secret places', is that a request ostensibly as simple as that of an *exact* copy of the Veronica posed more than a little difficulty even for a pope to agree to. The nature of this difficulty Paul carefully explained in a letter to Constance, the text of which Grimaldi dutifully copied into his archive:

Pope Paul V to Constance Queen of Poland, Our

107

dearest daughter in Christ, greetings . . . We have delayed bringing you the solace you wanted, because for a long time we were in doubt how we could satisfy your pious wish. Please understand that we could not employ any ordinary craftsman, since only canons of the venerable basilica [St Peter's] are allowed to approach the place where the precious treasure [i.e. the Veronica] is kept. But we were willing to try any means, and it has transpired that one within our own household is both a canon of St Peter's and a competent enough artist. Accordingly we have given him the task of making the closest possible copy of the most holy image, and he is very pleased with it. We now send this to you enclosed in a silver frame that is likewise nearly identical to the one in which the most holy Veronica veil is itself kept, which you will readily guess from the crude and simple way in which it has been made . . . Given at Sta Maria Maggiore, Rome on 7 September 1616.[5]

Now for us this is most fascinating information, not least because after all our frustrations over the fraudulent Heaphy, here for the first and indeed only time in history we have a properly documented 'behind the scenes' account of the making of a truly exact Veronica copy, as distinct from the more imaginative versions that had been commonly produced by artists.

Thus, evoking the very same mystique already established as surrounding the 'secret places', we learn that only canons of the basilica could have the access to the Veronica by which such a true facsimile copy could be made from it. Small wonder, therefore that Protestant Englishman Heaphy did not have any success gaining access. And given that the only recourse was to a canon with artistic abilities, this almost certainly explains the amateur quality we noted back in the last chapter of the special copy made back in the late fifteenth century to help plague-ridden Venice, and which has now become the 'holy face' of Alicante. Most likely this was made by a counterpart to Strozzi at that time.

We also learn that features in the form of forehead, eyes and bloodstains were still visible on the Veronica as it existed in 1616. Grimaldi was particularly at pains to attest to Strozzi's accurate recreation of these in the copy he made:

108

In the year 1606 the holy sweatcloth was on open display while being transferred to the new St Peter's on account of the destruction of the old. On that occasion I, Jacopo Grimaldi, a miserable sinner, had the opportunity of close viewing the true, most holy face with my own unworthy eyes, and can vouch for the aforesaid copy having the closest resemblance to this.[6]

Equally valuable is Grimaldi's information that the copy as given to Queen Constance even faithfully replicated the 'crude and simple' silver frame in which the original was enclosed. Could this give us the clue to the strange 'cut-out' shape we noted on the most authentic pre-1527 copies.

Clearly then, for us a great deal of interest centres on this copy made in 1616. If it could be located, potentially it could provide us with precisely what we had so vainly looked for in Heaphy's work, a copy created quite specifically to be as exact a replica as possible.

It was in the late summer of 1989 that I first came across Grimaldi's mention of Constance of Austria's copy, and at that time nothing answering its description was known to me. The only early seventeenth-century Veronica referred to and illustrated in scholarly literature was a clearly different one made in 1621 for the Duchess Sforza, and which the Duchess donated to Rome's then recently built Jesuit church, the Church of Gesù.[7] This was made during the pontificate of Paul V's successor, Gregory XV, and from photographs [pl. 20, below right] it seemed an uninspiring work, with closed eyes, and a modern wooden frame, rather than any replication of the 'crude and simple' silver one referred to in Grimaldi.

But while still pondering on the possibility that Constance of Austria's copy might have survived somewhere, there came the vague recollection of a letter that had been sent to me eleven years before remarking on an obscure Veronica copy in Vienna. On rereading this letter, from a Mrs Dorothy Piepke of East Aurora, New York, it suddenly assumed a new significance:

I was surprised to notice you omitted [in your book *The Shroud of Turin*] to refer to the 'relic' in the possession of the Hofburg Palace in Vienna. Upon visiting the Schatzkammer [Treasure Chamber] of Sacred and Secular Treasures of the Hapsburg rulers in Vienna two years ago I remember such a cloth, claimed to be the 'Cloth of Veronica'. At the time I was rather surprised to see it in a very unobtrusive location on a lower display area of the sacred treasures.[8]

Back in 1978, never once having come across this particular 'Veronica' copy, I had supposed this to be merely a late work of little relevance to my main interest, the 'shroud'. In the light of Grimaldi, however, it now occurred that it might actually be the same one as that given to Constance, perhaps having passed back into her Hapsburg family through inheritance. A Viennese acquaintance, Professor Hans Rohsmann, promised to make enquiries for me, and thanks to his help, and that of the Kunsthistorisches Museum, Vienna, in December 1989 there arrived in my mail a startling photograph of the very cloth described by Mrs Piepke [col. pl. VII].

Particularly startling was that while the outer frame was relatively modern, inside was a discordantly roughly-made inner frame strikingly corresponding both to the 'crude and simple' one referred to in Paul V's letter, and to the very same sharply 'cut-out' appearance hypothesized from the more 'authentic' artists' copies made before 1527.

Even more remarkable was the face on the cloth inside this cut-out. It was hardly distinguishable as a face at all, scarcely more than a series of blotches in the midst of which there seemed just distinguishable a crude, overlong nose, a broad transverse brush-stroke in token of a mouth, and the vaguest suggestion of closed eyelids. Instead of the traditional Veronica face as popularized by artists of the Middle Ages, here was something much more credible. It even made sense of the nineteenth-century descriptions of there being no visible image. Quite clearly someone had tried to make an honest, tone for tone, blotch for blotch duplicate of a highly impressionistic, outlineless original. Whatever the ultimate relationship it was even unavoidable not to see here an image strikingly reminiscent of Turin's 'shroud'. Indeed this was the very view that had been expressed by Constance of Austria herself.

According to Grimaldi:

> Constance . . . is said to have remarked that she recognized in it [the Veronica copy] the same likeness

(Above): *Holy Year
pilgrim with Veronica
badge on his cap. Detail
of the fresco 'the Church
Militant' by Andrea da
Firenze, in the Spanish
chapel of the Church of
Santa Maria Novella,
Florence;* (left): *More
examples of medieval
pilgrims' badges of the
Veronica, as retrieved
from the mud of the Seine,
Musée de Cluny, Paris*

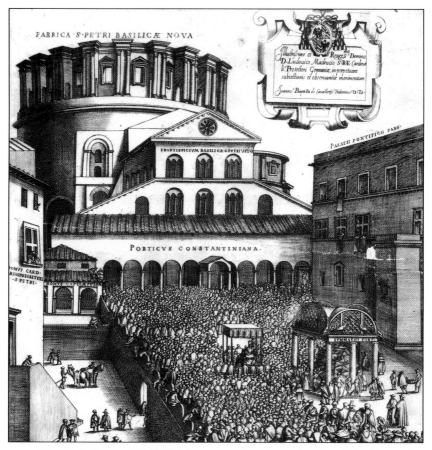

*The Holy Year of 1575, from a contemporary engraving. This shows the atrium of old St Peter's crowded with pilgrims, while Michelangelo's dome can be seen well under construction behind*

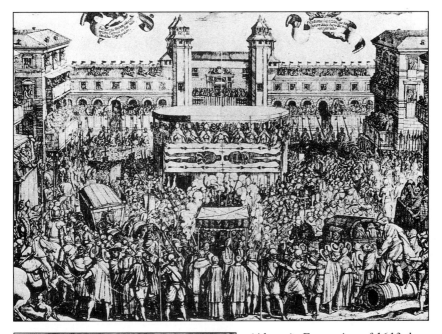

(Above): *Engraving of 1613, by Antonio Tempesta, showing exposition of the shroud in the courtyard of Turin's Royal Palace. Imperceptibly, popular enthusiasm seems to have shifted from the Veronica to the shroud at around this time;*
(left): *'Holy face' preserved at the church of Manoppello, near Pescara. Measuring 24 x 17cm, this has been painted on cloth with a very transparent paint. Some scholars believe it to be the original of the Veronica, surreptitiously transferred to Manoppello in the early seventeeth-century*

(Above): *The nineteenth-century English artist Thomas Heaphy the Younger, who made a special study of the 'holy faces'. From a self-portrait made in 1831, the year of his first visit to Rome, as preserved in the National Portrait Gallery, London;* (below, left): *Heaphy's 'copy' of the Archeropita 'holy face' of the Sancta Sanctorum chapel, Rome, from the album of his sketches as preserved in the Print Room of the British Museum;* (below, right): *Actual appearance of the same 'holy face'* (see also *col. pl. III*). *Note the inaccuracy with which Heaphy has conveyed the base of the halo, also the harmony of the eyes and nose in his portrayal, compared to the crudeness of the original*

(Above): *'Holy face' which in Heaphy's time was preserved in the church of S Silvestro, Rome (*see also col. pl. IVc), with (left): Heaphy's 'copy' from the album of his sketches in the Print Room of the British Museum. Although the halo indicated as part of the cloth background in Heaphy's sketch suggests he saw this work with the cover entirely removed, there is available in the public domain no modern information by which this can be checked*

(Above): *'Holy face' of the church of S Bartholomew of the Armenians, Genoa, showing this within its Palaeologuan-period Byzantine frame (see also col. pl. IVd), with (right): Heaphy's 'copy' of this same. Note how Heaphy has conveyed the ends of the hair and beard pointing in the very reverse direction to the actuality - raising a suspicion that he never saw the original*

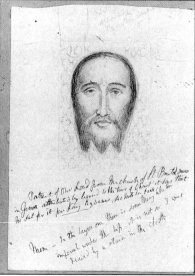

(Above): *The Genoa 'holy face' with the Palaeologuan frame removed, as photographed during a definitive examination of this icon in 1969, with* (left): *Heaphy's claimed 'copy' of the 'holy face' in this same state. The substantial disparity between Heaphy's 'copy' and the actuality can only be attributed to Heaphy having created his 'copy' largely from imagination*

(Above): *'Copy' of the Veronica 'holy face' made* circa *1240 by the English chronicler Matthew Paris, with text of Pope Innocent III's Veronica prayer below.* (Below): *Second 'copy' of the Veronica 'holy face', also by Matthew Paris and dated* circa *1250, from fol. 49v. of the* Chronica Majora *manuscript (ms 16) preserved at Corpus Christi College, Cambridge. Neither these, nor related English examples, seem to have been based on any direct knowledge of the Veronica's actual appearance*

of the holy face of Our Lord and Saviour Jesus Christ
as that imprinted on the cloth preserved with the most
universal veneration at Turin in Savoy.[9]

Nonetheless a first, crucial question was whether this was the
actual Veronica copy that Pietro Strozzi had made for Constance
of Austria? Here the accompanying information sent by Professor
Rohsmann and the Kunsthistorisches Museum seemed to pose a
set-back. The copy unquestionably dates from the time of Pope
Paul V. His name is incised onto the silver-gilt of the inner frame,
together with a sentence of excommunication against anyone
making unlicensed copies. But it bears the date 1617, one year
after the making of the copy for Constance. And according to the
Schatzkammer catalogue[10] it was acquired by the Hapsburgs only
in 1720, having previously been owned by the powerful Savelli
family of Rome.

Any possible disappointment evaporated, however, with the
application of a magnifying glass to the bottom right-hand corner
of the inner frame. This revealed the unmistakable signature of
P. Strozzi,[11] Paul V's secretary, the very man who, according
to Grimaldi, made Constance's copy. And since we learn from
Grimaldi that Strozzi made five further copies in 1617, before
Pope Paul V banned the making of any more, we may confidently
identify the Vienna copy as one of these. The Savellis, like the
Colonnas, were just the sort of powerful ecclesiastical Roman
family who might have snatched at the chance of owning such a
copy before Paul V's ban came down.

So while the Vienna copy is most likely not Constance's, we
may nonetheless be confident that it is as near the same as makes
no difference. And we have thus at last been provided with what
we have been seeking all along, our best available guide to the
Veronica appearance, at least as at the year 1617.

Now as already remarked, the first sight might seem more
than a little unprepossessing, although in the outlineless blotches
at least we have confirmation of precisely that 'impressionistic'
appearance we independently surmised from the works of Fouquet
and Pontormo, also from the remarks of the nun Julian of
Norwich. But studied a little more carefully, the whole work
reveals considerably more than might at first appear.

For instance, a useful comparison can now be made between the
facial image on this, the Strozzi copy, and the already mentioned

one made in 1621 that is now in the Church of Gesù [pl. 20, below right]. The most marked difference between the two is that the latter exhibits meaningful outlines to the nose, the mouth, and the eyelids. Since prehistory, artists have been naturally inclined to provide such outlines, but because Strozzi's version features no such delineation, and carries Grimaldi's attestation of accuracy, it, rather than the Gesù version, is arguably the more faithful to the characteristics of the original.

And since the two copies date from only four years apart, it is equally useful to study the elements in which they correspond. Here we need to return to the subject of the incidental blemishes discussed in the last chapter. For among several such marks that recur between each other are first: a repeated transverse stain at the top right-hand corner of the forehead; and second: a repeated prominent 'droplet' just below the left-hand eye. Immediately we may recall that there were identical such marks on the late fifteenth-century 'holy face' of Alicante, the second of these being its famous '*lagrima*' or teardrop.

The significance of this is obvious. If the copyists of 1617 and 1621 observed exactly the same marks as the artist who copied the Veronica in the late fifteenth century, then arguably the cloth all three were copying was one and the same original, i.e. the true Veronica. So the Veronica that pilgrims trampled each other to see in the Middle Ages *did* survive the Sack of Rome of 1527. Similarly the true Veronica could not have been stolen and taken to Manoppello in 1606, as has been argued by Professor Heinrich Pfeiffer. Since the Manoppello copy exhibits none of the crucial markings it can now safely be dropped from any further consideration.

Accordingly with such greatly enhanced grounds for accepting the Strozzi copy as our most reliable guide to the appearance of the Veronica as in its Middle Ages heyday, it is useful to turn our attention once again to the curious, 'cut-out' inner frame surrounding the face.

In the light of our confidence that this is an essentially exact copy from the original, one immediately striking feature is its close correspondence to the inner frames on the two other prominent 'holy faces'. These are none other than the most secret ones that were the focus of Heaphy's fakery: that of Genoa [col. pl. IVd], and that formerly in the Church of S. Silvestro [col. pl. IVc], which is now in the pope's private chapel. And it soon becomes apparent that this resemblance is more than superficial.

First, as has been noted by the renowned Italian art specialist Professor Carlo Bertelli,[12] all three inner frames have near identical dimensions, roughly eleven and a half inches by eight inches to the nearest half-inch. Even without the Strozzi copy in Vienna, we independently know this to be true of the Veronica as still preserved in St Peter's for the scholar A. de Waal gave these same approximate dimensions following his examination of this latter in 1894.[13]

Second, there is the closest possible correspondence in the way on all three 'holy faces' the inner frame has been cut to correspond to the shape of the hair and beard. Although the S. Silvestro one is today kept in a lavishly baroque frame made by the silver/goldsmith Francesco Comi in 1623, and has also never been fully explored, there does exist a photograph of this with Comi's frame removed [pl. 13, above]. This reveals a crude inner metal plate studded with nails at some thirty points surrounding the face and beard. Put a tracing of this side by side with a similar tracing from the Genoa 'holy face' and from the Strozzi Veronica copy [fig. 10], and it can be seen quite unmistakably that all three belong to the same 'family'.

Furthermore, thanks to the exhaustive study made of the Genoa 'holy face' by Colette Dufour Bozzo,[14] some form of

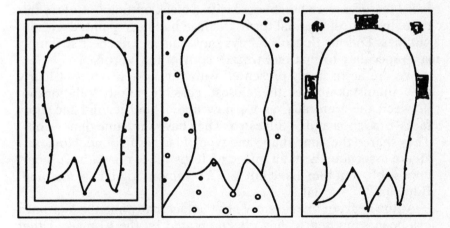

*Fig. 10. Outlines of the 'cut-out' surrounds of the S. Silvestro (a), Veronica (b), and Genoa (c) 'holy faces', showing clear 'family' relationship*

113

history of the plating with the 'cut-out' shape can be ascertained. The plating visible at the present-day on the Genoa 'holy face' is more sophisticated than those of the Veronica and S. Silvestro, and from the delicate filigree of its workmanship it has been reliably dated to the late thirteenth/early fourteenth century,[15] that is, to the Palaeologue period of Byzantine history.

But as Colette Dufour Bozzo has shown, this was but the last of a series of phases this particular work went through in the course of its history. Immediately prior to the Palaeologue refurbishment, it had been dressed in a simple cut-out silver plate much more closely corresponding to those of the Veronica and the S. Silvestro 'holy face'. This earlier appearance can be clearly seen depicted in the tiny panels with which the Palaeologue frame was illustrated [pl. 24, scenes f–i]. Before there had been a period when the face had been surrounded by pearls, the holes from which, although subsequently filled in, clearly showed up under X-ray [pl. 21, above]. Yet even this very pearl decoration still followed the same cut-out shape.

Equally compelling were revelations from Colette Dufour Bozzo's X-rays and accompanying tomographic work [pl. 21, left], in respect of the face. Its appearance as at the present day was found to be the product of several retouchings from even before the Palaeologue cover was imposed. The most marked of these were at the time when the pearl decoration was affixed, when the facial features were heightened with a black outlining. Before this time, in its most original form, the face had been painted without outlines. Dufour Bozzo's X-rays show this as a likeness strikingly corresponding to that on Strozzi's copy of the Veronica.

We are accordingly presented with yet more mystery. Clearly now unmistakable is the closest possible family relationship between the Veronica, as we now understand it, and the 'holy faces' of Genoa and S. Silvestro. They have the same dimensions. They shared the same shape and type of facial surround. Not least, all are associated with an image of Jesus's face on cloth. It seems impossible that they have not had a common origin in something. But what?

At the heart of this mystery lies the fact that while the Veronica has been supposed to have been created by the woman of that name rushing forward with her veil at Calvary, the Genoa and S. Silvestro 'holy faces' purportedly owed their origins to a quite independent Eastern tradition that Jesus imprinted a likeness of

114

himself on cloth for a king of the ancient principality of Edessa. The 'holy face' of Laon [pl. 8, above], it will be recalled, derived from this same Eastern tradition. While both eastern and western traditions, and the cloths with which they are associated, date back well before the fourteenth century, the date carbon dating has ascribed to the 'shroud', one of the most fundamental questions we face is exactly how far back can they be traced? And which is the original 'relic' from which the others sprang? Is it one of these 'big three' holy faces – or another yet to be identified?

Since we have managed to learn so much about the Veronica from our examination of its history dating after Innocent III's 'opening of the window' in 1207, it is now time to attempt the more difficult task of trying to trace its origins before that year. Exactly how far back can we trace it as a physical cloth relic preserved in Rome? Exactly what are the earliest origins of its accompanying legend of the woman Veronica? As we are about to find, once again Jacopo Grimaldi, our conscientious notary from the seventeenth century, will act as a most helpful guide.

## Chapter Ten

# PROBING FURTHER BACK IN TIME

*On the night of the nativity of Our Lord . . . we process to the sweatcloth of Christ, signing the 'Te Deum Laudamus'*

Instructions in anthem book, 1100 AD

To help us probe the Veronica's origins prior to 1207, it is a useful introduction to let our notary friend Jacopo Grimaldi recreate for us something of the historic Byzantine chapel that was its home during the earliest centuries of its recorded existence. For ironically it is thanks to Grimaldi's descriptions and sketches that we are rather better informed about the appearance of where the Veronica was kept during its time in old St Peter's, than we are of anything of its 'secret place' within the Veronica pier at the present day.

As already established, the Veronica chapel lay immediately inside the Guidonea doorway, the furthest right-hand one of the old St Peter's. If the demolition men of 1606 left any vestiges of its foundations these must lie very approximately below where Michelangelo's *Pièta* is displayed in the present-day St Peter's. We know from Grimaldi that the chapel was composed of a boxing-in of part of the line of columns that formed the old basilica's furthest right-hand nave. As evident from his drawing[1] of the inside of the basilica façade [pls. 22–23], the visitor had to walk the length of the chapel to its far end, where lay an arched doorway decorated with two Parian marble columns of the same twisted variety that also guarded the shrine of Peter at the high altar.

Separate detailed drawings by Grimaldi [fig. 11, also fol.

116

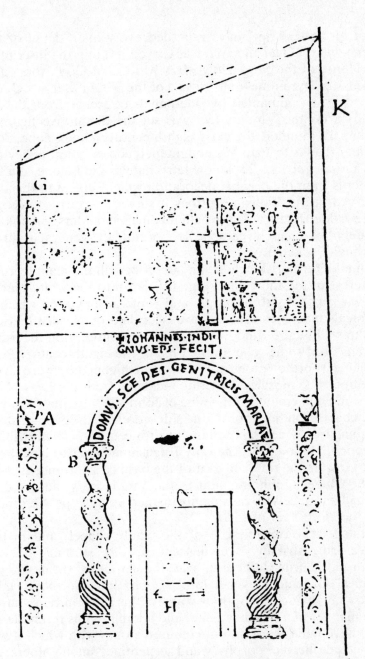

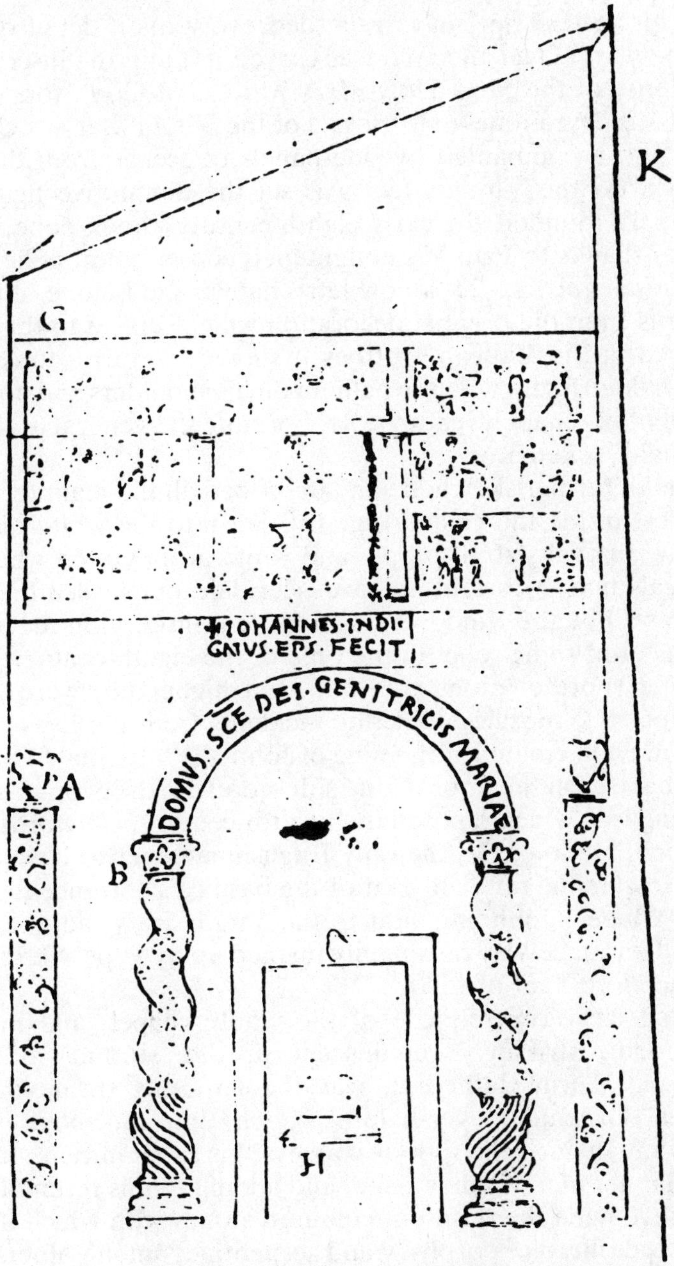
K
G
+IOHANNES·INDI·
GNIVS·EPS·FECIT
DOMVS·SCE DEI·GENITRICIS MARIAE
A
B
H

*Fig. 11. Grimaldi's sketch of the entrance-way to the Veronica chapel in old St Peter's, showing the twisted columns and the mosaic panels above the arch*

104 of his manuscript] have recorded every main detail of this entrance-way.[2] Over the arch was carved in Latin the inscription 'The House of the Most Holy Mary Mother of God', topped by an over-size Byzantine-style mosaic of the Virgin Mary as Queen of Heaven, accompanied by side-panels of scenes from the life of Christ. At the Virgin's feet was set the diminutive figure of the chapel's founder, the early eighth-century Greek pope, John VII, and thanks to Paul V's enlightened conservation policy this latter mosaic [pls. 22–23, below left], happens to be one of a few fragments from the original decoration which survive to this day. Preserved in the Vatican grottoes it shows John as a tonsured, square-haloed figure with the pallium on his shoulders and holding a model of his chapel, readily corroborating the general accuracy of Grimaldi's sketch.

Grimaldi further sketched[3] and described all the main features of interest inside the chapel [fig. 12]. Set into the white marble floor was an oval slab of purple-and-white porphyry on which St Veronica's body was said to have been laid out in death. Built into the wall by the window was an ancient inscription recording the transfer of some relics in the time of the eighth-century Pope Hadrian I. Further along this wall, but higher up, were lively Byzantine-style mosaics depicting incidents from the lives of Sts Peter and Paul, created at the time of John VII's original founding of the chapel. On the floor to one side stood a red Egyptian-stone sarcophagus in which reposed the twelfth-century, Hertfordshire-born pope, Hadrian IV, the only Englishman ever to have been pope. Gracing the far wall, that of the basilica's entrance façade, was the chapel's founding altar to the Virgin Mary, adjoined by the small entrance-way mistakenly opened up by Pope Alexander VI in the Holy Year of 1500.

But the clear centre-piece of the whole chapel, and in this arrangement, strikingly reminiscent of the 'shroud' altar in present-day Turin Cathedral, was the imposing shrine of the Veronica. Grimaldi's ever-helpful sketch[4] [pl. 23, above right] and accompanying description[5] conveys this as set in tiers, rather in the manner of a wedding-cake, and adding to this resemblance would have been the different coloured stones with which it was constructed, marble, porphyry and serpentine, among others. At ground level, surrounding an altar decorated with a sixteenth-century painting of St Veronica with Sts Peter and Paul, there stood on square bases four eight-foot-high white marble columns. These supported a platform perhaps twelve feet across, topped by a deep plinth with columned sides, and ornamented with a medallion-style half-length representation of St Veronica.

On top of this second tier, now well above human height and presumably accessible only by ladder, stood a further, smaller platform supporting two columns of the twisted variety. These flanked a heavy iron grille guarding two bronze doors. Only once behind these bronze doors could there be reached the silk-lined interior in which reposed the silver casket containing the Veronica, and even this latter was protected by two different locks.

Now Grimaldi, conscientious though he was, of course had few

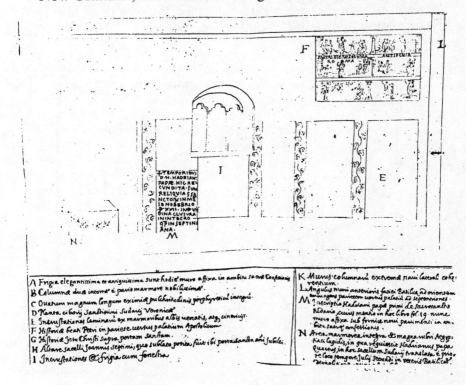

Fig. 12. Grimaldi's sketch of the interior of the Veronica chapel, showing wall decorations (E); mosaic scenes of the lives of Sts Peter and Paul (F); window (I); inscription of the time of the eighth–century Pope Hadrian I (M); and sarcophagus of the twelfth-century English pope, Hadrian IV (N)

of the critical skills of twentieth-century historical training. Accepting the legend that the Veronica had been brought to Rome by Veronica herself back in the first century AD, and noting that the chapel was quite indisputably built by John VII (besides the image of John as donor, there was a corroborative inscription over the doorway),[6] he not unreasonably assumed that John must have built the chapel specifically to house the Veronica. And since John's pontificate was between AD 705 and 707, to Grimaldi it seemed self-evident that the Veronica's shrine and its preservation in the chapel must date at least as far back as this time.

For our part, although we can make no such assumptions, this does not mean that we need to abandon the wealth of historical information that Grimaldi puts at our disposal.

*Fig. 13. Grimaldi's sketch of the engraving on the casket of the Veronica, as it existed in the early seventeenth century. It is unknown whether this is still preserved*

120

Only from Grimaldi, for instance, do we have any information about the Veronica's silver casket as it existed in the seventeenth century.[7] His square-shaped drawing of this [fig. 13] shows it as engraved with a 'holy face' flanked by the figures of Sts Peter and Paul, and with the tiny figure of the donor, a 'Master Matthew', kneeling below. Grimaldi tentatively identified this 'Matthew' as Matteo Massaroli, canon of St Peter's around the year 1360, but whatever the accuracy of this, the little that can be gauged of the casket's style suggests it is of too late a date to help our research into the Veronica's origins. Nonetheless, like Marco Polo's asbestos, it is another of those objects that would be well worth examination if, as is most likely, it still exists somewhere behind the scenes in the present-day Veronica pier.

Much more positively datable from Grimaldi's information are the bronze doors which protected the Veronica's inner sanctum on the topmost tier of its shrine, and which likewise may still be preserved. Grimaldi reproduced an inscription[8] [fig. 14] that was apparently removed from the Veronica shrine at the time of its destruction, on which was written in Latin:

Celestine III had this work done in the seventh year of his pontificate; Hubert of Piacenza made the doors.

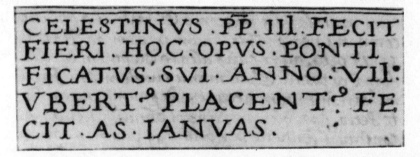

*Fig. 14. Grimaldi's transcript of the Celestine III inscription on the Veronica shrine*

Although this leaves slightly unclear whether the 'work' being referred to was the whole shrine, part of the shrine, or just the doors, nonetheless it firmly establishes the completion of the Veronica shrine's topmost section, inclusive of the doors, as

121

by not later than 1198, the seventh and last year of nonagenarian Celestine's pontificate. It also checks out with the earlier noted information that Celestine III conducted a special showing of the Veronica for King Philippe Auguste of France in 1191.

Taking us further back in time, although Grimaldi provided no information as to why the English pope, Hadrian IV, should have chosen to be buried in the Veronica's chapel, he found an attestation of an English contemporary of Hadrian's, Peter Mallius, that the Veronica was certainly housed in the chapel at least as early as the mid-twelfth century. According to Grimaldi, Mallius, who was a canon of St Peter's in 1161, wrote a *History of St Peter's* in which he remarked of the altar in the chapel built by John VII:

> Before this altar is the Sudarium of Christ which is called Veronica.[9]

In a separate passage, enumerating the many candles used to illuminate old St Peter's, Mallius listed:

> Before the Veronica, ten lamps, day and night.[10]

Grimaldi also found and quoted other documentary references which unquestionably push the Veronica's arrival in St Peter's yet further back. For the year 1131, he traced in the writings of Benedict, a canon of St Peter's, mention of Pope Innocent II carrying out a special ceremony of incensing all the altars of St Peter's. According to Benedict, after performing this rite on various others, Innocent

> . . . went to the sweatcloth [sudarium] of Christ which is called Veronica, and similarly to the altar of Holy Mary.[11]

For the year 1100, Grimaldi found a gradual, or anthem book, written on ancient parchment, in which could be read:

> On the night of the nativity of Our Lord . . . we process to the sweatcloth of Christ [i.e. the Veronica] singing the 'Te Deum Laudamus'. . .[12]

Furthest back of all, dating to the year 1011, the truly Dark Age pontificate of Benedict VIII, Grimaldi located 'an ancient pension grant written in Lombard script, listed in the Basilica archives as folio 346, bundle 223, container 61.' The crucial feature of this document was that it was drawn up by a scribe who identified himself as:

> + John, humble scribe and caretaker of Holy Mary in Beronika [i.e. Veronica] [fig. 15, below].[13]

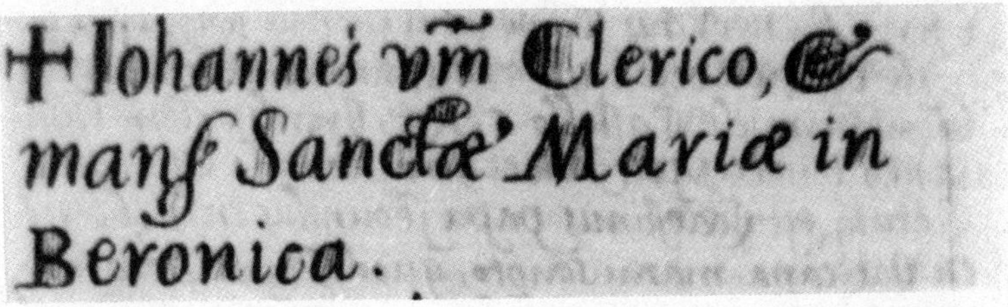
+ Iohannes vm̃ Clerico, & mans Sanctæ Mariæ in
Beronica.

*Fig. 15. The earliest-known reference to the Veronica as preserved in John VII's chapel in St Peter's, Grimaldi's transcript of a document dating from the year 1011*

From all this it is reasonable to infer that the Veronica cloth, in the form that we have so laboriously reconstructed from Pietro Strozzi's copy, was certainly an extant relic in St Peter's as early as the year 1100, and almost certainly as early as 1011 given that John VII's chapel already carried the Veronica name in that year.

But how much earlier was it brought to St Peter's? This is far more difficult to establish. As already mentioned Grimaldi believed the Veronica to have been there at least as far back as the 705–7 time of Pope John VII. In support of this Grimaldi even noted two tablets with John's name that were found in the Veronica shrine at the time of its demolition.[14] But even if valid, this is not necessarily evidence that John ever built the shrine for the Veronica, or knew of this latter's existence. Although he may have constructed a part of the shrine, this might simply have been as a canopy for his altar to the Virgin Mary, this altar when the Veronica came to Rome simply being switched to one side so that the Veronica could take up prime position under the canopy.

Particularly strongly suggesting that the Veronica was not brought to St Peter's in John VII's time is the fact that the chapel's original mosaic decoration, which John unquestionably commissioned in his lifetime (indicated not least by the square halo on his portrait), conveys not the slightest hint of the existence of any Veronica cult alongside that of the Virgin Mary. Although Grimaldi sketched and listed every scene, including those of Christ and the Virgin from over the doorway, and those of Sts Peter and Paul inside on the wall by the window, yet these embody nothing either of the Veronica story,[15] or of Jesus creating any imprint of his face on cloth.

Furthermore there is an otherwise inexplicable silence on the part of those writers of around this time who might have been expected to mention the Veronica, had it been in existence. One such was the sixth-century Frankish historian Gregory of Tours, who had a particular love of the miraculous, and told umpteen stories of objects and places of this kind. Yet his writings indicate no knowledge of the Veronica cloth. Similarly the eighth-century Venerable Bede, directly contemporary with Pope John VII, would undoubtedly have been fascinated by the idea of Jesus having left an imprint of his face on a cloth preserved in Rome. Yet it is quite clear from his writings that he likewise knew nothing of any such kind.

Not least, when on two occasions a serious danger threatened Rome during the century and a half following John VII's time – the first the arrival of a Lombard army in 754,[16] the second when a snake caused panic in Rome's city centre in 846 – it was the Sancta Sanctorum Acheropita [col.pl. III], not the Veronica, that was carried in procession to reassure Rome's citizens of their guarantee of divine protection.

Accordingly, on the basis of documentary and artistic sources, the only reasonable inference is that whenever, and from wherever, the Veronica arrived in Rome, it was most likely not before 846, the time that the Acheropita was clearly still pre-eminent, and not after 1011, when we have the first reasonably certain indication that the Veronica was now present in Rome.

Before accepting this as all that can be learned of the Veronica before 1207, there is, however, another avenue of enquiry open to us. It may be recalled from our earlier chapter featuring the redoubtable Gerald of Wales, who of course was alive in 1207, that there was a perceptible shift in the story of the woman Veronica as understood in his time, compared with that of two centuries later.

Thus whereas around 1380 the internationally popular book, *Meditations on the Life of Christ*, carried the supposedly 'traditional' story of Jesus's face being wiped as he toiled towards Calvary, Gerald, as we established, believed the image to have been created sometime before Jesus's arrest, on an occasion when he was leaving the Temple. Furthermore, as if to convey that even around 1207 there were still uncertainties as to how the image had originated, Gerald also remarked:

> . . . some maintain, playing upon the name, that the Veronica is so called from *vera iconia*, that is to say, 'true image'.[17]

The question accordingly arises that if such variations in popular understanding of the Veronica's origin could occur after 1207, might there have been any similar shifts during the preceding centuries? And indeed there were. Writing in the early 1900s the erudite Belgian Benedictine monk Dom Henri Leclercq, grappling to create a suitably authoritative 'Veronica' entry for his fifteen-volume dictionary of Christian archaeology,[18] exasperatedly spoke of an 'imbroglio of legends' when he tried to trace the whole history of the evolution of the Veronica story.

Thus from around the middle of the twelfth century Peter Mallius, the already-mentioned English canon of St Peter's, conjectured that the Veronica's creation might have been at the time of Jesus's 'bloody sweat' in the Garden of Gethsemane:

> . . . when his sweat became as drops of blood flowed to the ground.[19]

Clearly Mallius had in mind here the passage in the gospel of Luke 22: 44:

> In his anguish he prayed . . . and his sweat fell to the ground like great drops of blood.

Not much earlier than Mallius, however, a variety of manuscripts dating from the eighth to eleventh centuries, one entitled *The Healing of Tiberius*,[20] another, *The Vengeance, or Avenging of the Saviour*,[21] revealed quite a different understanding. In these Veronica was identified as the 'woman with the issue of blood'

125

who had been healed by touching Jesus's garment, as related in the gospel story of Matthew 9: 20–22; Mark 5: 25–34, and Luke 8: 43–48. But instead of this Veronica or anyone else receiving a cloth imprinted with Jesus's features, she was simply accredited with owning a 'portrait' of Jesus, the important feature of which was that it could cure disease. With this she was described as first healing an Aquitainian king called Titus, or Tyrus, then, as the highlight of the story, none other than the Roman emperor Tiberius himself.

Furthermore, seemingly confounding Gerald of Wales's suggestion that the name Veronica might simply have derived from the description 'vera iconia', or 'true likeness', the actual name Veronica (or Berenice, as in some versions), has proved to be traceable back as far as the fourth century, again in association with the woman with the issue of blood. She figures thus, without either portrait or imprinted cloth, in a work known as *The Acts of Pilate*[22] of which there survive versions in Latin, Coptic, Syrian, and Armenian.

And to complicate matters yet further, the ecclesiastical historian Eusebius of Caesarea, in his authoritative *History of the Church* written as early as AD 325, spoke of the woman with the issue of blood (he did not name her as Veronica), as having erected a *statue* of Jesus in gratitude for her cure.[23] Indeed, Eusebius and other authors of the next two centuries[24] described having seen this statue with their own eyes at Paneas, or Caesarea Philippi, supposed to have been the home town of the woman with the issue of blood. There are even at least two catacomb frescoes[25] that seem to convey this statue's appearance [pl. 23, below right].

Accordingly, if for no better reason than to clear our minds of so many complications, it may be helpful to look at a highly simplified summary of the legend's stages of development as follows:

1400 Veronica's cloth was an impression of Jesus's features made as he toiled towards Calvary. It is preserved in Rome. [Stations of the Cross; *Meditations on the Life of Christ*]

1200 Veronica's cloth was an impression of Jesus's features made sometime before his Passion. It is preserved in Rome. [Gerald of Wales; Peter Mallius]

1000 Veronica, the woman with an issue of blood,

had a portrait of Jesus which could heal the sick
[*Avenging of the Saviour; Healing of Tiberius*]

400 [Version 1] The woman with an issue of blood
was called Veronica [*Acts of Pilate*].
[Version 2] The woman with the issue of blood
had a statue of Jesus [Eusebius]

100 An unidentified woman was cured by Jesus of an
issue of blood. [Matthew 9: 20–22; Mark 5: 25–34;
Luke 8: 43–48]

From this it seems then quite evident that only sometime after the
year 1000 did there emerge arguably the two most salient features
of the Veronica: first, that it was some form of imprint of Jesus's
features on cloth; and second, that it was an actual physical relic
preserved in Rome. It would seem that with the coming to Rome
of the piece of cloth imprinted with Jesus's likeness there simply
became grafted onto it the earlier, but hitherto unrelated story of
the woman Veronica. Just as remarked by Gerald of Wales, the
assonance between Veronica and vera icon', 'true likeness' may
well have helped this process of grafting.

But what was it that could have caused this crucial development
around AD 1000 and, as we have good reason to believe, the
coming to Rome of the image-bearing cloth that Pietro Strozzi so
interestingly copied in the early seventeenth century?

As it happens, and as Dom Leclercq and many other scholars
were not slow to recognize, there is in fact very little mystery
concerning this. From the sixth century the one legend that most
Christians all over Europe took far more seriously than anything
to do with the woman Veronica was the Eastern story of Jesus
imprinting his likeness on cloth, the very one with which the Genoa
and S. Silvestro 'holy faces' were associated. According to the
most general form of this – and it is one equally as tangled in its
development as that of the Veronica – there was a first-century king
called Abgar, toparch of the independent principality of Edessa,
who was suffering from an incurable disease, and sent a messenger
to Jerusalem to ask Jesus to come and heal him. Jesus was either
unable or unwilling to go to Edessa himself, but instead arranged
for the sending after his death of a disciple called Thaddaeus,
or Addai, who brought to Abgar a cloth imprinted with Jesus's
likeness. When Abgar saw this he was cured of his disease, and
immediately asked to be instructed in the Christian faith.

Immediately evident is the similarity of this story to the basic pre-1000 elements of the Veronica story, with Abgar in place of Tiberius, and Thaddaeus/Addai in place of Veronica. The links between the two become even more apparent when we learn that in an early form of the Abgar story, the fourth-century *Doctrine of Addai*,[26] what was brought to Abgar was not a cloth, but a painted portrait, just as in the *Avenging of the Saviour*. Furthermore, according to Eastern tradition Thaddaeus's place of origin was Paneas/Caesarea Philippi, the very same where, according to Eusebius and others, Veronica/the woman with the issue of blood had her home.

Furthermore, with regard to priority, there can be no doubt that the Eastern, or Edessa version was by far the senior of the two strands of legends. Its concept of Jesus having imprinted his likeness on cloth could be dated back at least as early as the sixth century, easily five centuries before the equivalent development in the Veronica story. During the eighth-century iconoclastic dispute great Byzantine writers such as John of Damascus quoted the story of Abgar of Edessa as one to be taken totally seriously.

But of even greater importance, the Edessan 'holy face' that was the centre-point of this story was quite unquestionably a real-life historical cloth 'relic' that could likewise be dated at least as far back as the sixth century. Regarded as too holy for public gaze, it was kept in the strictest seclusion in Edessa, but then in AD 944 transferred in triumph to Constantinople. Specially restricted copies were made of it, just as later of the Veronica. But again just as in the case of the Veronica, there were no public expositions right up until the time of the Crusader Sack of Constantinople in 1204. What thereafter became of it is uncertain, the 'holy faces' of Genoa and S. Silvestro both, among others, being claimed as the original.

Given then the already established close similarity between the Veronica, as known from Strozzi's copy, and the Genoa and S. Silvestro original/copies of the 'holy face' of Edessa, the Veronica seems most likely to have originated as a 'vera icon', or exact copy of the Edessa 'holy face' that was almost certainly specially made for Rome not long after the Edessa image's arrival in Constantinople in 944. The period between 944 and 1011, the year of the first indication of the Veronica's presence in Rome, was one of the darkest and least well-recorded in Rome's history. Furthermore it was one of several diplomatic missions between

Rome and Constantinople just before the Great Schism between the eastern and western churches that took final effect about 1009. The Veronica may well have been brought as a gift of such a mission, and indeed is unlikely to have been brought after 1009 because of the very breakdown in relations between the two churches following that year.

We have established, then, that the Veronica as a physical cloth relic, in the impressionistic, outlineless form known to us from Strozzi's copy, certainly dates back to around the year 1000. We have also established that even at that early time it was a copy of something yet older, the Edessa 'holy face'. In this respect it would seem to have been for the 'holy face' of Edessa precisely what Strozzi's copy would be to the Veronica some six hundred years later – a 'true likeness' or 'vera icon', that is, as exact a copy as it was humanly possible to make. Also, looked at another way, Strozzi's copy was effectively a copy of a copy of whatever the 'holy face' of Edessa might have been, or might continue to be.

For the overall purposes of our study, there is a crucial significance to all these deductions. They unequivocally set the concept of Jesus imprinting an outlineless 'impression' of his features on cloth to far earlier than the very earliest date allowed for the Turin shroud by carbon dating. Furthermore they now equally firmly establish the 'original' of this idea as not the Veronica, but instead the 'holy face' that was brought from Edessa to Constantinople in 944.

Yet all this, in its turn, only presents us with yet a new problem: what was or is the 'holy face' of Edessa? Does it exist today as the 'holy face' preserved at Genoa? Or as the S. Silvestro one that is now in the pope's private chapel? Was it perhaps, as some historians have argued, a cloth that was kept in Paris up until 1792, only to be destroyed during the French Revolution? Or is there yet another alternative?

As we are about to discover, the true identity of the 'holy face' of Edessa lies at the very heart of the whole mystery.

## Chapter Eleven

# A CRUCIAL QUESTION OF IDENTITY . . .

*The chief point, that the Saviour's face was impressed on the cloth by some miracle, is agreed by all*

Author of Byzantine Feast Sermon, Constantinople, AD 945

In the quest for whatever the Edessa 'holy face' may have been, or may continue to be, it is perhaps first helpful to gain some idea of the exalted 'secret place' in which it was kept while in Constantinople up to the time of the Crusader Sack of the city in 1204.

The present-day visitor to Istanbul, if at all tempted to wander to the site of the former Great Palace of the Byzantine Emperors, will see little more than squalid hovels, pot-holed roadways and weed-covered, refuse-littered stumps of former buildings.

But a thousand years ago, here on the banks of the Sea of Marmora, there glistened a palace complex with few equals either before or since. Amidst a cluster of buildings inclusive of an orderly barracks, a huge hippodrome, and magnificent baths complex, rose an imperial living quarters and audience chamber that no foreign invader had sullied since the Emperor Constantine's first foundation of the city back in the fourth century. Those who sought business with the emperor would watch him rise and descend in dazzling robes on a mechanically controlled golden throne, surrounded by mechanical roaring lions and mechanical singing birds on a golden plane tree. Perfumed and bejewelled officials would fuss around him like exquisite puppets.

And somewhere not far from the audience chamber lay the Sacred, or Pharos Chapel that enshrined a collection of relics of

Jesus so complete that by contrast those in Rome seemed second-rate. According to the list as given by a crusader in 1204:

> . . . two pieces of the True Cross as large as the leg of a man . . . the iron of the lance with which Our Lord had his side pierced, two of the nails which were driven though his hands and his feet, the tunic which he wore and which was taken from him when they led him to the Mount of Calvary and . . . the blessed crown with which he was crowned.[1]

Quite incontestably a matter of historical fact is that throughout the years 944 to 1204 there reposed in this collection in Constantinople, as by no means its most insignificant item, the 'holy face' cloth imprinted with Jesus's likeness that the Byzantines variously referred to as the Holy Image of Edessa, the Holy Acheiropoietos ('made without hands'), and the Holy Mandylion, or 'mantle'. Despite not having a Grimaldi to sketch the scene, we nevertheless know that it was set in the chapel on the right-hand side, facing the east.[2]

But hanging like a pall of mystery over the exact identity of this cloth is the fact that it was regarded as so holy, and the security surrounding it so tight, that just as in the case of the Veronica before 1207, there is no clear record of it ever being exhibited publicly throughout its entire time in Constantinople. Those allowed to view it would seem to have been only the emperor and the highest clergy, and even then on very special occasions. In the words of a Byzantine hymn:

> How can we with mortal eyes
> contemplate this image, whose celestial
>   splendour
> the host of heaven presumes not to behold?
> He who dwells in heaven condescends this day
> to visit us by his venerable image;
> He who is seated on the cherubim
> visits us this day by a picture,
> which the Father has delineated
> with his immaculate hand,
> which He has formed in an ineffable manner,

and which we sanctify by adoring it
with fear and love.[3]

Furthermore this same attitude would seem to have prevailed even before this 'holy face' arrived in Constantinople, while it was still at its first home, the eastern city of Edessa, now Urfa in Eastern Turkey. According to a tenth-century Byzantine document describing the ceremonial accorded to it while in Edessa:

> The archbishop alone was permitted to go near the holy and immaculate Image, to worship and to kiss it, and after this to remove the white cloth that lay upon it, and to wrap it in another of purple colour.[4]

And elsewhere in the same document:

> . . . no one was allowed to draw near or touch the holy likeness with his lips or eyes. The result of this was that divine fear increased their faith and made the revered object palpably more fearful and awe-inspiring.

So exactly what can we retrieve from early sources that may help us recognize and identify the 'holy face' of Edessa? Unquestionably it was thought to be very old even when first brought to Constantinople in 944. In this regard the gold relief scenes studding the Palaeologue frame [col. pl. IVd] of the Genoese candidate convey the general Byzantine idea of its origins, as already very briefly sketched in the last chapter.

Running anti-clockwise round the frame commencing at the lower right-hand side, the scenes [pl. 24] show first King Abgar of Edessa, sick in bed, sending out a messenger, Ananias, in the hope of persuading Jesus to come to Edessa to cure him (scene a). In Jerusalem we see Ananias trying unsuccessfully to paint Jesus' portrait (scene b), then Jesus, after washing himself (scene c), imprinting his likeness on the cloth with which he had dried himself, and giving this to Ananias, together with a message to take back to Abgar (scene d). On Ananias' return to Edessa, we find Abgar miraculously cured by the 'holy face' (scene e), accepting conversion to Christianity and throwing down the city's pagan idols (scene f). Then after Abgar's death there apparently occurs a pagan backlash, for a Christian bishop is portrayed hiding the 'holy face' (scene g) in an apparent attempt to ensure its safety during a time of persecution of Edessa's Christians.

Theoretically the events of these scenes occurred in the very first Christian century, and although inevitably semi-legendary they at least have as a basis of fact that there was a King Abgar V (AD 13–50) directly contemporary with Jesus; also that Christianity had certainly become established and officially tolerated in Edessa as early as the late second century, during the reign of Abgar VIII (AD 179–212).[5]

The frame's next two scenes jump chronologically several centuries, for there follows the 'holy face's' purported rediscovery by an Edessan bishop during a siege of Edessa by the Persians (scene h); and its miraculous routing of the Persians shortly after (scene i). This siege of Edessa by Persians is historically known to have taken place in the year 544, and from this point on the 'holy face's' existence is quite uncontestably historical, with many documentary references to its existence in Edessa. In the final scene (scene j) there occurs a further substantial chronological jump, the 'holy face' shown being brought in triumph from Edessa to Constantinople in 944. By way of demonstration of the continuance of its healing power this scene shows the cure of a madman simultaneous with the 'holy face's' arrival in the Byzantine capital.

Now suffice it to say that this illustrated story of the 'holy face's' origins is but one of several slightly differing versions that prevailed and indeed continue to prevail in the world of the Eastern Orthodox Church. The consistent feature is the 'holy face's' arrival at Edessa sometime while this was ruled by kings with the name Abgar (up to AD 214), but exactly what happened at this time has to be considered more of the stuff of legend than of history.

Quite definite, however, is that immediately upon the 'holy face's' apparent rediscovery in the sixth century – it was described as sealed up in a niche above the gate of the city – there emerged the specific idea of its image being some form of watery impression of Jesus' features. The so-called *Acts of Thaddaeus* of this century recounted that Jesus had:

> . . . asked to wash himself, and a towel was given to him, and when he had washed himself he wiped his face

133

with it. And his image having been imprinted upon the linen, he gave it to Ananias . . .[6]

Dating no later than 560 a Syriac hymn extolling the then newly built Cathedral of Edessa likened the mottling of the cathedral's marble to 'the image not made by hands'.[7] The late sixth-century chronicler Evagrius, mentioning the image's part in routing the Persians during the siege of 544, spoke of it as 'the divinely wrought image, which the hands of men did not form.'[8]

In all history these are the earliest documented instances of the idea of Jesus having imprinted some form of likeness of himself on cloth, predating by four to five centuries anything equivalent relating to the Veronica. They are also in all history the earliest known instances of this idea being associated with anyone. Not even among the diversity of Greek myths is there anything that might even remotely be considered some form of inspiration. Arguably, therefore, the idea that the 'holy face' was created on the cloth by Jesus washing himself can only have arisen from some sixth-century direct observation of the apparently visibly watery mode of its composition.

Equally interesting, furthermore, is that from the time of the 'holy face's' arrival in Constantinople in the tenth century, the author of an official sermon[9] to mark the event felt obliged to introduce a slightly differing account of how the imprint might have been created, again seemingly as a result of direct observation. While repeating the old 'Jesus washed himself' version, and stressing that 'the chief point, that the Saviour's face was impressed on the cloth by some miracle, is agreed by all', he recounted at length an alternative version which he claimed to be 'neither incredible nor short or reliable witnesses.' This he offered because 'it would not be at all surprising if the facts had become distorted in view of the time that has elapsed.' According to this:

They say that when Christ was about to go voluntarily to death he was seen to reveal his human weakness, feel anguish, and pray. According to the Evangelist, sweat dropped from him like drops of blood. Then they say he took this piece of cloth which we see now from one of the disciples and wiped off the drops of sweat on it. At once the still visible impression of that divine face was produced. Jesus gave the cloth to Thomas, and

134

instructed that after his Ascension to heaven he should send Thaddaeus with it to Abgar . . .[10]

Immediately recognizable here is exactly the same idea of the image's creation that Peter Mallius recounted two centuries later of Rome's Veronica. This adds further support to the Veronica's origin as a copy of the Edessa 'holy face' dating from after the latter's arrival in Constantinople, acquiring the 'updated' story of its origin at one and the same time.

But it also seems evident that this new version of the 'holy face's' origin was inspired by someone's direct viewing of the holy face after its arrival in Constantinople, and their observation that the imprint seemed not just to be a simple wateriness, but something more along the lines of a 'bloody sweat'. Further attestation to this same quality to the imprint is also to be found in a quite independent work of this time, the eleventh-century Old French version of the *Life of Saint Alexius*, in which the story's hero, the 'Man of God' Alexius was described going as a humble penitent to:

> . . . the city of Edessa
> in which there was preserved a blood-stained
> image of the Lord
> Not made by hands.[11]

The inevitable question that therefore arises is whether similarly interesting data of the Edessa holy face's appearance can be gleaned from the various early Byzantine artistic copies made of it. Here unfortunately, just as in the case of the Veronica, the initial problem is the copies' diversity, even among the relatively few that survive from around or before 1204.

First it is to be noted that there have survived no even remotely direct copies – that is, representations of the face as on some form of cloth – that can be dated with any certainty to before the 'holy face's' arrival in Constantinople in 944.[12] The reason for this may have been that earlier copies were destroyed during the period of iconoclasm, or image-smashing that rent the Byzantine world during the eighth century. Alternatively, while in Edessa the original may have been considered too holy to be represented directly. Further consideration will be given to this in a later chapter.

But even those copies surviving from between 944 and 1204 vary one from the other in aspects that plainly betray them as conveying the spirit rather than necessarily the actuality of the original.

Thus two eleventh-century-manuscript miniatures (one in the Vatican[13] [pl. 25a], one in Alexandria[14] [pl. 25b]), two twelfth-century frescoes (one in Gradac, Serbia [pl. 25c]; one at Spas Nereditsa, near Novgorod[15] [pl. 25d]), together with Jacques Pantaléon de Troyes' early thirteenth-century 'Holy Face of Laon' icon[16] [pl. 8, above], all represent the Edessa cloth as covered with some form of trellis pattern.

Yet this feature is absent from a late tenth/eleventh century fresco from Sakli, Cappadocia [pl. 25e], from an icon of this same period in St Catherine's monastery, Mount Sinai[17] [pl. 25f], from two twelfth-century representations in Cyprus[18] [pl. 25g & 25h], and from a Russian fresco [pl. 25i] of this same date.[19] So was this a representation of some form of grille through which the 'holy face' was viewed, and which some artists omitted from their copies? We simply do not know.

Similarly, while the Alexandria miniature and Spas Nereditsa fresco show the cloth of the 'holy face' as fringed at its two sides, but not at top or bottom, the Vatican miniature shows it fringed top and bottom, but not at the sides, and the Laon and Sinai icons as fringed only at the bottom. While the Sinai icon and the Vatican and Alexandria miniatures represented Jesus as disembodied, but with a neck, all the rest represented him as still disembodied, but without a neck. Although the Sinai icon, the Gradac, Cyprus and Sakli frescoes and the two miniatures depict Jesus as with relatively straight-down hair, the Laon fresco and Spas Nereditsa show the ends of his hair as sharply splayed out at the sides. Not least, only the Vatican miniature and Laon icon show the background cloth as squarish; the rest show it as landscape aspect, and in most instances, quite largish.

All we seem to gain from these is the general impression that the Edessa 'holy face' was a disembodied, front-facing head of Jesus on cloth. And perhaps we should not expect more, for the Byzantines simply did not have any concern for the sort of accurate reproduction of the original we tend to regard as automatic at the present day. Their attitude is best conveyed by a famous story of a sixteenth-century Greek Orthodox priest who rejected a work he had commissioned from the renowned Renaissance painter Titian on the grounds 'Your scandalous figures stand quite out from the canvas: they are as bad as a group of statues!'[20] We should similarly not expect realistic direct representation of any bloodstains; the idea of artists even daring to represent the real Blood of Christ lay well into the future.

But as we have already noted, certain extant and non-extant 'holy faces' have been claimed to be the original of the 'holy face' of Edessa, so what of these? The very fact of a choice of claimants, no less than two owned by the Roman Catholic Church, suggests more than a little uncertainty surrounding the exact identity of the original. So is there any way of working through this difficulty?

Of the two just mentioned Roman Catholic claimants, per-haps the foremost, and the one to which we have already given the greater attention, is the 'holy face' of Genoa [col. pl. IVd], which reposes inside an ornate marble tabernacle atop a balconied marble shrine set to one side of the nave of Genoa's Church of St Bartholomew of the Armenians. With white columns set below the balcony and tabernacle area, the shrine is strikingly reminis-cent of the Veronica shrine in old St Peter's. And throughout the immaculate and modest-sized church there are sixteenth- and seventeenth-century paintings illustrating the story of the cloth being brought to Abgar of Edessa.

Furthermore, unquestionably this 'holy face' came from Con-stantinople. Not only is its already-described Palaeologue frame a thoroughly Byzantine one, there is little reason to doubt the popular tradition that it was a gift to Genoa's Doge Leonardo Montaldo from the Byzantine Emperor John V Palaeologus, whom Montaldo had helped against the Turks. To many, also particularly signatory is the 'holy face's' Greek inscription, TO ΑΓΙΟΝ ΜΑΝΔΥΛΙΟΝ 'The Holy Mandylion', one of the most popular appellations of the Edessan 'holy face'.

In fact this latter argument is quite a flimsy one. Many copies, including a seventeenth-century one owned by Her Majesty Queen Elizabeth II at Buckingham Palace,[21] carry the same Greek inscrip-tion. It is no more indicative of the original than the name 'Mona Lisa' on a Louvre Museum souvenir postcard.

Nonetheless, quite clearly this particular 'holy face of Edessa', whether it was or was not the original, genuinely seems to have been a work of major importance. This is evident not least from the various phases of its development revealed during the already

137

mentioned examination by the art specialist Colette Dufour Bozzo in 1969.

Thus according to Ms Dufour Bozzo's reconstruction the 'holy face's' earliest form seems to have been what we may best term the Natural Phase. In this the face was simply painted on a gold background onto a panel of cedar that was probably wider than the present-day dimensions. As discernible from X-rays and tomography, it seems to have been depicted without outlines and without any accompanying lettering, and to have remained in this form at least sufficient time to become darkened by candles and incense.

Then there occurred the second phase, which we will call the Pearl Phase. In this the more diffuse features of the face were heightened with black outlining, and the identifying letters IC XC painted into the upper corners. Pearls were affixed all round the entire outline of the face, the traces of these being clearly revealed by the X-ray. Other gems were probably added to decorate the arms of a cross painted behind the head. Also at this same time a cross was painted on the reverse side.

Sometime later there occurred what may be best described as the Cloth Phase. The surround of pearls and precious stones was stripped away, the holes left in the wood filled in. The original painting of the face was then partly covered over with an approximately six-inch by ten-inch piece of cloth (only two-thirds the size of the full panel), and sealed down with gesso, on which was painted the face that is now visible. This was then covered over with a 'cut-out' silver plate or plates of the kind we have already established as the common link between it and the Veronica and the S. Silvestro images.

Only sometime after this cloth phase was the image restored and represented in the silver-gilt case that we may term the Palaeologue Phase.

Now this careful reconstruction by Colette Dufour Bozzo enables two important deductions. First, if the 'holy face' began merely as a panel painting on wood, and was only partially covered over with a piece of cloth at the third or Cloth stage of its development, then it is most unlikely to have been the original. Diverse as the surviving copies are, they consistently indicate a face on a substantial size piece of cloth. The inclusion of a mere six-inch by ten-inch portion of cloth as late as the third of the 'holy face's' phase of development suggests that this feature was no more than

138

a token or symbol of the universally agreed fact that the original was on cloth.

The second deduction derives from Dufour Bozzo's finding that it was as late as the third or Cloth phase that the Genoa 'holy face' received its 'cut-out' silver plate framing the face, the type that we have already established it to have shared with its Veronica and S. Silvestro counterparts (see page 113). If this was the case, and if, as we have also established, the Veronica had most likely already arrived in Rome framed in this way as early as 1011, then the Genoa 'holy face's' two earlier phases arguably must predate 1011. Accordingly, even though it was not the Edessa original, the Genoa 'holy face' in its earliest phase, just visible via X-ray and tomographic techniques, would seem to have been a particularly early and important copy, almost certainly made while the original was still in Edessa.

The second 'holy face' claimed as the original of the one of Edessa is that which was in Rome's Church of S. Silvestro up to 1870,[22] and which is now kept in the Matilda Chapel, the pope's private chapel within the Vatican Apostolic Palace adjoining St Peter's. Although never seen publicly, photographs [col. pl. IVc] show this to be housed in a magnificent baroque frame/reliquary known to have been donated by one Sister Dionora Chiarucci,[23] and to have been completed in 1623 by the silver/goldsmith Francesco Comi. A late sixteenth-century fresco on the gable over the high altar of the S. Silvestro church conveys something of the frames in which it was housed preceding Comi's.[24] An outer one is Renaissance in style, while inside this is one with decoration suggestive of Gothic or late medieval craftsmanship.

But although the 'cut-out' innermost frame, the one shared with its Veronica and Genoa counterparts, suggests it to be at least as old as the eleventh century, and we have earlier suggested it to have been acquired about the time of Margherita Colonna, this 'holy face's' actual historical documentation dates it back earlier than 1517 – when the nuns of S. Silvestro were forbidden to exhibit it for fear it might cause confusion with the Veronica.[25] Furthermore it has not been allowed anything of the intensive specialist internal examination accorded to the Genoa 'holy face'. When the Italian art specialist Professor Carlo Bertelli was allowed to view it in the sixties he reported it to bear at the rear a seal with a cardinal's arms, accompanied by 'a parchment scroll, folded and with traces of writing.'[26] But even he, as one of Italy's most distinguished academics, was not allowed to open this to discover what light it might throw on this holy face's earlier history.

However, it seems unlikely that this, in its turn, can be the original of the 'holy face' of Edessa for exactly the same reason as in the case of Genoa: that careful visual examination reveals it to have been painted partly over yet another ten-inch by six-inch 'token' piece of cloth pasted onto the backing board. This piece of cloth is of interest in its own right because, according to Professor Bertelli, where the paint has flaked off its weave seems to be herring-bone[27] the same as that of Turin's 'shroud'. The possible significance of this will become more apparent later.

Meanwhile, although the third, or Paris, claimant to identity with the original Edessan 'holy face' is one that no longer exists, it in fact needs to be taken perhaps even more seriously than the others because the case for its identity has been argued by some eminent historians, notably Sir Steven Runciman.[28]

The background to this particular claimant is that after 1204 Constantinople became ruled by a series of incompetent western Crusaders, prime among whom was Baldwin II de Courtenay, a man so incapable of managing his finances that between 1239 and 1246 he pawned the Imperial Palace's last remaining sacred relics of Christ. On being unable to redeem them he had to give them up to his Venetian money-lenders, who found a willing new owner in the saintly King Louis IX of France, at that time eager to acquire the very holiest of relics for the magnificent Sainte Chapelle he was building in Paris. Concerned to avoid any possibility that Baldwin might claim the collection back, Louis insisted on his signing a gold-sealed transfer deed, a Chrysobull, which in its list of the relics being acquired included a 'holy towel attached to a board.[29] Since the 'holy face' of Edessa was said to have similarly been mounted on a board, Sir Steven Runciman and others have not unreasonably identified this as one and the same as this relic ceded by Baldwin to Louis.

Regrettably, whatever the true identity of this 'holy towel' that went to Paris, it is now lost to us, for it was destroyed along with many other treasures of St Louis' Sainte Chapelle in 1792, during the worst excesses of the French Revolution. But despite Sir Steven Runciman's eminence, there is in fact cause for serious doubt that even this could have been the true 'holy face' of Edessa. This is for the reason that following its arrival in Paris it faded into virtually total obscurity, even repeatedly failing to be listed in formal inventories. As Professor Bertelli, among others, has argued, it seems incredible that a 'holy face' that had been so highly thought of in the Byzantine world could have attracted so little interest in the west, particularly just at the very time when the Veronica was beginning to capture public imagination.[30] In this same context it is important to note that the Baldwin–Louis Chrysobull does not even mention there having been a face on the 'holy towel'. I believe it fair to conclude, therefore, that it was not the true 'holy face' of Edessa.

But if we can identify none of the three principal claimants as the true Edessan 'holy face', is there anything else still in existence that it might possibly have been? Here at long last it becomes unavoidable mentioning the 'shroud' of Turin. While at first sight this might seem implausible, not least because we have so far understood the Edessa cloth to bear only the imprint of Jesus's face, there are a variety of clues that there may literally have been more to it than normally met the eye.

Earlier in this chapter, for instance, we quoted as one of the earliest mentions of the Edessa 'holy face' the passage from the sixth-century *Acts of Thaddaeus* that Jesus had:

> asked to wash himself, and a towel was given to him . . .
> And his image having been imprinted upon the linen,
> he gave it to Ananias.

Here the interesting feature is that in the original Greek text of this quotation the word translated as 'towel' is 'tetradiplon', meaning a cloth 'doubled in four'. It is a most unusual word, occurring in the entire corpus of Greek literature only in regard to the 'holy face' of Edessa, and it prompted me some twenty years ago to try 'doubling in four' a photograph of the 'shroud', just to see what might emerge.[31]

The result was more than astonishing. Doubled, then doubled twice again to give four times two folds, the 'shroud' face appeared disembodied on a landscape aspect cloth exactly as conveyed by the copyists of the Edessan 'holy face' pre-1204 [fig. 16]. From this and similar evidence I deduced that the 'shroud' had been one and the same as the 'holy face' of Edessa, which explained its otherwise unrecorded pre-fourteenth-century history. Why it had not been described as a 'shroud' during the Byzantine era

141

was simply because it had been folded and mounted on a board, so that only the face was visible.

Of course this was only a theory, and to most it very understandably seemed conclusively shattered when the carbon dating set the shroud's age as between 1260 and 1390, impossible to equate with the Edessa 'holy face's' certain historical existence between the sixth century and 1204.

But as recently as 1987 an Italian scholar resident in Rome, Professor Gino Zaninotto, happened to come across in the Vatican Library a Byzantine manuscript that had escaped all earlier studies of the Edessan 'holy face', both my own and even those of the formidable German scholar Ernst von Dobschütz whose profusely documented *Christusbilder* (The Face of Christ), published in

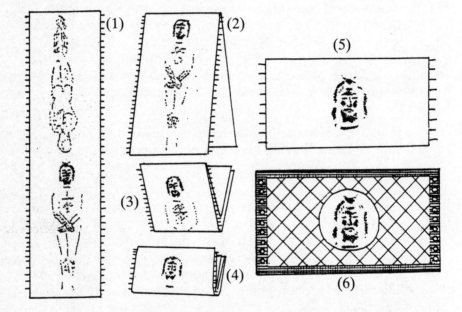

*Fig. 16. How the shroud may have been 'doubled in four' as the 'holy face' of Edessa: 1): The shroud full-length; 2): The shroud doubled; 3 & 4): doubled twice again, making 4 × 2 folds; 5): how the shroud face appears disembodied on a landscape aspect cloth when 'doubled in four in this way; 6): how the shroud may have appeared as the 'holy face' of Edessa, mounted on a board, and encased beneath a trellis-patterned cover*

142

(Above): *Late thirteenth-century depiction of the Veronica, of the Psalter and Book of Hours of Yolande de Soissons, as preserved in the Pierpont Morgan Library, New York;* (left): *The first-known depiction of the Veronica in a 'suspended cloth' form, from a late thirteenth-century* Apocalypse *manuscript, of English authorship, in the collection of the Gulbenkian Museum, Lisbon, Portugal;* (below left): *The first known depiction of the woman Veronica, dateable to 1353, which appears as an unobtrusive margin illumination on fol. 44v. of the British Library's Hours of Yolande of Flanders. Such depictions convey little confidence of any direct knowledge of the Veronica's actual appearance*

17

'St Veronica', early fifteenth-century panel painting by the so-called 'Master of St Veronica', as exhibited in the National Gallery, London. While this shows Jesus as without signs of suffering, another example, created by the same studio and preserved in the Pinacotheca, Munich, shows him anguished and crowned with thorns

(Left): *'St Veronica', early fifteenth-century drawing by the highly accomplished Master of Flemalle, which appears to have been a sketch for a panel painting in the Staedel Institut, Frankfurt. The drawing is preserved in the Fitzwilliam Museum, Cambridge;* (above): *'St Veronica' a tiny (13" x 9") but exquisitely detailed panel painting by the Flemish artist Hans Memling, created* circa *1470-80 and now preserved in the Samuel H. Kress Collection of the National Gallery of Art, Washington. Despite the artistic excellence of these fifteenth-century examples, they give little assurance of fidelity to the actual Veronica as preserved in Rome at this time*

(Right): *A more accurate fifteenth-century depiction of the Veronica cloth? Notable features are the sharply delineated hair and single-forked beard. From the early fifteenth-century Prayer Book of Philippe le Hardi, Duke of Burgundy;* (below left): *Another example of the sharply delineated type of Veronica. Mosaic of circa 1370, from scene of the Last Judgement at the south entrance to St Vitus's Cathedral, Prague;* (below right): *Veronica copy made in 1621 and preserved today in the Church of Gesù, Rome*

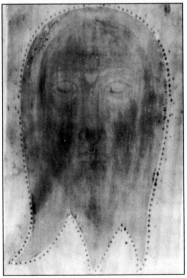

(Above): *The 'holy face' of Genoa (see also pl. 14), showing its earlier appearance as revealed under X-ray at the time of the specialist examination in 1969;* (left): *Tomographic photograph of the same icon also made during the 1969 examination. According to art specialists, the tomography seems to indicate that at the earliest stage of its development the face was painted without outlines*

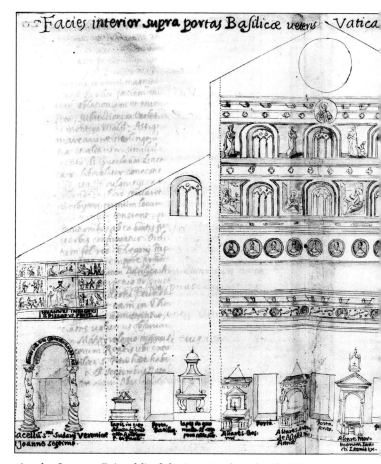

(Above): *Drawing by Jacopo Grimaldi of the interior facade of old St Peter's, showing the location of the Veronica chapel at far left. From Vatican Library manuscript Barberino lat 2733, fol. 120; (above right): Grimaldi's sketch of the Veronica shrine, the centre-piece of the Veronica chapel in old St Peter's. The inscription shows that Grimaldi believed it to have been constructed in AD 705, at the time of Pope John VII; (below left): Pope John VII, the Veronica chapel's founder. Mosaic fragment from the otherwise demolished entranceway to the original chapel, preserved today in the Vatican Grottoes; (below right): Jesus's cure of the 'woman with the issue of blood'. Fresco from the catacomb of Ss Peter & Marcellinus, Rome, thought to convey the appearance of a statue commemorating this cure extant at Paneas (now Banyas on Israel's northern border), up to the sixth-century AD. According to some sources, Veronica and the 'woman with the issue of blood' were one and the same person*

22

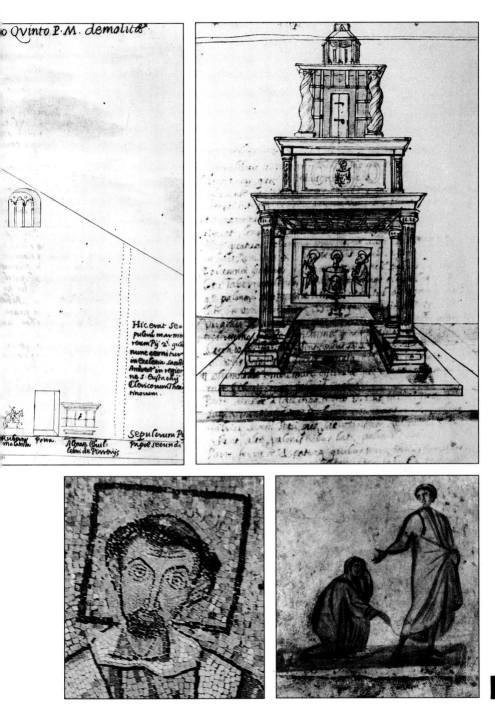

23

*History of the 'holy face' of Edessa, as depicted in the ten scenes that surround the frame of icon preserved in Genoa*

1899, remains to this day the master work on the subject. The manuscript is the Vatican Library's Greek Codex no. 511,[32] and as Zaninotto expertly deciphered the handwriting, he found it to be a sermon by one Gregory, Archdeacon at Constantinople's Hagia Sophia Cathedral at the very time that the Edessa 'holy face' was first brought to Constantinople in 944.[33]

In his text Gregory described himself as a 'referendarius' or notary – in effect, a tenth-century Grimaldi – and as having made very careful studies of all that was known in his time about the 'holy face' of Edessa, from sources both in Constantinople and in Edessa. In recounting the Abgar legend and the circumstances of the 'holy face's' apparent rediscovery at the time of the Persian siege, he revealed himself as a shrewd discarder of many of the more dubious elements that circulated around these stories.

But the real revelation to Zaninotto occurred in Gregory's account of how the 'holy face' had come to be imprinted on the cloth. Omitting any mention of the concept of Jesus having washed himself, Gregory spoke only of the idea of it having:

> . . . been imprinted with the drops of sweat from the agony [in Gethsemane], which flowed from the face of the Prince of Life like drops of blood.[34]

Then Gregory went on:

> And the image, since those flows, has been embellished by [blood] drops *from his very side*. The two [things] are full of symbolism, blood and water here, and there the sweat of the face.

Quite unmistakable here was the fact that Gregory, who would seem to have seen the Edessan 'holy face' for himself, was describing it as bearing the stain of Jesus's wound in the side. Gregory made no attempt to explain how a cloth purportedly imprinted by Jesus in life could bear the stains of an injury which could only have been inflicted at or after death. For the Byzantine such things could be shrugged away as mysteries that were not for mortal man to pry into. But for us the question is crucial. How could it be that this 'holy face' of Edessa was reported to bear the image of Jesus's wound in the side – unless it was a cloth that had wrapped his body after death, a cloth just such as we have in the

143

Turin 'shroud'? Could it be that despite the radio-carbon dating, the 'holy face' of Edessa might have been one and the same as the 'shroud', after all?

It is an appealing idea. Identity of the Edessan 'holy face' with the 'shroud' would make sense of so much, not least the watery and 'bloody sweat' characteristics described of the Edessa 'holy face's' imprint, the consistently disembodied manner in which this is depicted, the herring-bone weave on the cloth pasted to the S. Silvestro 'holy face', and the likeness to the shroud face exhibited by Strozzi's copy of the Veronica. The Veronica, from this point of view, would seem to have been a copy of the shroud face made while this was in Constantinople in the guise of the 'holy face' of Edessa.

But to carry conviction seriously to challenge the shroud carbon dating, much more evidence is needed. After all, the shroud's central feature is the figure of Jesus with crossed hands, laid out in death. If Zaninotto's Archdeacon Gregory had been able to view as much of the shroud as the wound in the side, surely someone must have seen the whole figure? As we are about to see, there is some considerable evidence that they did.

## Chapter Twelve

# THE MYSTERIOUS
# CROSSED-HANDS FIGURE

*Abgar reigned as toparch of Edessa. To him the Lord
Jesus sent a most precious cloth . . . This displayed to
those who gazed upon it the likeness and proportions of
the body of the Lord*

Ordericus Vitalis c. AD 1141

T he seventeenth-century notary
Jacopo Grimaldi, in his already so helpful 'Brief account of the
most holy Veronica', described one important, historic accompani-
ment of the Veronica that we have so far not mentioned. This was:

> . . . a very ancient and most noble *umbella*, woven
> throughout in gold and silver of very rich work, and
> full of gold because of its very great age . . . [which]
> used to be extended over the window of the shrine of
> the Veronica when it was shown to the people.[1]

An *umbella* is a large fabric covering or canopy that in
the Mediterranean world has been traditionally held over
distinguished personages and revered objects, and with his
characteristic thoroughness Grimaldi provided a most detailed
sketch[2] [pls. 26–27] of this particular one as used for the Veronica.
It was clearly of Byzantine origin, for besides transcribing the
Greek inscriptions to its various panels of embroidered scenes
from the life of Christ, Grimaldi also drew it as edged with the
figures of predominantly Eastern Orthodox saints: St Cyril, St

145

Basil, St Peter of Alexandria, St John Chrysostom, to name a few.

But the most fascinating feature of Grimaldi's sketch is the *umbella*'s central embroidered figure, larger than any of the rest, depicting Christ stretched out in death, the hands crossed over the pelvis in precisely the mode of Turin's 'shroud' [fig. 17, below].

Now clearly, particularly decorated with such a figure, the *umbella* would be of very considerable interest if it still existed to this day. And quite conceivably it does still exist, but is yet another item still kept away from normal human gaze in the so secret world inside the Veronica pier.

Baulked, however, of any opportunity to examine it at first hand, for us the crucial question is when it may have been made, and the extent to which it may still be possible to determine this from the visual and verbal data supplied by Grimaldi.

Grimaldi made clear that he was himself interested in this question, and remarked:

> It has depicted on it the same stories of our saviour Jesus Christ that Pope John VII . . . had made in mosaic in his Oratory [i.e. the John VII chapel in old St Peter's], and the said *umbella* is in the Greek style.[3]

For Grimaldi this was sufficient to date the *umbella* to John VII's time, i.e. to the early eighth century. However careful study simply of his own sketches reveals him to have been wrong in this judgement.

*Fig. 17. Shroud-like figure of Christ laid out in death, the central image on the Byzantine* umbella *used for showings of the Veronica. From then sketch by Jacopo Grimaldi*

146

Thus when his sketch of the Crucifixion scene among the mosaics above the entrance of John VII's chapel[4] is compared with his sketch of the Crucifixion scene on the *umbella*, it is immediately evident that in the former Jesus is dressed in a long robe, while in the latter he is in a loincloth [fig. 18].

Now in the case of the long-robe-type Crucifixion, as in the chapel mosaic, there is no problem identifying this to the eighth century. A nearly identical Crucifixion, unquestionably dating from John VII's time, is to be found as one of the murals in the Church of S. Maria Antiqua, which stands amidst the ruins of the Roman Forum.[5] Besides the long robe, features such as the feet nailed into the upright of the cross, the figures either side of Christ, a sun and moon set in the sky, etc., all readily correspond with Grimaldi's chapel mosaic sketch.

The loincloth type of Crucifixion, on the other hand, as on the *umbella*, seems to be of a significantly later date. One of the readiest parallels, and with many other features corresponding to Grimaldi's sketch, is to be found on a Byzantine mosaic diptych in the Museo dell'Opera del Duomo, Florence.[6] Of the twelve different scenes on this diptych, no less than seven, inclusive of the Crucifixion, closely match ones among the eight 'Life of Christ' panels on the *umbella*.

(a)                                                                 (b)

*Fig. 18. (a) As depicted, by Jacopo Grimaldi, scene of crucifixion from John VII chapel mosaics; (b) and from the* umbella *compared. The one on the left is characteristically* circa *eighth century*

147

But since this diptych is Palaeologuan, made between 1340 and 1400, this would date the *umbella* and its 'Christ laid out in death' figure to no earlier than the very period ascribed to the 'shroud' by carbon dating. And there even existed within this period precisely the circumstances in which the *umbella* might have been brought from Constantinople to Rome. In 1369 the Byzantine emperor, John V Palaeologus, desperate for western help against the Turks, travelled to Rome for talks with Pope Urban V. The *umbella* is just the sort of diplomatic gift he might well have brought with him to present to the pope during the lavish ceremonial that accompanied the event. The loincloth type of Crucifixion does have artistic parallels earlier than the Palaeologuan period. One of this type is to be seen on a mosaic in the monastery church of Osios Loukas, near Delphi, Greece, dating from as early as AD 1,000.[7] But on its own the iconography of Grimaldi's *umbella* sketch fails to establish the incontrovertible antiquity for the *umbella*, and therefore for the crossed-hands type, that we need.

Nonetheless even if the *umbella* is Palaeologuan, the presence within it of such a 'crossed-hands' figure would suggest this had antecedents. So what were these? And how far can the origins of the 'crossed-hands' type be traced back?

First it is worthwhile noting an apparently well-established association between the 'holy face' and a shroud-like 'crossed-hands' type of figure that is to be found in certain eastern and western examples not particularly old in themselves, but unquestionably founded on a much more ancient type.

For instance, in the Russian Museum, Leningrad, a seventeenth-century icon features the 'holy face' of Edessa floating above a 'crossed-hands' figure of Christ seemingly rising out of a tomb. In this the hands are particularly characteristically in the 'shroud' mode. Two other eastern examples, slightly less characteristic, are one in the Church of the Prophet Elijah, Jaroslav, dating *circa* 1750, and another in the collection of George R. Hann of Sewickley Heights, Pennsylvania [pl. 28, above].

In the west a similar close association, this time between the Veronica and this same 'crossed-hands' type, is to be found in a mid-fourteenth-century manuscript, the *Omne Bonum*, in London's British Museum;[8] also, insofar as the two types of illustration are within the same manuscript, in the *Supplicationes Variae* manuscript of 1294 preserved in the Laurentian Library, Florence.

148

But the important feature is that this same half-length type of Christ with crossed hands is also a well-recognized one in its own right within Byzantine iconography, and quite definitely has yet more ancient origins. A classic example, created in miniature mosaic, is one of the most closely guarded treasures of Rome's relic-filled church of Santa Croce in Gerusalemme.[9] This bears the Greek title 'Ο ΒΑΣΙΛΕΥΣ ΤΗΣ ΔΟΞΗΣ' (The King of Glory), the name repeatedly given to this half-length, crossed-hands type representation, and is thought to have been brought from St Catherine's monastery, Sinai, towards the end of the fourteenth century. A fourteenth-century painted icon of this same kind, and with particularly shroud-like crossed hands, is to be seen in the Treasury of the Great Meteoron monastery, Meteora, Greece.

*Fig. 19. Shroud-like 'crossed-hands' type representation of Christ, from a twelfth-century Byzantine enamel that was in the Botkin collection, St Petersburg (now Leningrad) up to the time of the Russian revolution (redrawn from photograph of 1911). The present-day existence and location of this enamel is undetermined*

149

Between 1302 and 1310 the South Italian sculptor Giovanni Pisano carved a similar figure, looking tantalizingly as if on cloth, onto the lectern of the most elaborate pulpit he created for the Cathedral of Pisa[10] [pl. 28, below left]. As apparently the earliest western example, it is also to be found in a mid-thirteenth-century manuscript now in Munich, but thought to have belonged to the monastery of St Moritz, Hildesheim.[11]

Dating yet earlier in the east, this same crossed-hands type – and again a particularly shroud-like one – is to be found in a Byzantine enamel of the twelfth century from the Botkin collection, Leningrad [fig. 19].[12] And that it existed earlier still is indicated by an eleventh-century gold and enamel frame preserved in the Church of the Holy Sepulchre, Jerusalem. Although the icon itself has been lost, the frame carries the identifying inscription 'Ο ΒΑΣΙΛΕΥΣ ΤΗΣ ΔΟΞΗΣ' and the inclination of the halo on the frame clearly indicates it to have been made for an image of this same kind.[13]

Now this particular type differs of course, both from Grimaldi's *umbella* dead Christ, and the figure on the shroud, in being only half length. But there are in fact further examples, similarly ancient, that are specifically of the full-length variety.

For instance, from around the year 1300 there has survived a most shroud-like example on a Byzantine liturgical cloth known as an *epitaphios*, one traditionally used to represent the shroud of Christ during the Eastern Orthodox Church's Good Friday liturgy. The example in question,[14] a beautiful gold-embroidered specimen preserved in the Museum of the Serbian Orthodox Church, Belgrade [pl. 28, below right], has the same crossed hands and the same frontality as the Turin's shroud, differing only in that the lower half of the body has been discreetly covered with a rectangular modesty cloth. The name Milutin Uroš is included in the inscription at the feet, and this identifies it as a gift of the Serbian ruler Stephen Uroš II Milutin, whose reign was from 1282 to 1321.

Although this is one of the earliest *epitaphioi* known, there is a consensus among scholars that it must have had antecedents, as is certainly indicated by the same type of figure being found in other art forms.

A particularly notable example occurs in a work entitled the Funeral Oration, forming part of the Pray manuscript[15] preserved in the National Széchényi Library of Budapest. Four pages of pen and ink drawings accompany a text that is among the very earliest in the Hungarian language, and in one of these, fol. 28 [pl. 29, above], we see Jesus's body being laid out full length on a shroud, entirely naked, and with the hands crossed over the pelvis in precisely the manner so characteristic of the Turin 'shroud' image.[16]

This drawing can be accurately dated, being reliably thought to have been made at the ancient Benedictine monastery of Boldva in Hungary between the years 1192 and 1195. And according to the specialist of Hungarian medieval manuscripts, Ilona Berkovits:

> . . . the style of its miniatures shows resemblance to the art associated with the middle of the [twelfth] century. It is not impossible that the miniaturist followed the illumination of an earlier, more elaborate manuscript, from the end of the eleventh or the beginning of the twelfth century, which has since been lost, and copied its compositions.[17]

Furthermore, even earlier examples are to be found, albeit without the so shroud-like total nudity of the Pray drawing. Among the wealth of icons in the Hermitage Museum of Leningrad is a magnificent specimen with gold relief and cloisonné enamel.[18] This comprises a crucifixion surrounded by figures of saints, with at the foot of the cross an image of Jesus with the familiar crossed hands, and with a rectangular modesty cover exactly as on the Milutin Uroš *epitaphios*. It carries the inscription, 'Christ lies in death, manifesting God', and its date is thought to be as early as the eleventh century.

Also from the eleventh century are several Byzantine ivories of the so-called Threnos, or Lamentation scene of Jesus being mourned as he is laid out in death. In perhaps the finest of these, in the Victoria & Albert Museum, London [pl. 29, left][19] Jesus' hands can yet again be seen crossed at the wrists in the so peculiar 'shroud' manner. He is also shown specifically lying on something like a shroud or a mattress.

Now it might already seem to be more than coincidence that it was at this very point, within a century of the 'holy face' of Edessa's arrival in Constantinople, that we come to the earliest to which this 'crossed-hands' type can be traced in art. Although there are earlier depictions of Jesus's entombment, including some from the end of the ninth century, these show him wrapped with mummy-style bands. So why the change? And why the sudden crossed-hands type?

151

If we look to scholars for help with this difficulty, we find no clear explanation. Princeton University's Professor Kurt Weitzmann, who has made a special study of the Lamentation theme in Byzantine art,[20] has suggested that it was inspired by classical representations of the Bewailing of Actaeon, the Greek huntsman whom the goddess Artemis caused to be torn to pieces by his own dogs because he had come across her bathing naked. But while it is possible that the scene's ancillary figures may have been so influenced, classical art offers no known antecedent of the crossed-hands figure itself that is the central feature of our interest.

Nor does it account for why, even in the representation of other scenes associated with Jesus's burial, we see from the eleventh century and after the curious inclusion of a large double-length shroud, where previously mummy-style bands had been imagined. Clear examples of this occur in a representation of the Deposition in the tiny Byzantine church of Nerezi, Macedonia, datable to 1164, and another of this same subject in the twelfth-century Chapel of the Holy Sepulchre in England's Winchester Cathedral.

Furthermore, if we ask whether, quite aside from Professor Zaninotto's discovery of the Gregory manuscript, there might be any direct evidence that the 'holy face' of Edessa was more than just a face on the cloth, we find that this is indeed the case.

For instance, interpolated sometime before 1130 into the text of a sermon attributed to the eighth-century Pope Stephen III was the following remark concerning the 'holy face' of Edessa:

> For this same mediator between God and men, in order that in all things and in every way he might satisfy this king [i.e. Abgar] spread out *his entire body* on a linen cloth that was white as snow. On this cloth, marvellous as it is to see or even hear such a thing, the glorious image of the Lord's face, and *the length of his entire and most noble body*, has been divinely transferred . . . [italics mine].[21]

Following on from this, about the year 1141 the English monk Ordericus Vitalis wrote in his *Historia ecclesiastica*:

> Abgar reigned as toparch of Edessa. To him the Lord Jesus sent . . . a most precious cloth, with which he wiped the sweat from his face, and on which shone

152

the Saviour's features, miraculously reproduced. This displayed to those who gazed upon it *the likeness and proportions of the body of the Lord* [italics mine].[22]

Equally explicit is a mention of the 'holy face' of Edessa by the well-travelled and somewhat underrated English raconteur Gervase of Tilbury. In his *Otia Imperialia*, completed shortly before his death in 1218, Gervase first quoted words allegedly spoken by Jesus to King Abgar:

> If indeed you desire to see my physical appearance, I send you a cloth on which the image not only of my face but of my entire body has been preserved.

Then Gervase went on:

> The story is passed down from archives of ancient authority that the Lord prostrated himself *with his entire body on whitest linen*, and so by divine power there was impressed on the linen a most beautiful imprint of not only the face but the entire body of the Lord.[23]

Now a frustrating feature of all these references is that they make no attempt to explain how and why Jesus might have imprinted his entire body on the cloth that went to Edessa.

Complicating the issue yet further is the fact that from as early as 958 there occur the first of several subsequent mentions of a burial *sindon* or shroud being among the imperial relic collection in Constantinople, without the slightest accompanying whisper of how this might have come to the city. The earliest, the 958 reference, comes from a letter of the Emperor Constantine VII Porphyrogennitus sent to his troops campaigning around Tarsus, telling them that he was sending them holy water consecrated by:

> the precious wood [of the Cross], the unstained lance . . . the reed which caused miracles . . . the *sindon* which God wore, and other symbols of the immaculate Passion.[24]

Constantine, who is known to have directly viewed the 'holy face' of Edessa on its arrival in 944, made no mention of this latter in the

153

958 letter, and if we might be tempted to assume from this that he now preferred to describe it in its full form as a burial *sindon*, the evidence of subsequent references by no means conclusively supports this. This is particularly because there are certain accounts that list both the shroud and the 'holy face' of Edessa as seemingly separate objects.

For instance an English pilgrim of *circa* 1150 mentioned a gold 'capsula' containing 'the *mantile* which, applied to the Lord's face, retained the image of his face', and also itemized a *sudarium* which was over his head.'[25] An inventory of 1190, by an unknown author, mentions 'a part of the linens in which the crucified body of Christ was wrapped'; a 'syndon'; and 'the towel [*manutergium*] sent to King Abgar of Edessa by the Lord, on which the Lord himself transferred his image.'[26]

But while in these two instances neither writer is likely to have seen either item with his own eyes, this could not have been the case with Nicholas Mesarites, a man who was none other than *skeuophylax*, or overseer of the holy relic collection and other treasures of the Great Palace of Constantinople.

In 1201 Nicholas was obliged to defend the Imperial collection at risk of his life when there was a palace revolution led by John Comnenus. He subsequently described how, completely unarmed, he stopped a bloodthirsty mob from breaking into the imperial collection by reminding them of the sacredness of the treasures that lay within. According to his own words as allegedly spoken at this time,[27] he told them first of the 'holy crown of thorns, which . . . remains intact because it took on incorruptibility from touching the sacred head of Jesus', then 'the holy nail . . . preserved today . . . just as it was . . . when it penetrated the most holy and merciful flesh', then 'the flagellum', and fourth 'the burial shroud [*sindones*] of Jesus.'[28] Then a little later he went on to mention 'the towel' (*cheiromaktron*) with a 'prototypal' image of Jesus 'as if by some art of drawing not wrought by hand.'[29]

Now it might seem that the only conclusion to be drawn from this and from a subsequent mention by Robert de Clari is that the shroud/*sindon* and something along the lines of the 'holy face' of Edessa were indeed preserved in Constantinople as the separate objects.

But in actuality this by no means necessarily implies that the latter was one and the same as the relic that had arrived in Constantinople as the 'holy face' of Edessa in 944. Given the closely guarded secrecy that prevailed in Constantinople's inner sancta, as in Rome, it is quite possible that once someone had discovered the true 'holy face' to bear a full-length image of Jesus, this quietly became the collection's *sindon* or 'shroud' (thus explaining the lack of documentary mention of the coming of this to Constantinople). Then in order not to cause public questioning of what had become of the Edessan 'holy face', a copy of this was substituted for the original, one most likely exactly along the lines of the Veronica made for Rome. This latter would have been the 'holy towel' referred to by Nicholas Mesarites.

Now while we can only conjecture that this is the explanation of the double mentions, quite incontrovertible is that from Mesarites we have one of the most tantalizing indications that there really was a full-body imprint, *à la* Turin shroud, on the shroud preserved in Constantinople's imperial collection. As Mesarites, according to his own account, continued his description of the shroud when confronting the mob:

> It is of linen, a cheap and easily obtainable material, still fragrant with myrrh. And it is imperishable because it covered the uncircumscribed, naked and myrrh-perfumed dead body after the passion.[30]

Besides describing the material of the shroud as linen, exactly the same as that of the Edessan 'holy face', Mesarites also most interestingly describes the body as *aperilepton*, 'uncircumscribed', or 'outlineless', tantalizingly suggesting the outlineless quality of the Turin shroud. Also, he referred to the body as 'naked', raising the question of why he should volunteer such information unless this nakedness was somehow evident on the *sindon*?

Now although on its own Mesarites' reference is insufficiently explicit to persuade us that the shroud in the imperial relic collection really did bear a Turin-shroud type imprint, as it happens, from just two years later there is another and even more persuasive eyewitness to be called upon.

This was a comparatively humble knight from Picardy in France, Robert de Clari who, as a member of the Fourth Crusade in 1203, toured Constantinople as a guest after having helped depose the Byzantine usurper Alexius III. Goggle-eyed at the wonders he saw around him, out-dazzling anything in western Europe, de Clari wrote an account of it, a *History*

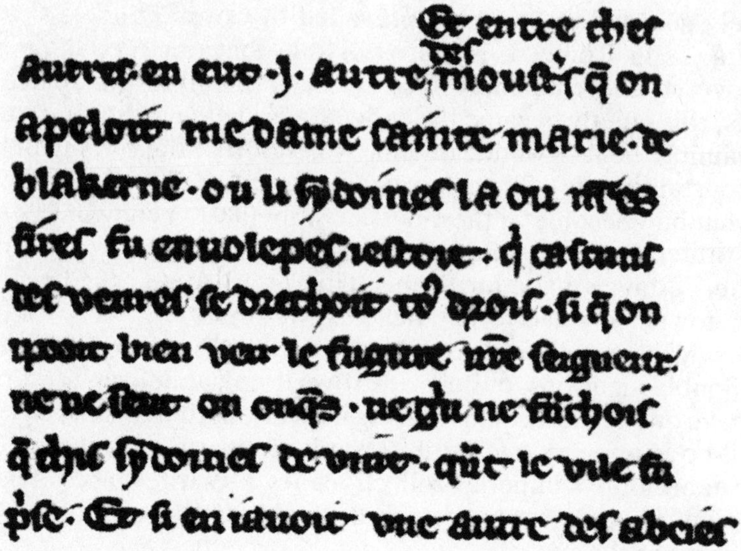

*Fig. 20. The crucial passage in Robert de Clari's manuscript, describing a 'shroud . . . on which one could see the figure of Our Lord.' Copenhagen, Royal Library, MS 487, fol. 123*

*of those who Conquered Constantinople*, which survives in a single manuscript in the Royal Library, Copenhagen.[31] In this he noted:

> . . . about the other marvels that are there [in Constantinople] . . . there was another church called My Lady St Mary of Blachernae, where there was the shroud [*sydoines*] in which [lit. where] Our Lord had been wrapped, which every Friday raised itself upright, so that one could see the *figure* of Our Lord on it [lit. there] . . . [fig. 20], above].[32]

Particularly in the light of the shroud carbon dating, for us this is one of the most crucial documents of any we have considered. Writing in the third person, Robert de Clari insisted 'he may not have recounted in as fair a fashion as many a good author would have done, yet he always told the strict truth,' and there is nothing in his book to suggest otherwise. Authoritatively and unequivocally he tells us that as early as 1203 there existed in Constantinople a shroud with an imprint of Christ's body – thus corresponding in all essential features to the one that carbon dating and Bishop d'Arcis would have us believe was so cunningly forged in France a century and a half later.

Now one puzzle posed by de Clari is that he set the showing of this shroud at the Church of St Mary of Blachernae, when theoretically all the major relics, including the Edessa 'holy face' and/or the burial shroud, were kept in the Pharos chapel within the imperial palace. Also if what was being shown was the Edessa holy face/shroud, why was it suddenly being shown publicly after so many centuries of being kept shut away from ordinary human gaze?

In actuality both questions can quite easily be answered by the special circumstances prevailing in 1203, when for the first time in their history the cultured and perfumed citizens of Constantinople came face to face with large numbers of uncouth and well-armed western foreigners actually within their midst. To show the Byzantine citizens the 'true likeness' of Christ as possessed by their emperor would have been a powerful way of persuading them that God was on their side. And since it would have been quite impractical to admit large numbers into the imperial palace for this purpose, the Church of St Mary of Blachernae, the people's traditional rallying-point in times of danger, would have been the logical alternative.

But the crucial point of interest is what was being shown? For historians de Clari's account has represented a most uncomfortable puzzle. While the reference to a cloth with an imprint has suggested to some that de Clari might have had in mind the Edessan 'holy face', his use of the word *figure* simply cannot be forced into referring to an impression of only the face. Although *figure* can mean 'face' in present-day French, scholars of Old French are well aware that it has only had this alternative meaning since *circa* 1650.[33] In Robert de Clari's time *figure* meant precisely the same as in present-day English. It has sometimes been concluded therefore that de Clari must have become muddled.[34]

There is one alternative, however, that makes complete sense of all the available facts. This is that what Robert de Clari saw was indeed the Edessan 'holy face', revealed for the first time publicly as a full-length, image-bearing shroud, exactly as understood of

157

the present-day shroud of Turin. It is even possible to put some sense to his description that the cloth 'raised itself upright', vividly conveying an image of Jesus rising out of the tomb, exactly as in the 'ΒΑΣΙΛΕΥΣ ΤΗΣ ΔΟΞΗΣ' or 'King of Glory' representations noted earlier in this chapter. Had there been contrived some gadgetry to make the cloth rise upright out of its casket, just as the emperor was made to whirl aloft before those who sought an audience with him in his golden throne-room?

Clearly de Clari was fascinated by what he saw, sufficient to note that:

> . . . no one, either Greek or French, ever knew what became of this shroud when the city was taken.[35]

This suggests, perhaps because it had so recently come to be kept at Blachernae, that the Edessa 'holy face'/shroud, was not with the other major relics when the Crusaders launched their full-scale sack of Constantinople in 1204. And this therefore at least allows the possibility that it became secreted away to emerge 150 years later as the cloth we now know as the Turin shroud.

But although we have now seen some compelling evidence that the 'holy face' of Edessa may have borne the imprint of a full-length, shroud-like figure, still this does not mean that it can be identified with any certainty as one and the same as *the* shroud that we know today in Turin. Seriously to challenge the carbon dating, we still need some almost finger-print-type means of determining that it was this very same shroud, and none other, that was around in the early centuries as the original of all the 'holy faces' that followed. Yet as we are about to see, even something very much along the lines of a finger-print-type identification may not be totally beyond our reach.

## Chapter Thirteen

# A MAN FRIDAY
# FOOTPRINT?

*Certain peculiarities were evident in the shroud –
peculiarities that were really accidental imperfections in
the image or the fabric itself, and that served no artistic
purpose. Yet . . . these very oddities appeared again and
again in a whole series of ancient art works, even though
artistically they made no sense. Surely, this could mean
only one thing: ancient artists had taken their conception
. . . from the image on the shroud, and had included
the anomalies because of a feeling that they were in
some mysterious way connected with the earthly
appearance of Jesus.[1]*

Author John Walsh, on the iconographic researches of Paul
Vignon

Earlier in this book we showed
how the Veronica of the Middle Ages almost certainly survived
at least until 1621. We established this from noting how certain
damage marks evident on a special copy of the Middle Ages were
repeated in Pietro Strozzi's copy of 1617 and in the Church of
Gesù's one of 1621. We were also able to expose the falsity of
Heaphy's claim to have examined the Genoa 'holy face' without its
cover by showing that the wear marks and holes he indicated on
his purported 'copy' simply do not exist in the original.

Clearly it would be most helpful to be able to use this same
method to establish whether the shroud, as preserved in Turin, was
around well before the fourteenth century. But nothing quite so

159

easy is available to us. This is not least because the earliest-known direct copy of the shroud in its full-length form, the pilgrim's badge of Lirey, dates no earlier than the mid-fourteenth century, the very same period as indicated by the carbon dating. Furthermore, even if we accept the hypothesis that during the earlier centuries the shroud was one and the same as the 'holy face' of Edessa, we face the problem that direct copies of this latter survive only from the tenth century, and these exhibit so many variations that none can be considered truly reliable.

Also, while it might be very compelling if an early copy reproduced the distinctive shape of one or more of the bloodflows visible on the shroud face, we should not expect any such depiction in Byzantine art. Byzantine art abhorred naturalistic portrayal of Christ's sufferings of the kind that became so popular in the medieval west. While Jesus's wound in the side could sometimes be depicted as a discreet fountain, truly realistic portrayal of his bloodstains is extremely rare.

Despite these difficulties, however, all is by no means as unforthcoming as might at first appear. For instance, long recognized on the shroud as preceding the very distinctive scars of the 1532 fire are four sets of triple burn holes that derive from some unrecorded damage incident that was certainly before 1516, as the marks are clearly visible in a painted copy of that year.[2] The four sets back each other up, indicating that the damage was sustained when the cloth was folded in four, and they appear almost as if a sputtering red hot poker was thrust through the cloth three times, the topmost of the three holes having next to it an extra one, as if created by a stray spark.

In 1986 French Dominican monk Père A. M. Dubarle,[3] a former scholar of the Jerusalem École Biblique, was corresponding on the subject of the shroud-like figure on the Pray manuscript of 1192 [pl. 29, above] when his correspondent drew his attention to some curious holes indicated on the illustration below this figure. Clearly visible on the sarcophagus in the scene of the three Marys visiting the Empty Tomb was a line of three holes, with an extra one offset to one side [fig. 21a].

Even more curious, though almost vanishingly tiny, was a similar set of three holes to be seen on the shroud or napkin-like cloth depicted rolled up on the sarcophagus [fig. 21b]. Could these have been intended to represent the 'poker hole' marks that the artist of 1192 knew to be on the Christ shroud of his day, the

160

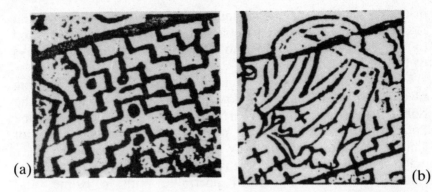

(a)

(b)

*Fig. 21. Shroud-derived 'poker-holes' indicated on the Pray manuscript of 1192 (see pl. 29, above) (a) on the sarcophagus; (b) on the 'rolled-up' shroud or napkin*

one preserved in Constantinople? If this could be believed, then even on its own it would at a stroke set the shroud's date nearly a hundred years earlier than the very earliest date allowed by carbon dating.

Realistically such a claim has to be recognized as rather over-optimistic. Had the holes been represented in their correct relative position on a full-length shroud, a suitably greater significance might be attached to them, but this is not the case.

However, well over half a century before this particular observation by Dubarle and his correspondent, another French-man had been fired by the self-same idea that something along these lines was the way to establish that the shroud really was around during the early centuries. This was Paul Vignon, who as early as 1900 had been shown the shroud photograph by Paris anatomy professor, Yves Delage. Although a biologist by training, Vignon became launched into decades of enthusiastic research into every aspect of the shroud.

Late in his life, however, the topic that particularly absorbed him was the incidence in early Byzantine portraits of the Christ Enthroned/Christ Pantocrator type of curious facial markings seeming to derive from equivalent features on the shroud. To present his findings, Vignon compiled a beautifully produced book, *Le Saint Suaire de Turin devant la Science, l'Archéologie, l'Histoire, l'Iconographie, la Logique* (The Holy Shroud of Turin

161

in the light of Science, Archaeology, History, Iconography and Logic).[4] But the potential impact of this was tragically blunted by the outbreak of the Second World War within a few weeks of its publication.

Even before examining Vignon's specific arguments relating to the markings, there is a lot to suggest that he was on the right track in surmising a powerful association between Byzantine Pantocrator/Christ Enthroned portraits and those of the face of Christ on cloth, as in our 'holy faces' and on the shroud.

Particularly indicative of this are two very ancient Christ Enthroned/Christ Pantocrator portraits, both in Rome, and known from the earliest as Acheropita, or images 'made without hands'. The first of these is the now familiar Acheropita of the Sancta Sanctorum Chapel of the Lateran [col. pl. III], which our old friend Gerald of Wales spoke of on equal terms with the Veronica, and which, as we have established, was in Rome at least as early as 754, more than two centuries before the earliest recorded existence of the Veronica. Although to this day it remains concealed behind the same ornamental exterior casing with which Innocent III had it covered in Gerald of Wales's time, at the beginning of this century the German Jesuit art specialist Monsignor J. Wilpert was allowed to examine what lies beneath,[5] with some unexpected insights.

Intriguing, for instance, was that the Christ face as visible through the metal cover proved not to be part of the original, but to have been crudely painted on to a piece of linen pasted over the top part of the walnut-wood panel that carried the badly-worn original painting. Since Pope Alexander III (1159–81) is recorded to have 'restored' the Acheropita, this superimposition of the piece of linen almost certainly happened in his time, and itself reinforces the Acheropita's relationship to 'holy faces' of the cloth variety.

Wilpert further found that such had been the ravages of time, probably through the painted panel having been carried in procession in all weathers, that the original painting was all but effaced. It took some energetic cleaning (with methods that would probably horrify today's conservators), before he was able vaguely to discern a figure of Christ enthroned, holding a scroll in his left hand, and with his right held in front of his chest [fig. 22]. The cruciform halo around Christ's head indicated it to date sometime after the mid-fifth century. Since it would

*Fig. 22. Acheropita 'holy face' of Rome's Sancta Sanctorum chapel (see col. pl. III) with all forms of later covering removed; (left): plan of the vestiges of image that had survived at the time of examination; (right): approximate reconstruction of the original image as a sixth-century Christ Enthroned*

163

seem to correspond closely to the 'likeness of Our Lord and Saviour painted on a board' recorded to have been carried by St Augustine when he evangelized Kent in AD 597,[6] the late sixth century may be the better approximation of the date. However, if it ever had any interesting Vignon-type facial markings, these have long been erased.

The second 'Acheropita', even more unconvincing as having been 'made without hands', is the already mentioned Christ Pantocrator head in mosaic [pl. 30, above] set in the apse of the basilica of St John Lateran, just across the piazza from the Sancta Sanctorum chapel. Over-size, this is readily visible to every basilica visitor, and the Christ countenance is replete with some most distinctive markings, particularly on the forehead.

Unfortunately, however, it is impossible to impart much significance to these for the reason that in its present form the mosaic is only a little over a hundred years old,[7] the whole apse of which it forms part having been dismantled and rebuilt in 1883. We know there to have been an even earlier restoration, in 1291, when the mosaic head, clearly already ancient at that time, was found to have been prefabricated on its own independent bed of Travertine marble. It would seem thus to have been a mosaic equivalent of the Veronica heads that we earlier noted to have been pre-prepared and pasted into the Matthew Paris, and related manuscripts. In its original form it most likely dates as far back as the late sixth century, for the reason that the basic iconographic type of a Christ bust superimposed on a cross is closely paralleled in relief designs on *ampullae* or holy oil containers,[8] that were sent at the end of the sixth century by Pope Gregory the Great to the vivacious Queen Theodolinda of the Lombards.

Now while this makes all the more frustrating that we can place no reliance on the markings, nevertheless these two 'Acheropita', both with 'holy face' associations, and both dating back to the sixth century (the time of the apparent rediscovery of the 'holy face' of Edessa), point to a very clear relation between the Christ Enthroned/Pantocrator iconographic type, and the 'made without hands' holy face on cloth.

This is further indicated by the fact that when in 945 the Byzantine Emperor Constantine VII celebrated the first anniversary of the 'holy face' of Edessa's coming to Constantinople, he issued a clearly commemorative gold coin with a Christ Pantocrator bust on its reverse.[9] There are also several references to the 'holy face' of Edessa being set on a throne and being accorded imperial honours. Effectively, Christ Pantocrator/Christ Enthroned portraits from the sixth century on would seem to have been representations of the 'holy face' of Edessa, merely in a translated form. And this serves to reinforce the significance that Paul Vignon attached to Byzantine Christ Pantocrator/Christ Enthroned portraits as embodying facial markings derivative from the shroud.

Now to find a classic example of the Vignon type – even though Vignon himself appears not to have been aware of this particular one – we need look no further than a well-preserved and strongly Byzantine Christ Enthroned [col. pl. VIII, above] that to this day looks down from the apse of the Basilica of Sant' Angelo in Formis, a church sited among ancient ruins five miles north of Capua in central Italy. Because it is in fresco this particular example has not suffered the retouchings and alterations that so often beset panel paintings and mosaics. It dates from *circa* 1050, and immediately evident are a variety of markings to the face, including several identified by Vignon as derivative from the shroud. Notable among these are a transverse line across the forehead, a raised right eyebrow, an upside-down triangle at the bridge of the nose, heavily delineated lower eyelids, a strongly accentuated left cheek, a strongly accentuated right cheek, and a hairless gap between the lower lip and beard.

Although most such markings tend to come and go between one portrait and another, indicative inevitably of artists working at several hands removed from the hypothetical master-original, the one deserving of special attention is the upside-down triangle clearly indicated between the eyebrows. Particularly important is that unlike several other of the markings it has no logic as a natural feature of the face, making all the more interesting its recurrence in several other key works. Thus we see it particularly distinctively on the awe-inspiring eleventh-century mosaic Pantocrator [pl. 30, below left] that glowers down from the dome of the church at Daphni, near Athens. In this, even more decisively than in the Sant'Angelo in Formis fresco, its occurrence simply cannot be dismissed as fanciful, for the reason that pieces of black mosaic have been specially selected and arranged into the shape of a triangle in order to convey it.

Equally significantly, we see it very prominently and distinctively on several early copies of the 'holy face' of Edessa, notably the one on the twelfth-century fresco at Spas Nereditsa [pl. 25d;

pl. 31a], and on the Genoa 'holy face' [pl. 21, above; pl. 31b], where importantly it appears on the oldest image, that is, the one underlying that visible at the present day, as revealed by X-radiography. Most crucially, of course, it is also on the Turin shroud itself [pl. 31d], where its incidence, though unmistakable, seems to be the entirely natural one of some anomaly of the weave. It is hard to believe that it was not the incidence of this feature on the shroud that caused it to be repeated by so many copyists.

Of course it is also arguable that such a single feature as this might be better attributable just to some trick of the eye, or at best to coincidence. This would be hotly refuted, however, by one distinguished American physician, Dr Alan Whanger, professor of psychiatry at Duke University, North Carolina. Introduced to the subject of the shroud at the time of its exposition in 1978, Whanger became so fascinated by the numerous parallels he observed between Byzantine Christ portraits and the shroud face that he invented his own special twin projector/polaroid overlay method in order more scientifically to compare the markings one against the other.[10]

For as Whanger quickly discovered, just to set up twin projectors, one with a slide of the shroud face, the other with a suitable-looking Christ portrait, was inadequate to make a suitably precise comparison. He therefore added polaroid filters, a vertical one in the first projector, a horizontal one in the second, giving the viewer a third filter for manual rotation in front of the projected image. This enabled the observation and mapping of the points of similarity with a quite remarkable ease and precision. And with the aid of this method Whanger found some instances of a hundred or more points of similarity, or congruity between a Christ portrait and the shroud face, well over anything that could possibly be attributed to chance.

Particularly astonishing have been the numerous points of congruity he identified in an icon Christ Pantocrator of the sixth century, from St Catherine's monastery, Sinai [pl. 30, below right], also in the first ever coins to feature the Christ Pantocrator image,[11] superb gold *solidi* minted by the Byzantine Emperor Justinian II, and thereby precisely datable to about the year AD 692. As a result of these and similar researches Whanger has become personally convinced that the shroud, in the guise of the 'holy face' of Edessa, has to have been in existence and known by

Byzantine artists a full eight centuries before the earliest ascribed to it by carbon dating.

Now Whanger's assurance has only come by many hours of patient studying of one image against another, experience which it is impossible for the reader fully to appreciate without going through very similar endeavours for himself. However there is a simpler way, one arising from our earlier deduction from certain distinctive markings on Pietro Strozzi's Veronica copy that it must have been copied from the same source as the much earlier Alicante 'holy face'. The question raised is whether there is anything, besides the already-mentioned upside-down triangle, that might offer a similar vehicle for deduction in respect of the Christ Pantocrator/Christ Enthroned type portrait and the face on the shroud?

In this regard perhaps no more distinctive and unnatural a feature is to be found on the shroud face than a sharply geometric topless square immediately between the eyebrows, just above the afore-mentioned upside-down triangle [pl. 31d]. As in the case of the triangle, its actual nature on the shroud is again uncertain. Although Whanger has thought it to be a Jewish phylactery, it is perhaps safest to regard it, as in the case of the triangle, as some accidental flaw or anomaly of the weave.

Worthy of note is that a somewhat reminiscent feature can be seen on the Sant'Angelo in Formis Christ Enthroned [col. pl. VIII, above] on the Daphni Pantocrator [pl. 30, below left] and several others (including the Acheropita apse mosaic in St John Lateran [pl. 30, above]. In each case, however, these are somewhat stylized, more rounded than on the shroud, as if having been rendered more naturalistic by artists copying this feature at second or third hand.

But there is one example that is almost spectacularly different. Out on the Via Portuense, which runs south-westwards out of Rome, there lies one of Rome's least-known catacombs, the Catacomb of S. Ponziano, or St Pontianus. It goes unmentioned even by the authoritative *Blue Guide* to Rome, and can only be visited by special permission from the Pontificia Commissione di Archeologia Sacra, the Pontifical Commission of Sacred Archaeology. Importantly, since the whole catacomb was closed down after AD 820, any decoration inside it almost inevitably has to be of an earlier date.[12]

On one wall, slightly damaged, but its colours still fresh, is to be seen a very fine fresco [col. pl. VIII, below] of Christ Pantocrator iconographically so close to that of the coins of Justinian II that its date is almost certainly the same, the end of the seventh century.

But its real feature of interest is the one which lies between Christ's eyebrows, and would be well nigh impossible to convey on anything as small as a coin. This is a sharply delineated topless square [pl. 31c] exactly corresponding in shape and positioning to that so unnatural mark between the eyebrows on the shroud.

Now there can be no question of this feature perhaps being the result of some later tampering with the fresco. Not only did Vignon feature it in his book of 1939[13], thus dating it back at least fifty years, there are many indications that it was the work of the original seventh-century artist. Throughout the work, for instance, the artist used only a very limited range of colours, and it can be seen to have been painted in one of these. Furthermore, it has been created in fresco, thereby having been made integral to the original wall plaster, and can be adjudged as such by any expert.

And if this originality is accepted, its significance in relation to the shroud's date is difficult to over-estimate. Just as the viewing of a single footprint on fresh sand provided for Robinson Crusoe the conclusive evidence that there was another human being (later revealed as Man Friday) on his island, so the presence of this topless square on an indisputably seventh/eighth-century fresco virtually demands that the shroud must have been around, somewhere, in some form at this early date. Since that form can have been scarcely other than the 'holy face' of Edessa, the shroud's history is effectively established at least as far back as the sixth century, with the Abgar story offering a glimmer of how it may have arrived in Edessa back in the first.

Of course, there is one alternative scenario that may occur to the more dogged sceptic. It is the inevitable chicken-and-egg one. Perhaps the hypothetical forger, in addition to his brilliance in creating the photographic quality of the shroud image, and his rendering of its bloodflows with such exactness, also knew of the strange markings on Christ portraits in art, and added these for yet more convincing effect?

While such a possibility has to be acknowledged, it is equally important to stress its unconvincingness. As in so much else in his methodology, the hypothetical forger would have been alone among fourteenth-century artists, eastern and western, in taking an interest in these markings. Even in the Byzantine world the incidence of them fell away markedly following the Sack of Constantinople in 1204. Furthermore he would have had more than a little difficulty even finding out about the marking on the Ponziano catacomb fresco, for there seems no evidence that anyone knew of this catacomb's existence from its closure in 820 to the time the Italian archaeologist G. B. de Rossi began systematic excavation of all catacombs in 1852. Effectively, while there is a great deal to suggest that in the seventh/eighth century the Ponziano fresco artist might have taken his inspiration from a 'holy face' cloth such as the shroud, there is absolutely nothing to suggest that in the fourteenth century the hypothetical shroud forger would or could have known anything of the Ponziano catacomb.

Overall then, we have satisfied all the main requirements for confidence that something answering all the essential characteristics of the shroud was in existence as the 'holy face' of Edessa between the sixth century and 1204. We have seen that the idea of Jesus imprinting the likeness of his face on cloth, and the physical existence of a cloth corresponding to this idea, goes back at least as far as the sixth century. We have found that the idea of Jesus imprinting wounds from his dead body (notably the wound in the side) onto this cloth, dates back at least as far as the tenth century. We have established that the idea of Jesus imprinting the full imprint of his body on cloth dates at least as far back as the twelfth century. Not least, we have identified markings that virtually fingerprint the shroud to having been in existence at least as early as the eighth century.

Against all this we have been able to add virtually nothing to the credibility of the hypothetical fourteenth-century forger. So was there in the fourteenth century a brilliant unknown individual who transmuted the undeniably pre-existent idea of Jesus imprinting his image on cloth into the extraordinary reality that is the Turin shroud, embodying in it features it was virtually impossible for him to know of? Or could the accuracy of the shroud carbon dating somehow be not quite all that has been claimed of it? It seems long overdue that we take a closer look at this latter alternative.

## Chapter Fourteen

# THE SHROUD: CAN CARBON DATING LIE?

*. . . whereas all the Oxford samples come out consistently in the 1st century AD, the Harwell samples come out consistently in the 5th century AD . . . The archaeological world waits with bated breath to see how this problem is resolved*

*Current Archaeology*, August 1986

While our earlier findings clearly demand a reconsideration of the carbon dating as carried out on the shroud in 1988, this does not mean that we should even remotely call into question either the competence or the integrity of those scientists who took part in this exercise. All were and still are highly respected nuclear physicists. Knowing that the eyes of international media were upon them, the procedures they employed were meticulous. Being from three different countries, they represented a suitably balanced international spread. The presence among them of at least one Catholic (Donahue) and one Quaker (Damon) ensured a suitable religious balance. And from a personal acquaintance with some, and having been treated by them with unfailing courtesy, I totally deplore the machinations of those, such as the French priest, Bruno Bonnet-Eymard, who have argued that either they, or Dr Tite as invigilator, were involved in some form of sample-switching plot.

Instead the true point at issue is whether the whole science of carbon dating, as a spin-off from nuclear physics, quite justifies the air of infallibility that the media have certainly imparted to it, and that archaeologists equally certainly had once hoped-for from it.

By way of re-cap, we should remind ourselves that radio-carbon dating was a by-product of the atomic age, developed by Professor Willard F. Libby of the Chicago Institute of Nuclear Physics within the very decade of the bombing of Hiroshima and Nagasaki.[1] As such it inevitably became mentally associated with all the high-precision technology of this latest wonder-science, understandable not least from the ingenious principle upon which it is based.

According to this principle, neutrons generated by cosmic rays bombarding the earth's stratosphere change some of the upper atmosphere's nitrogen atoms into the mildly radioactive form of carbon known as carbon 14. On descent into the lower atmosphere this becomes incorporated into the carbon dioxide taken in by plants and trees via photosynthesis. Since animals eat plants, and human beings eat both, all living organisms take in carbon 14 while they are alive, and cease to do so at death. Their carbon 14 thereupon 'decays', like all radioactivity, at a seemingly highly precise rate through time. It seemed good science therefore, to Libby, that with the aid of a Geiger counter measuring the proportion of carbon 14 to carbon 12, he should be able to determine the death date of any organic object, just as if he was reading this from an atomic clock.

Now as at the present the method has been developed for some forty years, and in this time has become widely and routinely used for archaeological materials of organic origin – wood, bone, shell, leather, parchment, flax, cotton, food remains, and the like. Furthermore its accuracy has undoubtedly been improved. Everyone knows that it is possible to tell the age of a tree by the number of its rings, but fewer are aware that the thicknesses of rings vary according to the climatic vicissitudes of different years. In the case of very long-lived specimens, such as the up to four thousand year old bristlecone pines of the White Mountains in California, it is possible by overlapping one specimen against another accurately to plot the variations of thickness back over thousands of years.[2]

Thus specimens of known age of this kind, if carbon dated, can act as a most useful cross-check on carbon dating's accuracy. Checks of this type resulted in the discovery that special adjustments, or calibrations, were needed to be made to carbon dating calculations, in order to take account of the different times in the earth's history, such as the atom bomb tests of the 1960s, in which

171

the carbon 14 intake has fluctuated. These calibrations are now a routine part of any and every carbon-dating test.

A further development to carbon dating took place from 1977 when Professor Harry Gove of the University of Rochester, New York State, devised an improvement on the old method of reducing the sample to gas, and counting the beta particles emitted. With the aid of an accelerator generating very high voltages, Gove's method enabled the isolating of the actual number of carbon 14 atoms in any given sample. This had the major advantage of requiring considerably less sample than had been needed hitherto. By 1985 several laboratories had adopted the method, enabling an intercomparison trial on samples of known date which showed that in terms of reliability of results there was little to choose between the old Libby proportional counter method, and the new accelerator mass spectrometer one. Accordingly, because of the much smaller sample size needed, it was laboratories using Gove's accelerator mass spectrometer method, specifically those of Tucson, Oxford and Zurich, who were eventually selected as the ones to work on the Turin shroud.

Listen to most physicists talking about the accuracy of carbon dating, and you may be led to believe that it is about as inviolable as the high-society world of 1912 thought the *Titanic* unsinkable, and that therefore the shroud dating result should be accepted without question.

But listen to many an archaeologist, the actual users of carbon dating, and it is a different story. Years before the submission of the shroud to carbon dating, Bill Meacham, an American archaeologist with the Hong Kong Museum of History warned of the dangers of regarding carbon dating as an arbiter on the shroud.[3] Among a long list of individuals whom Meacham chided for putting too great a reliance on carbon dating was myself, who in 1978 rather rashly and over-confidently wrote that it should settle 'once and for all . . . the question whether or not the shroud is a fourteenth-century forgery.'[4]

The fact is that for any layman one of carbon dating's most misleading features is the seemingly very precise margin of error claimed: in the case of the shroud a quoted 95 per cent probability or 'confidence limit' for it dating sometime between 1260 and 1390. Too rarely understood is that these margins represent hypothetical statistical concepts, rather than necessarily the actual parameters of the true date.

172

For there can be no doubt that even the most recent archaeology is littered with examples of such widely variegated results that the quoted margins of error can only be regarded as very seriously misleading.

One example concerns the massive Bronze Age volcanic eruption of the Aegean island of Thera, or Santorini, which overwhelmed the port of Akrotiri and other settlements on Thera itself, and may well also have precipitated the demise of the Minoan civilization of Crete, sixty miles away. Historically the event has been thought to have happened *circa* 1500 BC. But when organic materials preserved by the eruption were carbon dated, the dates calculated produced more confusion than clarification. According to the present-day excavator, Professor Christos Doumas:

> The application of the radio-carbon method of dating . . . has unfortunately not been a success . . . During the decade 1967–77 a whole series of samples were processed . . . and a wide range of dates acquired . . . Samples taken were divided into two classes: long-lived (charcoal or wood) and short-lived beans, grains, shrubs), and in both cases dates have been produced for the destruction of Akrotiri with discrepancies ranging from about 1100, plus or minus 190 years BC, to 2590, plus or minus eighty years BC. Some specialists think that the discrepancies may be due to gas emanating from the volcano.[5]

Another example concerns one of the British Museum's most recent acquisitions, Lindow Man [pl. 32, below], the well-preserved upper torso of a neatly-manicured man in his mid-twenties who in 1984 was unearthed in a peatbog in Cheshire, England, and who appears to have been the victim of a Celtic human-sacrifice ritual. According to a 1986 report in the British journal, *Current Archaeology*:

> . . . there are continuing problems over his [Lindow Man's] date. Three sets of radiocarbon dates have been obtained. Firstly there are those obtained by conventional methods from the peat that surrounded him, which has been dated both by Harwell and by the British

173

Museum at dates around 300 BC, and this is the date they are adopting for publication. The other dates are done by the two new super-duper small measurement laboratories at Harwell and at Oxford, which can date minute samples of the body itself, of the hair, bones and skin. However, whereas all the Oxford samples come out consistently in the 1st century AD, all the Harwell samples come out consistently in the 5th century AD. At one time they thought that the difference might be due to the differing pre-treatment at the laboratories, so they swapped samples following pre-treatment, but the resulting measurements came out within the respective series for each laboratory. The archaeological world waits with bated breath to see how this problem is resolved.[6]

In fact, the problem still remains unresolved. In the British Museum's very latest publication on radiocarbon dating, Dr Sheridan Bowman, the new keeper of the Museum's Research Laboratory remarks: 'This is surely a mystery equal to that of the motive for the murder itself'.[7] And needing maximum emphasis in respect of this is that all the sets of radiocarbon dates, fourteen centuries apart in the case of Thera and eight centuries apart in the case of Lindow Man, have their own margins of error quoted at plus or minus *circa* one hundred years. Even just these two examples give the lie to the radiocarbon laboratories' stated margins of accuracy having anything like the precision they claim for them.

But the deep-seatedness of the problem is further evidenced from numerous examples in archaeology in which archaeologists have been given radiocarbon dates they have been unhappy with, but have had insufficient alternative data to be able to prove that the dates are wrong. The well-known British Egyptologist, Dr Rosalie David, for instance, cites Egyptian Mummy 1770 in her department's collection at the Manchester Museum, a mummy which she and colleagues very scientifically unwrapped in 1975 [pl. 32, above]. When she sent the bones and the bandages of the mummy off for dating, the British Museum radiocarbon laboratory produced the astonishing calculation that the bones were eight hundred to a thousand years older than the bandages.[8]

*Early depictions of the 'holy face' of Edessa,* (a): *eleventh-century Vatican Codex;* (b): *eleventh-century Greek menologion;* (c): *twelfth-century Serbian fresco (Gradac);* (d): *twelfth-century Russian fresco (Spas Nereditsa);* (e): *tenth/eleventh-century Cappadocian fresco (Sakli);* (f): *tenth-century triptych, St Catherine's, Sinai; (g & h): twelfth-century frescos, Cyprus;* (i): *twelfth-century Russian fresco*

25

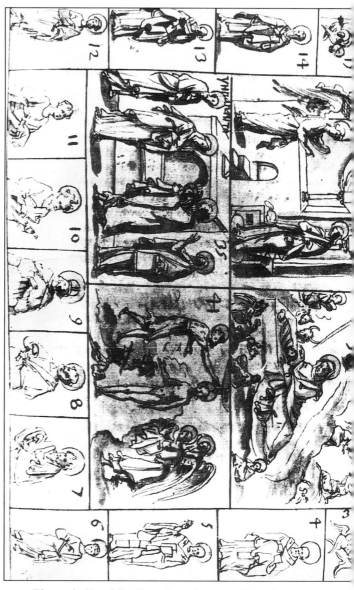

*The* umbella *of the Veronica, the magnificently-
embroidered Byzantine canopy used to protect and
ornament the Veronica during its expositions in the
Middle Ages and after, from the drawing made by
Vatican notary Jacopo Grimaldi in the early
seventeenth-century. (Biblioteca Nazionale,*

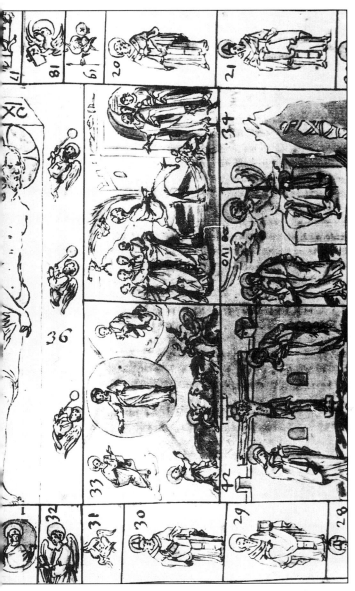

*Florence Ms. II III 173, fol. 114.) It is possible that the original* umbella *still survives somewhere within the so-inaccessible inner sancta of St Peter's. Particularly noteworthy is the figure laid out in death, as seen at the centre*

(Above): *Clear iconographic association of the Edessa 'holy face' and 'crossed hands' type figure seen on seventeenth-century Russian icon from the collection of George R. Hann, Sewickley Heights, Pennsylvania;* (below left): *Crossed-hands type figure on early fourteeenth-century lectern made for the pulpit of Cathedral of Pisa by the South Italian sculptor Giovanni Pisano. Staatliche Museen Preussischer Kulturbesitz, Berlin Dahlem;* (below right): *Superbly embroidered* epitaphios *of the early fourteenth-century as made for the Serbian King Milutin Uroš. This shows clear kinship to the Turin shroud figure*

*Early depictions of Jesus laid out in death, with crossed hands in typical 'shroud' pose; (above): from fol. 28 of the Pray manuscript, reliably datable to between 1192-5, National Széchenyi Library, Budapest; (left): From eleventh-century Byzantine ivory, Victoria & Albert Museum, London*

(Above): *'Acheropita' mosaic face of Christ, from the apse of the basilica of St John Lateran, Rome. Although a late nineteenth-century 'restoration', this is based on a much earlier mosaic, dating probably as far back as the sixth-century;* (below left): *Eleventh-century Pantocrator mosaic from the dome of the church at Daphni, near Athens, exhibiting markings strikingly reminiscent of incidental blemishes on the Turin shroud. Particularly noteworthy is the upside-down triangle at the bridge of the nose;* (below right): *Sixth-century Christ Pantocrator from St Catherine's monastery, Sinai*

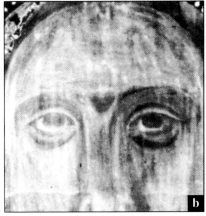

(a): *Detail from Spas Nereditsa fresco of Edessa 'holy face' (see pl. 25d), showing upside-down triangle at the bridge of the nose;* (b): *detail of X-ray image of earlier appearance of the Genoa 'holy face' (see pl. 21, above), clearly revealing similar, very distinctive triangle at the bridge of the nose;* (c): *detail from Ponziano catacomb Christ Pantocrator (see col. pl. VIII, below), showing equally distinctive topless square feature between the eyebrows;* (d): *detail of the face on the Turin shroud, natural appearance (see pl. 1, above), showing both the upside-down triangle and topless square. Given that the Christ portraits unquestionably date from well before the fourteenth-century, these peculiarities in them suggest, though do not prove, that the shroud was around substantially earlier than the date ascribed to it by carbon dating*

31

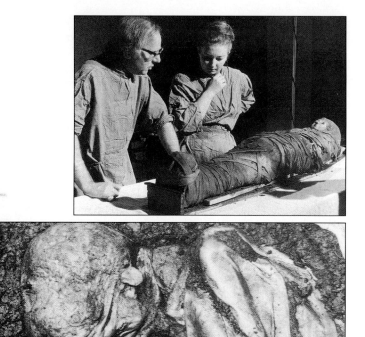

(Above): *Egyptologist Dr Rosalie David about to
undertake an exhaustive scientific examination of
Manchester Museum Egyptian Mummy no. 1770.
Carbon dating of this mummy by the British
Museum produced the astonishing calculation that
the mummy's bones seemed to be eight hundred to
a thousand years older than its bandages;*
(below): *Lindow Man, a victim of human sacrifice
excavated from a peat bog in Cheshire, England,
in 1984. Carbon dating findings have failed to
agree on whether he died in AD 500, AD 100 or
300 BC*

This caused Dr David to be torn between two hypotheses: first, that the mummy had perhaps been rewrapped eight hundred to a thousand years after death; the second that perhaps something in the resins and unguents used in mummification had acted in an as yet undetermined manner that interfered with a correct carbon-dating reading.

But to complicate the issue yet further, just at the time of this book being prepared for publication, the British Museum laboratory disclosed that there was a system error in all the datings it issued between 1980 and 1984 – inclusive of its work on Mummy 1770.[9] Apparently this was due to non-allowed-for evaporation in the modern control samples routinely used during this period. They stated that although in most cases the error amounted to only two or three hundred years, they were unable to issue any correction in the case of the Manchester Mummy – making yet more difficult Dr David's choice between the two alternatives.

That such examples are not mere isolated anecdote, but that there are some more fundamentally flawed aspects to carbon dating than yet conceded by the physicists, has been further demonstrated recently in an inter-comparison trial commissioned by Britain's Science and Engineering Research Council. Thirty-eight laboratories agreed to take part, representing both the conventional Libby method and the up-to-date accelerator mass spectrometer one, and each were given artefacts of dates known to the organizers, but unknown to the laboratories. The shock finding of this totally scientific trial was that the laboratories' actual margins of error were *on average* two or three times greater than the margins they claimed. Of the thirty-eight laboratories, only seven produced results that the organizers of the trial considered satisfactory, with those laboratories using the new accelerator mass spectrometer technique faring particularly badly.[10]

Somewhat shamefully, the Oxford laboratory (who of course worked on the shroud), adroitly avoided getting caught up in this controversy by declining to take part. In this light their subsequent claim that the errors 'should be laid at the doors of the laboratories that produced them'[11] can only be regarded as ringing more than a little hollow – somewhat akin to an athlete claiming he could have won an Olympic gold medal if only he had entered the race.

What seems unavoidable, as has been candidly pointed out by Professor Murdoch Baxter of the Scottish Universities Research and Reactor Centre, East Kilbride, is that 'other *unaccounted-for*

175

sources of error occur during the processing and analysis of samples [italics mine].'[12]

Just what those unaccounted for sources of error might be is undoubtedly the hardest question to answer. Quite definite is that there are varieties of contamination that can affect the reliability of carbon-dating readings. Although pre-treatment, involving cleaning of materials to be carbon dated, is standard procedure, and was certainly carried out with maximum possible thoroughness in the case of the shroud samples, doubts surround the extent to which this procedure can ever be 100 per cent effective, particularly in the case of highly porous materials, such as linen, which do not have the advantage of being able to be independently cross-checked by dendrochronology. As again remarked by Dr Sheridan Bowman, in her recent British Museum publication on radio-carbon dating:

> Many materials used for preserving or conserving samples may be impossible to remove subsequently: do not use glues, biocides, . . . [etc.]. Many ordinary packing materials such as paper, cardboard, cotton wool and string, contain carbon and are potential contaminants. Cigarette ash is also taboo.[13]

In the light of such concerns, the shroud's known history, that is, its universally accepted history subsequent to the mid-fourteenth century, provides an almost copy-book case of an object seriously unsuitable for carbon-dating. Quite aside from it having been subjected to centuries of smoke from burning candles, an equivalent surely to cigarette smoke, well-known also, not least from the scorches and patches it carries to this day, is that the shroud was involved in a serious fire in 1532.

In this latter it came so close to destruction that the silver of its casket melted, destroying one corner of the cloth as it lay folded inside. Knowing that this process could only have happened at temperatures in excess of 960°C, silver's melting-point, Manchester textile specialist John Tyrer has remarked:

> In these circumstances moisture in the shroud would turn to steam, probably at superheat, trapped in the folds and layers of the shroud. Any contaminants on the cloth would be dissolved by the steam and forced not only into the weave and yarn, but also into the flax

176

fibres' very lumen and molecular structure . . . [They would] become part of the chemistry of the flax fibres themselves and would be impossible to remove satisfactorily by surface actants and ultrasonic cleaning.[14]

Furthermore, two years after the fire the shroud was sewn onto a backing made up from three portions of sixteenth-century holland cloth. Inevitably this linen must contain carbon with equally as much contamination potential as the paper, cardboard and cotton wool mentioned by Dr Bowman. And it has now been in the closest contact with the shroud for over four hundred and fifty years.

Another area of concern derives from the fact that the sample as used for the 1988 carbon dating was taken from one edge of the shroud, precisely where the cloth would have received maximum handling from being held up during its many expositions in the sixteenth and seventeenth centuries. Nor would this have been the only contamination danger from such occasions. In 1615, for instance, St Francis de Sales was one of three bishops who held up the shroud before the people on a very hot day, and recorded how he was embarrassed to see perspiration from his forehead drip onto the shroud. Who knows how many similar instances have gone totally unrecorded?

Yet the force of these and similar contamination arguments has been fiercely contested by Professor Edward Hall, the recently-retired director of the Oxford laboratory. He has argued:

> Calculations show that a modern contamination amounting to 65 per cent of the mass of the shroud would be necessary to give a date of 1350 to a fabric originally dating from the time of Christ . . . We believe that any such contamination would have been less than 0.1 per cent.[15]

The weak point of Hall's argument, however, is that there still undoubtedly has to be *some* serious and as yet unaccounted-for explanation for the substantial discrepancies already noted in recent carbon datings like Lindow Man. Furthermore the Zurich laboratory is reliably known to have erred by up to a 1000 years in its dating of a sample during the inter-comparison trial conducted by the British Museum in 1985, an error that was apparently due to their failure to remove a certain unidentified source of contamination.'[16] So on the basis of Professor Hall's calculations, are we to suppose that a laboratory as scrupulous as Zurich could have left some 50 per cent contamination in this instance?

Also to be discounted is the argument that the credibility of the shroud carbon dating is hugely reinforced by having been arrived at by three theoretically independent laboratories. This is totally vitiated by the fact that as users of Gove's accelerator mass spectrometer technique all three laboratories are clones of each other. Furthermore, instead of having received samples taken from different areas of the shroud, they all received sections of a single portion taken from one edge of the cloth. Effectively they were almost bound to achieve the same result, a weakness of the original decision on the choice of laboratories as made in Turin.

All this is not to argue that contamination was *the* source of an error in the carbon dating, if indeed such an error occurred. Other possibilities have been cited, including the idea that if the image on the shroud was caused by the release of some form of energy at Jesus's resurrection, then this same energy-release may have altered the shroud's carbon 14 isotope content to make it appear younger than it is. In the words of one correspondent to the British journal *New Scientist*:

> If energy released in the resurrection process activated an extra 18 per cent of carbon 14 compared to that present naturally in the cloth, the shroud, although being 2000 years old, would appear to be only 650 years old. And it is certainly possible to produce that amount of carbon 14 via a short burst of high energy.[17]

Whether, therefore, there has or has not been some error in respect of the shroud carbon dating, what is undeniable is that the process of carbon dating, despite all the ultra-scientific precision with which it is associated, can and does err in its results. It should be regarded as tool, not arbiter, and should never be mistaken for the latter. As has been very cogently remarked by the former Biblical archaeologist Dr Eugenia Nitowski:

> In any form of enquiry or scientific discipline, it is the weight of evidence which must be considered conclusive. In archaeology, if there are ten lines of evidence, carbon

dating being one of them, and it conflicts with the other nine, there is little hesitation to throw out the carbon date as inaccurate . . .[18]

Which now ultimately leads us back to the very problem with which we started. After all that we have learned, what really was was the origin of the Veronica and its related 'holy faces'? Despite the carbon dating, could it have been the shroud, in the guise of the 'holy face' of Edessa? Is there any more information we could find out about the 'holy faces' that might enable us to be rather more sure that the shroud was around well before the fourteenth century, and was their progenitor rather than their successor? Although we may know enough to be sure that carbon dating can lie, whether it actually *has* lied remains an open question.

## Chapter Fifteen

# 'THEY OUGHT TO BE BROUGHT TO THE LIGHT OF DAY . . .'

*I do not know why Rome should persist in being a city of mystery. There are relics in it . . . which art and piety may demand to be made acquainted with, but which, unfortunately, one may either not see, or only see indistinctly. They ought to be brought to the light of day, and not withheld from fear of scoffing incredulity and sceptical ignorance. If these relics be really genuine, truth will be elicited . . . Piety may believe without seeing, but reason must see to believe*

Abbé Barbier de Montault *circa* 1854

In a sense this book has turned full circle, from looking away from the shroud to what its ancestor might have been among the Veronica and other famous 'holy faces' of history; to arriving back at the shroud having found that it remains the only logical source both of all the 'holy faces' and of the familiar Christ likeness as it has come down to us in art.

It is important, however, to remind ourselves that the shroud was never intended as the central subject of this book, and so there are many items of potentially supportive new evidence relating to it which rightly belong to a more concentrated independent study. For instance, in August 1981 a Leicester University archaeological team excavating at St Bees Priory, Cumbria, England, unearthed a coffin containing the well-preserved body of a late thirteenth-century knight wrapped in two shrouds,[1] which have since been expertly conserved. Compared with the Turin shroud these genuine medieval shrouds reveal quite different dimensions, and indicate a quite different method of enfolding the body. French medieval manuscript depictions of contemporary shroud burials similarly exhibit marked differences to the procedure indicated on the Turin shroud.[2] If the latter was the work of a medieval forger, he therefore seems to have thought out a funerary arrangement quite different from anything with which he might be expected to have been familiar. This is a hitherto neglected area of enquiry that needs considerable further study.

Along these same lines has been a study of the shroud's dimensions as recently made by an expert in early Syriac, Ian Dickinson, from Canterbury, England.[3] Curious at the shroud's, by British units of measurement, anomalous 14 foot 3 inch by 3 foot 7 inch overall size, Dickinson wondered if these dimensions might make more sense if converted to the cubit measure as prevailing in Jesus's time. Establishing that the first-century Jewish cubit was most likely to the Assyrian standard, reliably calculated at between 21.4 and 21.6 inches, Dickinson found that if he chose the lower of these measures there was an astonishing correlation, accurate to the nearest half-inch:

| | |
|---|---|
| Length of Turin shroud | 14 feet 3 inches |
| 8 cubits at 21.4 inches | 14 feet 3 inches |
| Width of Turin shroud | 3 feet 7 inches |
| 2 cubits at 21.4 inches | 3 feet 7 inches |

Such conformity to an exact 8 by 2 Jewish cubits is yet another piece of knowledge difficult to imagine of any medieval forger. It also correlates perfectly with the 'doubled in four' arrangement by which we hypothesized the shroud to have been once folded and mounted as the 'holy face' of Edessa, for the exposed facial area of this latter would have been an exact 1 by 2 Jewish cubits.

These and similar findings, so irreconcilable with the shroud radiocarbon dating, make all the more frustrating that the Veronica and other 'holy faces', although clearly closely linked with the shroud's origins, still remain so inaccessible. And in this regard the reader may well have been long wondering why, for the purposes of this book, this author has not made his own concerted attempt to penetrate the world of the secret places, particularly

181

in order to examine the Veronica and other items at first hand? Even if Heaphy failed in the nineteenth century to gain the access he claimed, surely it ought to be possible in the arguably more enlightened climate of the late twentieth century?

The plain answer, as the reader is entitled to expect, is that while shunning aggressive foot-in-the-door methods of investigative journalism, I have indeed attempted such access. Even as early as 1977, having made the acquaintance of Archbishop Bruno Heim, the Vatican's Apostolic Delegate in London, I broached in a letter to him the question of whether there might be any possibility of obtaining even merely a photograph of the Veronica. He declined to reply, and what had previously been a cordial correspondence abruptly ceased. Independently I learned that others, making similar enquiries to other individuals high in the Catholic hierarchy, had met similar stonewalling.

So on the commencement of this book, keenly aware that there were likely to be difficulties, I made careful and prolonged enquiries with a variety of individuals, in Rome and elsewhere, concerning whom best to approach in order to try to gain actual access to the Veronica and other holy faces. Should it be Heim's successor as Apostolic Delegate in London? Should it be Archbishop Silvestrini of the Vatican Secretariat of State? Should it be Archbishop Van Lierde, the Papal Sacristan? Might it even be best to make a direct approach to Pope John Paul II himself – particularly since one 'holy face' that I wanted to examine, the former S. Silvestro one, was actually in the pope's private chapel?

Eventually it was a Vatican correspondent, Peter Jennings of the American Catholic weekly *Our Sunday Visitor*, who persuaded me that an individual within Vatican circles who had always responded very positively to him was Monsignor Stanislao Dziwisz, the pope's most senior private secretary. The idea appealed, for arguably there is no man closer to the pope than Dziwisz. A fellow-Pole, he worked for the then Cardinal Wojtila for thirteen years before he became Pope John Paul II, and stayed on as his closest aide, to the extent even of being soaked in his blood, and protecting him with his own body, when Turkish gunman Ali Agca came so close to assassinating him in St Peter's Square in 1981. And since my first book on the shroud had been very warmly received in Poland, and I knew the pope to be deeply interested in the subject (he had had his own special showing on 13 April 1980), I hoped that this might serve as at least some introduction.

182

Fortuitously Peter Jennings happened to be accompanying the Archbishop of Canterbury's visit to Rome in September 1989, and so he kindly volunteered to use this opportunity to hand directly to Dziwisz a letter from me. This two-page letter explained the research I was involved in, and requested no more than a day's access both to the Veronica and to the S. Silvestro 'holy face', in order to document and study these in the company of a photographer and two key specialists. In the event it took until Christmas before a reply came, and then not from Dziwisz, but from Monsignor Sepe of the General Affairs section of the Secretariat of State. Disappointingly this was no more than a formal acknowledgement, stating in English, 'I am pleased to inform you that your request has been transmitted to the departments competent to give an answer.'

Several more weeks passed, then early in February came a letter in Italian from Archbishop Virgilio Noè. Although the name was not immediately known to me, some quick enquiries established that he was an important individual within the Vatican hierarchy, none other than the meticulously protocol-minded papal master of ceremonies who supervised the funerals of Popes Paul VI and John Paul I, and the conclaves which had elected John Paul I and John Paul II. As his letter made clear, however, he was writing as an official of the Fabbrica of St Peter's, the organization in charge of all matters behind-the-scenes at St Peter's, including control of the permanent work-force of 'sampietrini',' and, inevitably, access to the 'secret places'. Courteously but firmly he told me that, in common with previous similar applications, he could only give a negative answer to my request. The fundamental reason, he stated, was:

> the fact that the Veil [i.e. the Veronica], is in too precarious a condition for it to be advisable to open up the frame for examination purposes.[4]

Now emphatic as the letter was, this very statement in it seemed to open an opportunity not to take Noè for an answer. For if the Veronica was indeed in so precarious a condition, then surely someone within the Fabbrica must already have made a documentary photograph to record its appearance; just as any museum does of the more perishable items in its collection? Surely, in such circumstances, it would not be an unreasonable request to

183

be allowed to examine these photographs in lieu of the original? Furthermore, if conservation was the main concern, it ought to be permissible at least to view the location where the Veronica was kept, particularly to note the existence or otherwise of curios such as the Veronica casket sketched by Grimaldi, and the piece of asbestos brought for it from the East by the Polo brothers?

Within three days of receiving Noè's letter I sent by express mail a polite and professionally-translated response, making these points, and requesting at least an interview at any day and time convenient to himself. I suggested any time during the first three weeks of March as most suitable for myself. But unhappily the result was, and has continued to be, as studious a silence as that first received from Archbishop Heim.

Now in the event, such intransigence, though scarcely commendable, is not to be unexpected from Noè. As Vatican master of ceremonies he was so staunchly traditionalist, and steeped in protocol, that he is known to have severely disapproved when the genial, refreshingly humble and sadly short-lived Pope John Paul I rejected wearing the traditional papal tiara and similarly declined to style himself with the customary royal 'we'.[5] Reportedly Noè was similarly furious on hearing that the same pope had been spotted going for a solitary early morning stroll onto streets outside Vatican territory, actually reprimanding the non-plussed John Paul I for behaving in such a manner. For Noè, even a pope is expected to obey the rules and conform to tradition, and if anyone one day opens up the 'secret places' of St Peter's to the impious gaze of lay people, it is unlikely to be him.

But the irony, certainly in the case of the Veronica, at the very least, is that there is so little true holiness to what Noè and his like seem to be trying to protect. As the Roman Catholic Church has itself long recognized, there are serious doubts concerning the historical existence of any 'Saint Veronica' corresponding to the popular legend. The woman of this name goes unlisted in the Roman Catholic Church's official list of its saints. The continuance of a feast day for her (12 July), seems a mere sop to popular superstition. As for the cloth itself, we have already shown that it seems at best to have been a tenth-century artist's copy of the 'holy face' of Edessa, whether or whether not that was the present-day Turin shroud. Effectively what Noè is guarding is far more of art-historical than of religious interest, and ought to be available to everyone as freely as the *Mona Lisa* or the Bayeux Tapestry.

184

Absurdly, for instance, we still cannot even yet be sure that the cloth preserved today as the Veronica is genuinely one and the same as that exhibited to medieval pilgrims. Although we have already seen that it seemed to have survived to the early seventeenth century, the curiosity remains that while the copy made by Pietro Strozzi shows at least vestiges of a facial image, the existence of anything of this kind on the original has been denied by all who have examined it during the last century.

Thus Professor Pfeiffer of Rome's Gregorian University has informed me that he heard from a canon of St Peter's, Canon Krieg, that there is no visible image on the present-day Veronica. And this has been similarly attested by the only individual of my direct acquaintance who appears to have seen the original at first hand, Isabel Piczek, a highly talented Hungarian-born artist who specializes in church murals, stained glass and mosaic, and is now resident in Los Angeles, California.

Isabel Piczek's story is a particularly fascinating one. During the 1950s, when only thirteen, she fled from the communist suppression in Hungary, arriving in Rome, where her artistic abilities quickly won several awards, including a competition to create a fresco at the Pontifical Biblical Institute, across the road from the Gregorian University in Rome. It was this work which brought her into contact with several very senior individuals within the Vatican hierarchy, ones who could literally open any door. Isabel was not yet fourteen when one of these took her into St Peter's, entered the sacristy, and kept her waiting nearly an hour. Such was the secrecy insisted upon that to this day Isabel declines to make public the name of the individual concerned (though she has disclosed this to me). But to her astonishment the sacristy door suddenly opened, and the illustrious cleric and his companion were revealed a few feet inside holding a framed cloth that she was told was the Veronica. According to her description:

> On it was a head-size patch of colour, about the same as the [Turin] shroud, slightly more brownish. By patch, I do not mean that it was patched, just a blob of a brownish rust colour. It looked almost even, except for some little swirly discolorations . . . Even with the best imagination, you could not make any face or features out of them, not even the slightest hint of it.[6]

185

As she further recollects:

> The light was not that good at all, and there was glass
> on the object [i.e. the Veronica]. He did not bring it out
> in apparent fear that people would gather.

As an artist, Isabel feels strongly that despite the poor light, she would have been able to make out at least the semblance of a face, if there was anything there. And this certainly checks out with the German art historian J. Wilpert's insistence that he was unable to see a face even when the glass was removed in 1906.[7] Curiously, Isabel cannot recall seeing the 'cut-out' inner frame forming a surround to the face. This suggests that this may perhaps have been removed at the time of Wilpert's examination.

But whatever, visible image or no visible image, it should still be possible to establish whether the piece of cloth preserved as the Veronica is one and the same as that exhibited in the Middle Ages. We should be able to do this merely by checking for the damage marks as carefully recorded by Pietro Strozzi in his copy of 1617, and on the Church of Gesù's copy of a few years later. Furthermore, if the conclusion from this were affirmative, then modern techniques such as infra-red and laser photography should enable the retrieval even of a near totally effaced image. I have personally seen a very convincing demonstration of this at the Home Office Forensic Science Laboratory in London. It is possibilities such as these that continue to be blocked by Archbishop Noè's intransigence.

So what possible justification can there be for Archbishop Noè and his colleagues persisting in keeping the Veronica under such ultimately futile conditions of inaccessibility from the outside world? Why, furthermore, should there similarly be excluded from ordinary lay access items such as the piece of asbestos which the Polo brothers brought from the East for the Veronica's protection; the Byzantine *umbella* which used to be held over the Veronica when it was displayed (if this still exists); the medieval silver casket in which it was stored (and may still be stored); and whatever else, unknown to us, lies in the so tightly closeted world behind the Veronica pier? Why are serious scholars not even allowed photographs of such objects?

Not only are there no satisfactory answers to these questions, the blame cannot be set entirely at the door of traditionalist-minded men such as Noè. Had Pope John Paul II been so inclined,

Monsignor Dziwisz might at least have been able to respond positively in the case of the S. Silvestro 'holy face' in the pope's private chapel. This part of my request went totally ignored. Yet as in the case of the Veronica, there is no serious case for this 'holy face' being of any true 'holiness', for it is quite manifestly an icon. Its real interest is an art historical one, bearing as it does, an obvious close relationship to the Genoa and Veronica 'holy faces', carrying a 'token' cloth that may be of the same herring-bone weave as the shroud, and also bearing on its back an as yet unopened parchment potentially informative as to its early history. Not least with regard to this latter, it is quite absurd that it should be left to crumble unread towards its inevitable final disintegration, simply because secrecy and exclusion from lay access have so long been the tradition.

Effectively, in the interests both of potential relevance to the shroud and of the general furtherance of human knowledge, a new air of *glasnost* is needed to blow through the darker corners of St Peter's and the Apostolic Palace. Too much of what has been set down in this book has had, of necessity, to be derived from second- and third-hand information, its reliability unable to be 100 per cent because of the sheer inaccessibility of the central subjects. Given that an exhaustive specialist access has already been granted of the shroud – an object potentially of far greater holiness than any of the rest put together – there is simply no excuse for the same not being allowed of the 'holy faces' of the 'secret places'.

So what should be done? One example of just how useful comparative work can be, even from photographs, derives from the simple, amateur experiment of superimposing the outline of the Genoa image onto a photograph of the shroud. There is a remarkable match.[8]

But of course this is no substitute for expert study of all the 'holy faces' at first hand, preferably at one and the same time, and side by side with the shroud, so that instant comparison can be made. There should be no excuse for not including the Veronica in this. Even if it is in a very precarious condition, modern specialist conservation techniques should be able to stabilize it, arrest further decay, and enable careful handling by which its fabric characteristics can be determined. Analysis by textile experts should definitively establish whether this and the 'token' cloths on the Genoa and S. Silvestro 'holy faces' bear any relation weave-

187

wise to the shroud. The wood backgrounds of these same 'holy faces' may be suitable for dendrochronological or tree-ring analysis to date it with genuine precision. Dare one suggest it, tiny pieces both of wood and/or fabric might be allowed for carbon dating? There might also be allowed an ancillary public exhibition in which all the 'holy faces' could be brought together and displayed as historical objects, as never before in history.

But at the end of the day, what would all this be for? Certainly not any more to 'test' the shroud. Among believers and non-believers alike that was perhaps the greatest unspoken motivation – and the greatest mistake – behind the shroud carbon-dating exercise. We were all guilty of wanting a result corresponding to our expectations in order that this might, or might not be, seen as some form of proof of the hand of God.

We should have reminded ourselves of the gospel stories of Jesus's temptation in the desert during which he was exhorted to throw himself unharmed from a high parapet in order to prove his divinity to all men. Reproving his tempter, Jesus chose, unusually for him, to quote from Jewish scripture: 'You must not put the Lord your God to the test' (Deuteronomy 6: 16). When University of Arizona professors Paul Damon and Douglas Donahue drove with their shroud sample through the Sonora desert to their laboratory, in a very real sense they were aiming to demonstrate whether God had shown himself in the form of the Turin shroud. Is it too much to suggest that God might have pulled down the blinds?

No such reservations, however, need apply to the opening-up of the holy faces to now long-overdue scientific and art historical scrutiny. This would be no more than simple, open-ended expansion of ordinary human knowledge. Because we simply do not know where the investigations might lead, and because media-wise the shroud has already been so roundly written off, there need be little or none of the 'putting God to the test' connotations that so dogged the carbon dating.

But ultimately, in the light of the seemingly so much more pressing problems that beset the pope and other world leaders at this time, what might all this be for? It is important that we should not underrate this.

For however intangible it might seem, there is something very deep in the human psyche that is stirred by coming, in ordinary everyday life, face to face with what may or may not be *the* Holy Face. Back in the early thirteenth century, the poet Dante put into

188

the mouth of the pilgrim from Croatia the question: 'Lord Jesus Christ . . . was this then your true semblance?' While at that time Dante had of course in mind the Veronica of Rome, this same question persists to this day of its close relation, the face on the Turin shroud, even in the very teeth of the carbon dating: 'Was this truly you, Jesus of Nazareth. Was this what you really looked like?'

In this context, although there are many individuals who are quite happy to accept that the shroud was faked in the fourteenth century, and regard it as of supreme unimportance in their everyday lives, there are others, including myself, for whom the question 'Was this what you really looked like?' simply refuses to go away. Not only is the shroud as difficult to attribute to a fourteenth-century artist as the Sistine Chapel ceiling is attributable to Van Gogh, there is not even any comfort in not being able to dismiss it in such a way.

For if that face, however subjectively, seems as though it has transcended two thousand years, it is as if neither time, nor the grave, have any meaning. It bespeaks the very same questions as those that wracked the pilgrims to the Veronica: 'Were those the lips that spoke the Sermon on the Mount and the Parable of the Rich Fool?'; 'Is this the Face that is to be my judge on the Last Day?'

Even if this face were, after all, the work of some fourteenth-century artist, then even in my unbelief at this I can only marvel. For a human artificer of six hundred years ago, technologically unable ever to see the full fruits of his creation, to have given so many well-educated and self-critical twentieth-century people the inescapable feeling that they are in the presence of the Real Presence is the stuff of the very highest art. One could not even remotely call such a man a faker or a forger.

But the alternative, inevitably, is even more daunting. In the shroud we have a piece of cloth that men cast lots over when they put it to the test (remember the cowboy boots?). A piece of cloth they mocked when their instruments of destruction showed it, seemingly, as of mere human frailty. Is it not all strikingly evocative of what they did when they committed the body of Jesus himself to crucifixion and the grave? And did not something mind-blowingly unexpected happen to this, just when Jesus's followers felt at their most defeated? It all gives one the unnerving feeling that the shroud, even now, frail and discredited as it might seem, is part of a cosmic drama not yet played out.

189

# NOTES AND REFERENCES

## CHAPTER ONE

1 For an excellent and up-to-date description of the architectural features of the Capella of the Holy Shroud, see H. A. Meek, *Guarino Guarini and his Architecture*, Yale University Press, 1988, p. 61ff.
2 See Dorothy Crispino, 'The Report of the Poor Clare nuns, Chambéry, 1534', *Shroud Spectrum International*, no. 2, March 1982, pp. 19–27.
3 Bill McLellan, 'Secrets of the Shroud', *St Louis Post-Dispatch*, 15 May, 1988.
4 David Sox, *The Shroud Unmasked*, Basingstoke, Lamp Press, 1988, p. 147.
5 The full, exact text of the Cardinal's communiqué, as published on 17 October 1988 in the weekly English language edition of the official Vatican newspaper, *L'Osservatore Romano*, was as follows:

In a dispatch received by the Pontifical Custodian of the Holy Shroud [i.e. Cardinal Ballestrero] on 28 September 1988, the laboratories of the University of Arizona, of the University of Oxford and of the Poly-technic of Zurich which had conducted the tests for the radio-carbon dating of the cloth of the Holy Shroud, have finally communicated the result of their tests through Dr Tite of the British Museum, the co-ordinator of the project.

This document states that the cloth of the shroud can be assigned with a confidence of 95 per cent accuracy to a date between AD 1260 and 1390. More precise and detailed information concerning the result will be published by the laboratories and Dr Tite in a scientific review in an article which is in the course of preparation [see note 7].

For his part Professor Bray of the 'G. Colonetti' Institute of Metrology of Turin, which was charged with the review of the summary report presented by Dr Tite, has confirmed the compatibility of the results obtained by the three laboratories, whose certainty falls within the limits envisaged by the methods used.

After having informed the Holy See, the owner of the Holy Shroud, I make known what has been communicated to me. In submitting to science the evaluation of these results, the Church confirms her respect and veneration for this venerable icon of Christ, which remains an object of devotion for the faithful in keeping with the attitude always expressed in regard to the Holy Shroud, namely that the value of the image is more important than the date of the shroud itself. This attitude disposes of the gratuitous deductions of a theological character advanced in the sphere of a research which had been presented as solely and rigorously scientific.

At the same time the problems about the origin of the image and its preservation still remain to a large extent unsolved and will require further research and study. In regard to this the Church will show the same openness, inspired by the love of truth which she showed by permitting the radio-carbon dating as soon as she was presented with a reasonable and effective programme in regard to that matter.

I personally regret the deplorable fact that many reports concerning this scientific research were anticipated in the press, especially of the English language, because it also favoured the by no means objective insinuation that the Church was afraid of science by trying to conceal its results, an accusation in open contradiction to the Church's attitude on this occasion also when she has gone ahead resolutely.

Turin<br>13 October 1988<br>Cardinal Anastasio Ballestrero

On the basis of this carefully dispassionate communiqué London's *Daily Telegraph*, theoretically one of Britain's 'quality' newspapers, carried the headline 'Turin shroud is a forgery, says Catholic Church', followed by a first paragraph 'The shroud of Turin is not the burial cloth of Christ . . . the Roman Catholic Church said in Italy yesterday.'

6 Michael Sheridan and Phil Reeves, the *Independent*, Friday 14 October 1988.
7 P. E. Damon *et al.*, 'Radio-carbon dating of the shroud of Turin', *Nature*, v. 337, no. 6208, 16 February 1989, pp. 611–15.
8 *La Contre-Réforme Catholique au XXe Siècle*, no. 200, Christmas 1988.
9 Sheridan and Reeves, op. cit.
10 Thomas J. Phillips, 'Shroud irradiated with neutrons', letter to *Nature*, 16 February 1989, p. 594.
11 Robert Hedges, letter to *Nature*, 16 February 1989, p. 594.
12 Professor Paul Damon, personal correspondence with the author, 12 June 1989.

# CHAPTER TWO

1 Memorandum of Pierre d'Arcis, Bishop of Troyes, to anti-pope Pope Clement VII. Paris, Bibliothèque Nationale, Collection de Champagne, v. 154, fol. 138.
2 Translation by Revd Herbert Thurston, SJ, 'The Holy Shroud and the Verdict of History', *The Month*, CI, 1903, pp. 21–6.
3 Ibid., p. 22.
4 Ibid., p. 23.
5 For texts and discussion of these, see Luigi Fossati, SDB, *La Santa Sindone, Nuova Luce su Antichi Documenti*, Turin, Borla Editore, 1961.
6 See Stephen Murray, *Building Troyes Cathedral, The Late Gothic Campaigns*, Indiana University Press, 1987.

7 Clement both issued a bull and sent d'Arcis a personal letter. These and related documents are reproduced in the original Latin in Fossati, op. cit., pp. 205ff.

8 'Figura seu representacio sudarii Domini nostri Jhesu Christi venerabiliter conservatur.' The full text, from Vatican Archives Rg. Avign., 261, fol. 309 v. is reproduced in the original Latin in Fossati, op. cit., pp. 211–13. See also the same author's English language article, 'The Lirey Controversy', *Shroud Spectrum 8*, September 1983, p. 26.

9 For further details, see Barbara Tuchman, *A Distant Mirror: The Calamitous Fourteenth Century*, Penguin edition, p. 322:

> Cardinal Robert persuaded the men of Cesena to lay down their arms, and won their confidence by asking for fifty hostages and immediately releasing them as evidence of good will. Then summoning his mercenaries . . . from a nearby town, he ordered a general massacre 'to exercise justice'. Meeting some demurral, he insisted, crying '*Sangue et sangue!*' (Blood and more blood!), which was what he meant by justice . . . For three days and nights . . . the soldiers slaughtered . . . Trying to escape, hundreds drowned in the moats, thrust back by relentless swords. Women were seized for rape, ransom was placed on children, plunder succeeded the killing, works of art were ruined, handicrafts laid waste, 'and what could not be carried away, they burned . . .'. The toll of the dead was between 2,500 and 5,000 . . .

10 Musée du Petit Palais, Avignon.

11 M. Perret, 'Essai sur l'Histoire du S.Suaire du XIVe au XVIe siècle', *Mémoires de l'Académie des Sciences, Belles Lettres et Arts de Savoie*, IV, 1960, p. 66.

12 After the year 1388 Jeanne de Vergy instituted in the Church of Geneva an anniversary for the soul of Aymon of Geneva. See A. Sarasin, 'Obituaire de l'église cathédrale de Saint-Pierre de Genève', *Mémoires et documents publiés par la Société d'Histoire et d'Archéologie de Genève*, t.XXI, 1882, p. 267.

13 See Fossati, 'The Lirey Controversy', op. cit., p. 28.

14 See Fossati, *La Santa Sindone*, op. cit., p. 72.

15 Ibid, p. 193. The original document is in the archives of the French *département* of the Aube, Troyes, I, 17.

16 Archives of the French *département* of the Aube, Troyes, fonds de Lirey, 96, reproduced in Fossati, *La Santa Sindone*, op. cit., p. 194ff.

17 '. . . quod olim genitor ipsius Gaufridi zelo devocionis accensus, quandam figuram sive representacionem Sudarii Domini nostri Jhesu Christi sibi liberaliter oblatam.' Fossati, *La Santa Sindone*, op. cit., p. 205.

18 See Perret, op. cit., p. 81.

19 See Dorothy Crispino, 'Why did Geoffrey de Charny change his mind?', *Shroud Spectrum*, 1, p. 34, note 4.

20 The badge is displayed in the Musée de Cluny, Paris. It was first published in Arthur Forgeais, *Collection de Plombs Historiés trouvés dans la Seine*, Paris, 1865, where it was wrongly identified as the Holy Shroud of Besançon. Between 1848 and 1860 Forgeais retrieved a variety of similar objects from dredging and construction work carried out in the Seine. For a useful recent study of the badge, see Dorothy Crispino, 'The Pilgrim Badge of Lirey', *Shroud Spectrum International*, 25, December 1987, pp. 13–18.

21 Arthur Piaget, 'Le livre Messire Geoffroi de Charni', *Romania*, 1897, T.XXVI, pp. 394–411. At the time of this book going to press I have learned of a translation being made by the Oxford University Scholar Elspeth Kennedy.

22 For a full bibliography of the scientific work carried out in 1978, see my own book, *The Mysterious Shroud*, New York, Doubleday, 1986, pp. 154–6.

23 Walter C. McCrone 'Light Microscopical Study of the Turin "Shroud" ', I & II, *The Microscope*, vol. 28, no. 3/4, 1980; III, vol. 29, no. 1, 1981.

24 Charles Locke Eastlake, *Methods and Materials of Painting of the Great Schools and Masters*, London, Longman, Brown, Green & Longman, 1847, p. 94ff.

25 Quoted from interview with Peter Jennings, published under headline 'Shroud holds new mystery', *Birmingham Post*, Thursday 13 October 1988.

26 Luigi Fossati, SDB, 'Copies of the Shroud II & III', *Shroud Spectrum International*, 13, December 1984, p. 28.

27 Luigi Fossati, SDB, 'Copies of the Shroud I', *Shroud Spectrum International*, 12, September 1984, p. 20.

28 In his masterly survey of these copies, Fossati concludes, 'In all the copies, their manual origin is patent. Never do they

show a totally negative character, such as the shroud presents; they are a *mélange* of positive and negative, in which the positive obviously predominates. One can see the difficulty which the artists encountered: in trying to reproduce a reality which was not exactly what they were accustomed to, they represented the figure in ways and means which did not correspond to that reality.' Fossati, *Shroud Spectrum International*, 13, op. cit., p. 34.

29 Joe Nickell, *Inquest on the Shroud of Turin*, Buffalo, New York, Prometheus Books, 1983.

30 Peter Murray Jones, *Medieval Medical Miniatures*, London, British Library, 1984, p. 38.

31 J. M. Cameron, 'A pathologist looks at the Shroud' in Peter Jennings, ed. *Face to Face with the Turin Shroud*, Oxford, Mowbray, 1978, pp. 57–9.

32 F. Zugibe, *The Cross and the Shroud*, New York, Angelus Books, 1982.

33 Robert Bucklin, 'The Medical Aspects of the Crucifixion of Christ', *Sindon*, 7, 1961, pp. 5–11.

34 Michael Straiton, 'The Man of the Shroud: a thirteenth-century crucifixion action-replay', *Catholic Medical Quarterly*, XL no. 3, 243, August 1989, pp. 135–43.

# CHAPTER THREE

1 James Lees-Milne, *Saint Peter's, The Story of Saint Peter's Basilica in Rome*, London, Hamish Hamilton, 1967.

2 Giorgio Vasari, *The Lives of the Artists*, a selection translated by George Bull, Harmondsworth, Penguin, 1965, p. 387.

3 See Rudolf Wittkower, *Gian Lorenzo Bernini*, London, Phaidon, 1955, pp. 192–3.

4 Alta Macadam, *Blue Guide to Rome and Environs*, London and New York, Black & Norton, 1985, p. 296.

5 James Lees-Milne, op. cit., p. 254.

6 James Lees-Milne, personal communication, 25 December 1989.

7 Aubrey Menen, 'St Peter's', *National Geographic*, vol. 140, no. 6, December 1971, p. 878.

8 Revd Adrien Parvilliers, SJ, *La devotion des prédestinés, ou les stations de Jerusalem et du Calvaire pour servir d'entretien*

*sur le passion de Notre Seigneur Jesu Christ*. This appeared in fourteen editions between 1696 and 1892.

9  See, for example, Walter L. Strauss, *The Intaglio Prints of Albrecht Dürer*, New York, Kennedy Galleries & Abaris Books, 1976, pp. 192–3 and 234–5.

10  'Vultus Domini Nostri Jesu Christi quae Romae in sacrosancta basilica S.Petri in Vaticano, religiosissime asservatur et colitur.'

11  X. Barbier de Montault, 'Iconographie du Chemin de la Croix', *Annales Archéologiques*, vol. 23, 1863, p. 232.

12  M. Sanuto, *Diarii*, Biblioteca Marciana, Venice, MSS Ital. Cl. VII, vol. 45, col. 122.

13  Barbier de Montault, op. cit., p. 232.

14  Joseph Wilpert, *Römische Mosaiken und Malereien*, Freiburg im Breisgau, 1924, II, 2, p. 1123ff.

15  Werner Bulst, SJ/Heinrich Pfeiffer, SJ, *Das Turiner Grabtuch und das Christusbild*, Frankfurt, Knecht, 1987, p. 120; also Heinrich Pfeiffer, 'Una Visita a Manoppello', *Collegamento pro Sindone*, March–April 1986, pp. 35–8.

# CHAPTER FOUR

1  For useful biographical background to Gerald of Wales, see his autobiography, Giraldus Cambrensis, *Autobiography of Giraldus Cambrensis*, ed. H. E. Butler, London, Cape, 1937.

2  See Rodolfo Lanciani, *Pagan and Christian Rome*, London, Macmillan, 1892, p. 231ff.

3  Jacopo Grimaldi, *Descrizione della Basilica Vaticana*, Biblioteca Vaticana, Ms, Barb.lat. 2733, reproduced in the Metropolitan Museum of Art, New York, *The Vatican Collections, the Papacy and Art*, New York, Harry N. Abrams, Inc., 1983, p. 27.

4  Giraldus Cambrensis, *Speculum Ecclesiae* (Rolls Series) vol. IV, pp. 278ff. Translated Herbert Thurston, *The Holy Year of Jubilee*, London, Sands & Co., 1900, pp. 193–4.

5  Ibid., pp. 194–5.

6  Petrus Mallius, *Historia basilicae Vaticanae antiquae*, quoted in Von Dobschütz, *Christusbilder*, Leipzig, 1899, Belege zu Kapitel VI, 285.

7  'Et ostendit [Celestinus papa] regi Francie et suis capita

apostolorum Petri et Pauli et Veronicam, id est quemdem linteum, quem Iesus Christus vultui suo impressit; in quo pressura illa ita manifeste appareat usque in hodierum diem acsi vultus Iesus Christi esset, et dicitur Veronica, quia mulier cuius pannus erat dicebatur Veronica.' 'De gestis Henrici II et Ricardi I', in *Mon. Germ. Hist. Script.* XXVII, 131.

8 'On the Assumption of St Mary my Lord Pope, with all the Curia, doeth vespers and vigils of nine lessons in the Church of Santa Maria Maggiore. When this is done he returneth to the Lateran, and the cardinals and deacons, with all the people, take the Image of Jesus Christ from the Basilica of St Laurence (the Sancta Sanctorum) carrying it through the Lateran field . . . And when the Image is come to Santa Maria Novella, they put it down before the church and wash its feet with basil. Meantime in the church the choir do matins, to wit, of three lessons. And the people standing and blessing the Lord, take the image thence and carry it to S. Adriano, where they again wash its feet' and go to Santa Maria Maggiore.' Based on quotation from Thurston, *Holy Year of Jubilee*, op. cit., p. 193, after the *Politicus* of Benedict Canonicus in Mabillon, *Ordines Romani*, xi, cap. 72, *Mus. Ital.* ii. 151.

9 For a useful account, see Robert Brentano, *Rome Before Avignon, A Social History of thirteenth-century Rome*, London, Longman, 1974, p. 19. It is to be noted that some authors, following the English chronicler Matthew Paris, date the founding of the station to 1216. But more on-the-spot sources unequivocally date it to 1207.

10 S. J. P. Van Dijk and J. Hazelden Walker, *The Origins of the Modern Liturgy*, Maryland and London, Westminster, 1960, pp. 102–3 and 460–61.

11 Potthast, vol I, p. 450, ann. 1216, m. Jul. Innocent III, Regest X, 179; *Bull. Vat.* I. 90, 110, 133, quoted in La Favia, *The Man of Sorrows*, Rome, Edizioni Sangui, 1980.

12 See Suzanne Lewis, *The Art of Matthew Paris and the Chronica Majora*, Cambridge, Scolar/Corpus Christi College, 1987, pp. 126–30.

13 Ibid., p. 126: 'While the fortunes of the English king were in such a state of turmoil, Pope Innocent, whose unsteady hand upset the administration of the Church, according to custom carried the image of the face of the Lord, which is called the Veronica, in procession from the Church of St Peter to the

Hospital of the Holy Spirit. That having been done, this effigy, while standing in its place, turned around upon itself and was reversed in such a way that the forehead was below and the beard above. Very much taken aback, the pope sadly believed that a foreboding prophecy had occurred . . .'

14 For the full text of this letter, see André Grabar, 'La Sainte Face de Laon . . .', *Seminarium Kondakovianum*, Prague 1935, p. 8. Translation by Noel Currer Briggs, *The Shroud and the Grail*, London, Weidenfeld, 1987, p. 58.

15 Robert Brentano, op. cit., p. 174ff.

16 For a full discussion, see Carlo Bertelli, 'Storia e Vicende dell'Imagine Edessena', *Paragone*, no. 17, Arte, 1968, note 27.

17 See my own *The Shroud of Turin*, New York, Doubleday, 1978, p. 160.

18 See A. G. L. Christie, *English Medieval Embroidery*, Oxford, Clarendon Press, 1938, pp.89–92 and pls. XLII & XLIII.

19 *The Travels of Marco Polo*, modern translation by Teresa Waugh, New York, Facts on File Publications, 1984, p. 50.

20 See Maurice Collis, *Marco Polo*, London, Faber & Faber, 1950, p. 83.

## CHAPTER FIVE

1 Thurston, *Holy Year*, op. cit., p. 12ff.

2 For a balanced background, see T. S. R. Boase, *Boniface VIII*, London, Constable, 1933.

3 G. Villani, *Chroniche*, lib.viii, c.xxxvi, Trieste, 1857.

4 Ibid.

5 Ventura, 'Chron. Asti', in L. A. Muratori, *Rerum italicarum scriptores* (25 vols published between 1723 & 1751), vol XI.

6 Ibid., p. 191.

7 *Paradiso* 31, 103–8. Translation from *The Divine Comedy of Dante Alighieri*, trans. John D. Sinclair, III, *Paradise*, London, 1958, p. 451.

8 H. H. E. Craster and M. E. Thornton, *The Chronicles of St Mary's Abbey, York*, Durham, Surtees Society. 1934, 31, 132, 30.

9 Robert Brentano, op. cit., p. 54, after Pio Pecchiai 'Banchi e

botteghe dinanzi alla Basilica Vaticana nei secoli XIV, XV e XVI', *Archivi*, ser. 2, XVIII (1951, pp. 81–123, here especially pp. 91–5 and 99).

10  Louis M. La Favia, *The Man of Sorrows, Its Origin and Development in Trecento Painting*, p. 53, after A. H. M. Lepicier, *Indulgences, their origin, nature and development*, New York, 1928, p. 384, n. 2.

11  For a useful recent study of Clement VI's pontificate, see Diana Wood, *Clement VI, the Pontificate and Ideas of an Avignon Pope*, Cambridge University Press, 1989.

12  Petrarch, *Epistolarum Carmine Scriptarum*, book II, ep. 5.

13  Clement VI's Bull, *Unigenitus Dei Filius*, as translated in Herbert Thurston's *The Holy Year of Jubilee*, op. cit., pp. 56–7.

14  In the original Latin:
'Salve Sancta Facies Nostri Redemptoris
In qua nitet species Divini splendoris
Impresta paniculo nivei candoris
Dataque Veronica signu ob amoris'.

15  This indulgence was being quoted even at the beginning of the sixteenth century. See for instance the engraving of the head of Christ reproduced as no. 109 in the catalogue of the National Gallery of Art, Washington, *Fifteenth Century Woodcuts and Metalcuts from the National Gallery of Art, Washington DC*, ed. Richard S. Field, Washington DC, nd.

16  The text of this bull was printed by Ae. Amort, *De origine . . . indulgentiarum*, Vienna, 1735, p. 81ff.

17  Petrarch, *De Rib.Senil.* vii, 1.

18  Villani, lib. I, cap. 55. Translation from Herbert Thurston, *The Holy Year of Jubilee*, p. 58.

19  Translation from Anna Maria Armi, *Petrarch, Sonnets & Songs*, New York, 1968, p. 17, XVI.

20  Herbert Thurston, *The Holy Year of Jubilee*, p. 59.

21  M. Fagiolo and M. L. Madonna, *Roma 1300–1875, L'arte degli anni santi*, Catalogo Mostra Roma, Palazzo Venezia, 20 December 1984 – 5 April 1985, Milano, 1984, pp. 142–3.

22  A number of these are quoted in the manuscript of Jacopo Grimaldi, *Opusculum de Sacrosancto Veronicae Sudario Salvatoris Nostri Iesu Christi*, Rome, 1620, fols. 53–4, as preserved in the Biblioteca Nazionale, Florence. For further details of this manuscript see chapter 9.

23 See Henry Yates Thompson, *The Book of Hours of Yolande of Flanders*, London, 1905, p. 11 and folio 44A, verso.
24 See Burian & Hartmann, *Prague Castle*, pl. 37.
25 *The Vision of Piers the Ploughman*, ed. Skeat, London, 1867.
26 See Millard Meiss, *Painting in Florence and Siena after the Black Death*, Princeton, 1951, reprinted Harper & Row, 1964, p. 36 and fig. 44.
27 Another example is to be seen on the fifteenth-century sculpted head of a pilgrim in the Museum of Evreux, northern France, as published in P. Perdrizet, 'De la Veronique et de Sainte Veronique', *Seminarium Kondakovianum*, Prague, 1932, fig. 1.

# CHAPTER SIX

1 Jacopo Grimaldi, op. cit., p. 60 recto.
2 Ibid., p. 61 recto.
3 Ibid., p. 62 verso.
4 Ibid., p. 64 recto.
5 Paolo dello Mastro, *Chronache Romani*, as translated in Ludwig von Pastor, *The History of the Popes from the Close of the Middle Ages*, London, Kegan Paul, vol. II, pp.83–4.
6 Ibid., p. 84.
7 Ibid., p. 98.
8 This is in the Kunsthistorisches Museum, Vienna, see the Gallery catalogue, *Flämische Malerei von Jan van Eyck bis Pieter Bruegel D. Ä., Kunsthistorisches Museum, Vienna*, Vienna 1981, pp. 290–91.
9 See Claude Schaeffer, *The Hours of Etienne Chevalier, Jean Fouquet, Musée Condé, Chantilly*, London, Thames & Hudson, 1972, illumination no. 16. 'The Road to Calvary'.
10 For an English language translation, see F. M. Nichols, *The Marvels of Rome, or a Picture of the Golden City*, London, 1889.
11 For discussion of this woodcut, see A. M. Hind, *A History of Woodcut*, London, Constable, 1935, vol. 2, p. 403ff. The Wiegendruckgesellschaft of Berlin published a reproduction in 1925 in an edition edited by C. Hülsen. For an alternative version, see H. Pfeiffer, 'L'iconografia della Veronica', in M.

Fagiolo and M. L. Madonna, *Roma 1300–1875*, op. cit., fig. II, 7(b).

12 John Burchard, *The Diary of John Burchard of Strasburg*, translated by the Rt. Revd Arnold Harris Mathew, vol. I, 1483–92, p. 138.

13 Ibid., p. 291.

14 John Burchard, *Diarium*, ed. Thuasne, vol, II, p. 582.

15 Ibid.

16 L. Merlet and M. de Gombert, *Récit des funerailles d'Anne de Bretagne*, Chartres, 1858, p. 110.

17 See André Chastel, 'La Véronique', *Revue de l'Art*, 40, June 1978.

18 For two detailed accounts of the Sack of Rome at this time, see E. R. Chamberlain *The Sack of Rome*, London, B. T. Batsford, 1979; also André Chastel, *The Sack of Rome*, 1527, 26th. vol. of the A. W. Mellon lectures in the Fine Arts, Princeton University Press, 1983.

19 M. Sanuto, *Diarii*, Venice, 1879 seq. vol. 45: fol. 122.

20 Quoted, without exact source, in Chamberlain, op. cit., p. 175.

21 Wilpert, *Die romischen Malereien . . .*, op. cit., p. 1125.

22 Maurus Green, 'Veronica and her Veil: The Growth of a Christian Legend', *The Tablet*, 31 December 1966.

23 *Die Warthafftige und kurze Berichtung . . . (The True and Brief Account . . .)*, written in 1527 by one of the soldiers of Georg Frundsberg, Prince of Mindelheim. Quotation and translation from André Chastel, *The Sack of Rome, 1527*, p. 101.

24 Marcello Alberini, *I Ricordi*, published in D. Orano, *Il Sacco di Roma Studi documenti*, vol. I, Rome, 1911, quoted and translated in Chastel, ibid., p. 104.

25 E. Müntz, *Rome au temps de Jules II et de Léon X*, Paris, 1911, appendix, p. 442.

26 'Udi in S. Pietro la messa pontificale di Paolo III e riveri il Volto Santo e il sacro ferro della Lancia' F. M. Torrigio, *Le Sacre Grotte*, 2nd. ed., Rome, 1639, vol. II, p. 109.

27 Grimaldi, op. cit., fol. 74 verso.

28 Michel de Montaigne, *Journey into Italy*, quoted and translated in Thurston, *The Holy Year of Jubilee*, op. cit., p. 273.

29 Heinrich Pfeiffer, 'Una Visita a Manoppello', *Collegamento pro Sindone*, March/April 1986, pp. 35–8.

30 Donato da Bomba, *Relatio Historico, circa* 1640.

# CHAPTER SEVEN

1 For general background on both Thomas Heaphy the Elder and Younger, see their respective entries in the *Dictionary of National Biography*. Further information is to be derived from Redgrave's *Dictionary of Artists,* from *Athenaeum* no. 2390, 16 August 1873, also from an article by the Revd Cyril C. Dobson 'The Likeness of Christ – Early Portraits – Two Unpublished Copies' in *The Times*, 24 December 1932.

2 See the letters of Mrs Eliza Heaphy preserved in the British Museum Print Room's correspondence file for 1881.

3 Thomas Heaphy, 'An Examination into the Antiquity of the Likeness of Our Blessed Lord' part I, *Art-Journal*, 1 January, 1861, p. 1.

4 Ibid.

5 Ibid.

6 Ibid., p. 3.

7 Ibid. It is fair to point out that Heaphy's quoted words 'even of this last' do not in this instance specifically refer to the Veronica. Nonetheless his writings and sketches unquestionably led people to believe he had gained access to this, along with the rest.

8 Ibid., part V, 1 May 1861, p. 129.

9 Thomas Heaphy, *The Likeness of Christ, being an enquiry into the verisimilitude of the received likeness of Our Blessed Lord*, ed. Wyke Bayliss, London, 1880, pp. 49–50.

10 This consists of a leather-bound volume entitled *The Iconography of Christ*. Several of Heaphy's key 'holy face' sketches have been pasted in, without any information of the dates at which they were created. Very late in the volume is a pencil sketch of Mrs Esther L. Wynne, dated 1857. This essentially provides a likely *terminus ad quem* for the rest of the work.

11 Barbier de Montault. See note 11 for chapter 3.

12 A. De Waal, *Romische Quartalschrift für christliche Altertumskunde und für Kirchengeschichte*, 1893, pp. 293ff.

13 Thomas Heaphy, 'An Examination . . .', part I, *Art-Journal*, 1 January 1861, p. 4.

14 Ibid., part V, 1 May, p. 131.

15 Ibid., part I, p. 1.

16 Lionel Cust and Ernst von Dobschütz, 'Notes on Pictures in

the Royal Collections, article III, 'The Likeness of Christ', *Burlington Magazine*, September 1904, p. 521.

17  Heaphy, op. cit., part V, p. 130.

18  It is to be noted that this has at some stage become displaced in the album as preserved at the present day. But it is obvious enough where Heaphy had originally placed it.

19  Colette Dufour Bozzo, *Il 'Sacro Volto' di Genova*, Roma, Istituto Nazionale d'Archeologia e Storia dell'Arte, 1974.

20  Art. VII, Anonymous author, 'Portraits of Christ', *Quarterly Review*, Autumn 1867, p. 497.

21  *Athenaeum*, no. 2089, 9 November 1867. Heaphy's letter begins: 'In my capacity as a painter and occasionally as a writer I have had to stand my share of criticism: criticism too of all kinds and degrees, denunciatory as well as other. To these criticisms I never reply unless the critic ventures upon averments as to matters of fact that are at the same time erroneous and of a nature to do me injury. In the current number of *Quarterly Review* are some statements calculated to do me much hurt; and as it is of importance to me that I should give an early denial of them I venture to ask the favour of a portion of your valuable space to enable me to do so . . .'

22  For a reproduction of Heaphy's sketch, see Rex Morgan, *The Holy Shroud and the Earliest Paintings of Christ*, Manly [Australia], Runciman Press, 1986, p. 54 and pl. 2. Morgan's text should, however, be treated with caution.

23  See the Correspondence file for 1881 in the Print Room of the British Museum.

24  Cust & von Dobschütz, op. cit., p. 518.

25  Sir Wyke Bayliss, *Rex Regum, A Painter's Study of the Likeness of Christ from the Time of the Apostles to the Present Day*, London, S. P. C. K., 1905. In his Apologia, Wyke Bayliss records: 'Early in the seventies the late Mr Thomas Heaphy and myself were fellow-members of the Royal Society of British Artists and served on many committees. Our homes lay in the same direction, and after the close of a council we generally found ourselves walking together across the Park. It was during these walks, on summer evenings, or star-lit that we first exchanged thoughts on the question, profoundly interesting to us both, of the authenticity of the commonly received Likeness of Our Blessed Lord. Mr Heaphy, who was considerably my senior, had made it a special study; and had devoted much thought

203

and time and travel to its elucidation. He was, moreover, a portrait painter, so that he possessed exceptional facilities for recording his impressions with subtle insight and discriminating accuracy. In Italy and the South of France he made many exquisite facsimile drawings of the rarest and most remarkable examples . . .'

26 Joanne Snow-Smith, *The Salvator Mundi of Leonardo da Vinci*, Seattle, Henry Art Gallery, University of Washington, 1982, pp. 66, 67.

# CHAPTER EIGHT

1 See the 'Veronica' entry by Anatato Frutatz in the *Enciclopaedia Cattolica*. This strange order, which was certainly not fully implemented, may well have been to discourage the sort of multiplication of copies which occurred in the case of the Turin shroud during this same century.

2 British Library MS Arundel 157, fol. 2.

3 Suzanne Lewis, *The Art of Matthew Paris and the Chronica Majora*, Cambridge, 1987, p. 127.

4 Matthew Paris, *Chronica Majora*, Corpus Christi College, Cambridge MS 16, fol. 49 verso.

5 For example, Suzanne Lewis, op. cit., remarks of BL MS Arundel 157: 'a remarkably elegant but powerful style by a hand unmistakably that of Matthew Paris.'

6 Gervase of Tilbury, *Otia imperialia* 3, 25; quoted by Dobschütz, op. cit., pp. 292–3. According to an autobiographical note, Gervase was in Rome in the time of Pope Alexander III (1159–81). See Reinhold Pauli, *Nachrichten von der K Gesellschaft der Wissenkunden zu Göttingen*, 1882, p. 392.

7 Calouste Gulbenkian Foundation, *Apocalypse*, LA 139, fol. 13.

8 Laurentian Library, Florence, Codex *Supplicationes Variae*, Pluteo XV, n. 3, fol. 387 verso.

9 New York, Pierpont Morgan Library, M729, fol. 15 recto.

10 For a definitive study, see Karen Gould, *The Psalter and Hours of Yolande de Soissons*, Speculum Anniversary Monographs, vol. 4, the Medieval Academy of America, 1978.

11 Henry Yates Thompson, *The Book of Hours of Yolande of Flanders*, London, 1905, p. 11 and fol. 44A, verso.

12 London, National Gallery, Master of St. Veronica, 'Veronica and her Veil'.

13 Cambridge, Fitzwilliam Museum, Robert Campin 'St Veronica', no. 604.

14 See chapter 6, note 8.

15 National Gallery of Art, Washington DC, Samuel H. Kress collection, Hans Memling 'St Veronica'.

16 Brussels, Bibliothèque Royale, ms. 11035–7, fol. 8 verso.

17 Brussels, Bibliothèque Royale, ms. 11060–61, p. 8. See the comments of Millard Meiss in *French Painting in the Time of Jean de Berry*, Phaidon, 1967, p. 201: 'In 1960 Eisler and the writer pointed to the fact that the Veronica painted on leather glued to page 8 indicates that the manuscript was at the Burgundian court around 1420 . . . Lyna . . . in 1937 pointed to the devotion of the house of Burgundy to the Holy Face, and to the cult, fostered by Margaret of Bavaria, of St Veronica, who was customarily invoked against sudden death. Margaret, in whose possession the Hours given by the Duke of Berry to the Duke of Burgundy were last recorded, had lost her husband in 1419 by assassination, and her practice of adding Veronicas to her manuscripts seems appropriate. These were of an unusual type, painted on leather, and glued or fastened by threads into the manuscript . . .'

18 Brussels, Bibliothèque Royale, ms. 11035, fol. 98, illumination by the Rhénan illuminator, as published in Patrick M. de Winter, *La Bibliothèque de Philippe le Hardi, Duc de Bourgogne (1364–1404)*, Paris, Editions du Centre National de la Recherche Scientifique, 1985, pl. 137.

19 Detail of devotional image to the Most Holy Body and Blood of Christ, by Masters Friedrich and Johann von Villach, in the parish church at Mariapfarr, near Tannsweg, Salzburg, Austria, reproduced in Gertrud Schiller, *Iconography of Christian Art*, trans. Janet Seligman, vol. 2, London, Lund Humphries, 1972, pl. 774.

20 Birian and Hartmann, *Prague Castle*, op. cit., pl. 37.

21 I am deeply indebted to Professor Gino Zaninotto of Rome, who obtained access to the manuscript on my behalf, and sent me a detailed report; also to David Rolfe, who obtained a colour photograph of the Veronica illumination back in the 1970s.

22 Wallraf-Richartz-Museum, Cologne, detail of altarpiece with

cycle of the Life of Christ, by Cologne Master, reproduced in Schiller, op. cit., pl. 664.
23 Pinacotheca, Munich, Master of St Veronica, 'Veronica with her Veil'.
24 For source, see chapter 4, note 8.
25 Dom Roger Hudleston, OSB (ed.), *Revelations of Divine Love shewed to a devout ankress by name Julian of Norwich*, London, Burns Oates, 2nd. ed 1952, p.20.
26 See chapter 6, note 9.
27 See Padre Joseph Fabiani, *Disertacion historico-dogmatica sobre la sagrada reliquia de la Ssma. Faz de Nostro Señor Jesu Christo, venerada en la Ciudad de Alicante*, 1973, republished in facsimile edition 1974; also booklet by Baltasar Carrasco, *La Santa Faz, Breve reseña historica de la Veronica de Alicante*, Orihuela, 1943. I am deeply grateful to Dr Teresa Iglesias for her kindness in obtaining both these works and a modern photograph of the *Santa Faz*.

# CHAPTER NINE

1 Jacopo Grimaldi, *Descrizione della Basilica Vaticana*, Biblioteca Vaticana, Ms. Barb. lat. 2733, fol. 8 recto.
2 Jacopo Grimaldi, *Opusculum de Sacrosancto Veronicae Sudario Salvatoris Nostri Jesu Christi . . .*, Rome, 1620. Manuscripts: Rome, Archivio San Pietro, H.3; Florence, Biblioteca Nazionale II, III, 173; Milan, Biblioteca Ambrosiana, Ms. A. 168 inf. and in the Bibliothèque Nationale, Paris. All references here relate to the Florence manuscript, microfilm of which was kindly obtained for the author with the help of Mario Fusco of Rome.
3 Grimaldi, *Opusculum de Sacrosancto Veronicae Sudario . . .* fol. 54 verso.
4 Ibid., fol. 90 recto ff. Translation of this and other extracts from Grimaldi kindly made for the author by Bernard Slater.
5 Ibid., fol. 91 recto ff.
6 Ibid., fol. 91 verso.
7 Heinrich Pfeiffer, 'L'Immagine Simbolica del Pellegrinaggio a Roma: La Veronica e il volto di Christo', in Marcello Fagiolo and Maria Luisa Madonna (eds.), *Roma 1300–1875* op. cit., pl. II.6 (g).

8 Personal communication from Mrs Dorothy Piepke, dated 15 September 1978.
9 Grimaldi, op. cit., fol. 92 recto.
10 Manfred Leithe-Jasper and Rudolf Distelberger, *Kunsthistorisches Museum Wien I. Schatzkammer und Sammlung für Plastik und Kunstgewerbe*, München–London, 1982. The inventory number of the Veronica copy is D 108.
11 His name is sometimes rendered in Latin as 'Stroza' or 'Strozza'. Here I have adopted the Italian form in which he is referred to in Ludwig von Pastor's *The History of the Popes from the Close of the Middle Ages*, London, Kegan Paul, 1937, vol. XXV, p. 374.
12 Carlo Bertelli, 'Storia e Vicende dell'Imagine Edessena' *Paragone* no. 217 (Arte), 1968, pp. 14–15.
13 'A modern silver frame . . . 63cm high x 51cm wide, protects under glass an antique gilded-metal plate . . . Into this plate is cut the space for the 'holy face'. The plate is 31cm high x 20cm wide . . .' A. de Waal, *Römische Quartalschrift für christliche Altertumskunde und für Kirchengeschichte*, 1893, pp. 259ff.
14 See chapter 7, note 19.
15 'The type and design of the filigree are easily recognizable in works of the late thirteenth and early fourteenth century. Particularly similar to the Genoa filigree is that of a mosaic icon in the Grand Laura of Mount Athos, an icon by tradition attributed to the Emperor John I Zimiskes (956–76), but definitely of a much later date.' Carlo Bertelli, op. cit., p. 20. Translation for the author by Mrs Maria Jepps.

## CHAPTER TEN

1 Jacopo Grimaldi, *Descrizione della Basilica Vaticana*, Biblioteca Vaticana, Ms. Barb. lat. 2733, fol. 120.
2 Grimaldi, *Opusculum de Sacrosancto Veronicae Sudario . . .*, op. cit., fol. 99.
3 Ibid.
4 Ibid., fol. 106 recto.
5 Ibid., fol. 105, recto.
6 '+ IOHANNES INDIGNUS EPISCOPUS FECIT BEATAE DEI GENITRICIS SERVUS' 'John, an unworthy bishop, servant of the blessed mother of God, made [this]'.

7 Grimaldi, '*Opusculum* . . ., fol. 83 recto.

8 Ibid., fol. 29 verso.

9 Ibid., fol. 27 verso.

10 Ibid., fol. 27 recto.

11 Ibid., fol. 24 recto.

12 Ibid., fol. 24 verso.

13 Ibid.

14 Ibid., fol. 19 verso.

15 One careful qualification is needed here. Among scenes from the life of Christ is included the healing of the woman with the issue of blood [Matthew 9: 20–22; Mark 5: 25–34; Luke 8; 43–48]. Later in this chapter we will show this woman to have been identified with 'Veronica'. But this act of healing forms such a minor element in the scene in which it is portrayed that its inclusion seems no more than coincidental.

16 *Liber Pontificalis* I. 443 Stephanus II, n. 232: 'According to custom, processing offering prayers of supplication, with the most sacred image of Our Lord God and Saviour Jesus Christ, which is called Acheropsita [sic] . . .'

17 See chapter 4, note 5.

18 Fernand Cabrol and Henri Leclercq, *Dictionnaire d'archéologie chrétienne et de liturgie*, 15 vols., 1903–50.

19 '. . . quando sudor eius factus est sicut guttae, sanguinis decurrentis in terram', Peter Mallius, *Historia basilicae Vaticanae antiquae* as quoted in Dobschütz, op. cit., p. 285.

20 *Cura Sanitas Tiberii*. For English language summary of text see M. R. James, *The Apocryphal New Testament*, Oxford, Clarendon Press, 1953, p. 158. There are several Latin versions, and also an old Anglo-Saxon one.

21 For English language summary, see M. R. James, op. cit., pp. 159–60.

22 'And a certain woman named Bernice [Beronice, Copt . . ., Veronica, Latin], crying from afar off said: I had an issue of blood and I touched the hem of his garment, and the flowing of my blood was stayed which I had twelve years. The Jews say; we have a law that a woman shall not come to give testimony.' M. R. James op. cit., p. 102.

23 'As I have mentioned this city [Paneas, or Caesarea Philippi], I do not think I ought to omit a story that deserves to be remembered by those who will follow us. The woman with a haemorrhage, who as we learn from the holy gospels was cured

of her trouble by our Saviour, was stated to have come from here. Her house was pointed out in the city, and a wonderful memorial of the benefit the Saviour conferred upon her was still there. On a tall stone base at the gates of her house stood a bronze statue of a woman, resting on one knee and resembling a suppliant with arms outstretched. Facing this was another of the same material, an upright figure of a man with a double cloak neatly draped over his shoulders and his hand stretched out to the woman. Near his feet on the stone slab grew an exotic plant, which climbed up to the hem of the bronze cloak and served as a remedy for illnesses of every kind. This statue, which was said to resemble the features of Jesus, was still there in my own time, so that I saw it with my own eyes when I resided in the city . . .' Eusebius, *The History of the Church from Christ to Constantine*, trans. G. A. Williamson, Harmondsworth, Penguin, 1965, pp. 301–2.

24 Sozomen, *History of the Church* [continuation of that of Eusebius], 5, 21.
25 For example, the fresco from the crypt arcosolium lunette, catacomb of St Peter and Marcellinus, Rome, as reproduced Pierre du Bourget, *Early Christian Painting*, London, Weidenfeld & Nicholson, 1965, pl. 99.
26 This is known from a single manuscript, preserved in Leningrad, and translated into English by G. Phillips in *The Doctrine of Addai the Apostle*, 1876.

## CHAPTER ELEVEN

1 Robert de Clari, *The Conquest of Constantinople*, trans. E. H. McNeal, New York, Columbia University Press, 1936, p., 103.
2 Court of Constantine Porphyrogennitus, *De Imagine Edessena* (Story of the Image of Edessa), trans. Bernard Slater and published in I. Wilson, *The Shroud of Turin*, New York, Doubleday, 1978, p. 250.
3 As translated in Edward Gibbon, *The Decline and Fall of the Roman Empire*, abridged D. M. Low, Harmondsworth, Penguin, 1963, pp. 624–5.
4 From tenth-century Greek text as published in the supplement to Dobschütz, op. cit., pp. 110–14.

5 For the most definitive study of the history of Edessa, see J. B. Segal, *Edessa 'The Blessed City'*, Oxford, Clarendon Press, 1970. I have followed Segal's numbering of the dynasty of monarchs bearing the names Abgar and Ma'nu who ruled Edessa up to AD 216.

6 *Acts of Thaddaeus*, as translated in Alexander Roberts and James Donaldson, *The Ante-Nicene Fathers*, Grand Rapids, Wm B. Eerdmans, 1951, vol. VIII, p. 558.

7 Codex vaticanus syriacus 95, fol. 49–50, translated into French in André Grabar 'Une hymne Syriaque sur l'architecture de la Cathédrale d'Edesse', *L'art de la fin de l'antiquité et du moyen âge*, College de France Fondation Schlumberger pour des études Byzantines, 1968.

8 'τὴν θεότευχον εἰχόνα 'ἥν 'ανθρώπων μὲν χεῖρε ὀυκ ἐργάσαντο' Evagrius, Ecclesiastical History, Greek text in Migne, *Patrologiae graeca*, vol. 86, 2, 2748–9.

9 See note 2 of this chapter.

10 Translation from Wilson, op. cit., p. 240.

11 'Edisse [venit] in urbem
In qua sanguinea domini serva[ba]tur ymago
Non manibus facta'
Latin Code Monac. Aug. S. Ulr. 111, ed. Massman. It is interesting to note that the Bollandist version of the *Vita Alexius* uses the word *sindone*: 'an image of Our Lord Jesus Christ made without human work on a cloth' 'sine humano opere imago Domini nostri Jesu Christi in sindone', Acta Sanctorum, Julii, 4, p. 252. For an excellent study of the Old French, *Life of Saint Alexis*, see Linda Cooper, 'The Old French *Life of Saint Alexis* and the Shroud of Turin', *Modern Philology*, University of Chicago Press, vol. 84, no. 1, pp. 117.

12 One possible exception worth noting, even though it does not show the face on cloth, is a face of Christ in a roundel on a sixth-century icon of Sts Sergius and Bacchus, now in the Museum of Kiev. The face has the 'cut-out' characteristics of the Genoa, Veronica and S. Silvestro 'holy faces' and has been suggested as the earliest-known direct representation of the Edessa 'holy face'. See André Grabar, *Byzantium from the Death of Theodosius to the Rise of Islam*, London, Thames & Hudson, 1966, p. 186, fig. 201.

13 Vatican, Codex Rossianus 251, fol. 12 verso.

14 Alexandria, Greek Patriarchal Library, Codex 35, p. 286.

For discussion, see Kurt Weitzmann, 'The Mandylion and Constantine Porphyrogennetos', *Cahiers archéologiques*, XI, 1960, p. 170.

15 See André Grabar, *La Sainte Face de Laon* . . . , op. cit., pls. VI.6 & III.1.

16 Ibid., pl. 1.

17 See Weitzmann, op. cit., fig. 1 and accompanying discussion.

18 See Andreas & Judith Stylianou, *The Painted Churches of Cyprus*, London, Trigraph, 1985, plates 96 and 267, and accompanying discussion.

19 Grabar, op. cit., pl. III, 2.

20 Gibbon, op. cit., p. 625.

21 See Cust & Dobschütz, op. cit.

22 For the most thorough modern discussion, see Carlo Bertelli, 'Storia e vicende dell'imagine Edessena', op. cit., pp. 8–13.

23 Von Dobschütz, in Cust & Dobschütz op. cit., attributes the frame to 'Sordinora Larutia', and Morgan, op. cit., and others have followed this error, which has arisen from a misreading of the inscription on the frame. For the correct reading, see Ilaria Toesca, 'La Cornice dell'imagine Edessena di San Silvestro in Capite a Roma', *Paragone* 217 (Arte), 1968, p. 34.

24 For discussion with accompanying illustration, see Bertelli, 'Storia e vicende . . .', op. cit., p. 8.

25 'ob confusionem vitandam et ut maiori reverentia adhibeatur ill sancti Petri, prohibitum monialibus ipsis sanctae Clarae ne illud publice ostendant.' Fra Mariano da Firenze, OFM, *Itinerarium Urbis Romae*, 1517, republished and with an introduction and illustrative notes by P. Enrico Bulletti, OFM, Rome, 1931, *Studi di antichità cristiana pubblicati per cura del Pontificio Istituto di Archeologia Cristiana*, II, p. 215.

26 Bertelli, 'Storia e vicende . . .', op. cit., p. 11.

27 'Where a colour has flaked off – and that has happened in very limited areas – at the extreme left of the beard; a tiny piece is missing on the forehead; and there are two extremely small chips on the lower corner of the left eye – the cloth can be seen very well. It seems very fine and light, with a weave recognizable as herring-bone, which, if it were examined under the microscope, could offer some useful information on its origin and dating.' Bertelli, 'Storia e vicende . . .', op. cit., pp. 11–12, trans. Maria Jepps.

28 Steven Runciman, 'Some Remarks on the Image of Edessa, *Cambridge Historical Journal* 3, 1931, pp. 238–52.
29 De Riant, *Exuviae Sacrae Constantinopolitanae*, II Geneva, 1878.
30 Bertelli, 'Storia e vicende . . .', op. cit., note 13.
31 For fuller discussion, see my book *The Shroud of Turin*, Doubleday, 1978, chapter XIV.
32 Up to Zaninotto's discovery, the only publication this text had received was in *Biblioteca hagiographica graeca*, 3rd. ed. F. Halkin, 1957, vol. III, p. 111, 7g, in an appendix on the Edessa image and Christ, in the series *Subsidia hagiographica*, published by the Bollandists of Brussels.
33 Gino Zaninotto, 'Il Codice Vat. Gr. 511, ff. 143–50 verso: Una Conferma dell 'Identita tra l'immagine Edessena e la Sindone di Torino?', *Collegamento Pro Sindone*, March, April 1988, pp. 14–25.
34 ʽτο δε ; πᾶς ἔνθεασθήτω τῷ διηγήματι - μόνοις ἐναγωνίοις ἱδρῶσι προσώπου ζωαρχικοῦ, τοῖς ὡσεὶ θρόμβοι κατασταλάξασιν αἵματος, ἐντετύπωται καὶ δακτύλῳ θεοῦ· αὗται τὸ ἐκμαγεῖον ὄντως χριστοῦ αἱ χρωματουργήσασαι ὡραιότητες, ὅτι καὶ τὸ ἀφ' οὗ κατεσταλάχθησαν ρανίσι πλευρᾶς ἰδίας ἐγκεκαλλώπισται, ἄμφω δογμάτων μεστὰ αἷμα καὶ ὕδωρ ἐκεῖ, ἐνταῦθα ἱδρὼς καὶ μορφή, ὦ πραγμάτων ἰσότητος— ἐκ τοῦ ἑνὸς γὰρ ταῦτα κὰι τοῦ αὐτοῦ.' Ms. Vat. Graec. 511, fol. 149 verso.

# CHAPTER TWELVE

1 Grimaldi, *Opusculum de Sacrosancto Veronicae* . . ., op. cit., fol. 111 recto.
2 Ibid., fol. 114.
3 Ibid., fol. 111 recto.
4 Ibid., fol. 104 recto.
5 For historical background, see Gordon McNeil Rushforth, 'The Church of S. Maria Antiqua', *The British School at Rome*, vol. I, 1902.
6 See full colour reproduction in Kurt Weitzmann et al., *The Icon*, London, Bracken Books, 1982, pp. 74–5.

7 David Talbot Rice, *Art of the Byzantine Era*, London, Thames & Hudson, 1963, p. 97, pl. 82.

8 London, British Museum, Royal MS. 6. E. VI fol. 15r. In this example the two devices, slightly separated, occur as part of the 'Arma Christi', the Instruments of the Passion, a highly popular theme in the art of the high Middle Ages.

9 See Carlo Bertelli, 'The Image of Pity . . .', op. cit.

10 Michael Ayrton & Henry Moore, *Giovanni Pisano, Sculptor*, London, Thames & Hudson 1969, pl. 302, Berlin-Dahlem Museum.

11 Munich, Staatsbibliothek, Clm. 23094, fol. 7.

12 H. Schrade, 'Beiträge zur Erklärung des Schmerzensmann-bildes', in *Deutschkundliches, Friedrich Panzer zum 60. Geburtstag, Beiträge zur neueren Literaturgeschichte*, Heidelburg 1930, pl. II, fig. 1.

13 See *Byzantine Art*, catalogue of the 9th Exhibition of the Council of Europe, Athens, 1964, no. 475; also Hans Beltung, *The Image and its Public in the Middle Ages*, New York, 1990, p. 117, fig. 70.

14 Pauline Johnstone, *Byzantine Tradition in Church Embroidery*, London, Alec Tiranti, 1967, p. 94.

15 Budapest, Országos Széchényi Könyvtár (National Széchényi Library), MNY I.

16 Ilona Berkovits, *Illuminated Manuscripts in Hungary, XI–XVI Centuries*, trans. Zsuzsanna Horn, Shannon, Ireland, Irish University Press, 1969, pl. III.

17 Ibid., p. 19.

18 Leningrad, State Hermitage icon no. 211. See Kurt Weitzmann et al., *The Icon*, op. cit., p. 61.

19 Kurt Weitzmann, 'The Origin of the Threnos', *De Artibus Opuscula XL, Essays in Honour of Erwin Panofsky*, ed. Millard Meiss, New York University Press, 1961, fig. 15.

20 Ibid., pp. 476–90.

21 'Nam isdem mediator dei et hominum, ut ipsi regi in omnibus et per omnia satisfaceret, supra quoddam linteum ad instar nivis candidatum toto se corpore stravit, in quo, quod est dictu vel auditu mirabile, ita divinitus transformata est illius dominice faciei figura gloriosa et tocius corporis nobilissimus status, ut qui corporaliter in carne dominum venientem minime viderunt, satis eis ad videndum sufficiat transfiguratio facta in linteo', Dobschütz, op. cit., p. 134.

22 Ordericus Vitalis, *Historia ecclesiastica*, part III, book IX, 8, 'De Gestis Balduini Edessae principatum obtinet'.

23 Gervase of Tilbury, *Otia Imperialia* III, from *Scriptores rerum brunsvicensium*, ed. G. Liebnitz, Hanover 1707, I, pp. 966–7.

24 This document has been kindly brought to my attention by Dan Scavone, Professor of History at the University of Southern Indiana.

25 'Mantile, quod visui Domini applicatum, imaginem vultus eius retinuit . . . sudarium quod fuit super caput eius.' Comte Riant, *Exuviae sacrae constantinopolitanae*, Geneva, Société de l'Orient Latin, 1878, II, 211ff.

26 '. . . pars linteaminum quibus crucifixum Christi corpus meruit involvere . . . syndon . . . Manutergium regi Abgaro a Domino . . . Edesse missum, in quo ab ipso Domino sua . . . transfigurata est ymago.' Riant, *Exuviae* . . ., op. cit., 217.

27 August Heisenberg, ed. *Nikolaos Mesarites, die Palastrevolution des Johannes Komnenos,* Würzburg, Koenigl. Universitaetsdruckerei von H. Stuertz, 1907, p. 30.

28 Ibid., 'Ἐντάφιοι σινδόνες χριστοῦ'.

29 Ibid., 31: 'τὸν νομοξότην αὐτὸν ὡς ἐν προτοτύπω τετυπωμένον τῷ χειρομάκτρῳ καὶ τῇ εὐθρύπτῳ ἐγκεκολαμμένον κεράμῳ ὡς ἐκ ἀχειροποιήτω τέχνῃ τινὶ γρχφικῇ.'

30 Ibid., 30: 'αὗται δ' εἰσὶν ἀπὸ λίνου ὕλης εὐώνου κατὰ τὸ πρόχειρον, ἔτι πνέουσαι μύραι ὑπερτεροὺς, ὅτι τὸν ἀπερίληπτον νεκρὸν γυμνὸν ἐσμυρνημένον μετὰ τὸ πάθος συνέστειλαν.'

31 Copenhagen, Royal Library, MS 487.

32 'Et entre ches autres en eut un autre des mousters que on apeloit medame Sainte Marie de Blakerne, ou li sydoines la ou nostres sires fu envelopes, i estoit, qui cascuns desvenres se drechoit tous drois, si que on i pooit bien veir le figure nostre seigneur.'

33 See, for example, Walther von Wartburg, *Französisches Etymologisches Wörterbuch*, vol. III, p. 521; also an excellent article by Dr Peter F. Dembowski, 'Sindon in the Old French Chronicle of Robert de Clari', *Shroud Spectrum International* 2, March 1982, pp. 12–18. Dr Dembowski is Chairman of the Department of Romance Languages and Literature at the University of Chicago.

34 For example, by Robert de Clari's translator into English, E. H. McNeal, in Robert de Clari, *The Conquest of Constantinople*,

trans. E. H. McNeal, New York, Columbia University Press, 1936.

35 'Ne seut on onques ne Griu ne Franchois que chis sydoines devint, quant le vile fu prise'.

## CHAPTER THIRTEEN

1 John Walsh, *The Shroud*, London, W. H. Allen, 1964, p. 120.
2 Copy sometimes erroneously attributed to Dürer, preserved in the Church of St Gommaire, Lierre, Belgium.
3 Information derived from personal correspondence with Père Dubarle, and from a lecture given by him to the Simposio Internazionale, La Sindone e le Icone, Bologna, 6–7 May 1989.
4 Paul Vignon, *Le Saint Suaire de Turin devant la science, l'archéologie, l'histoire, l'iconographie, la Logique*, Paris, Masson, 1939.
5 Hartmann Grisar, SJ, *Die römische Kapelle Sancta Sanctorum . . .*, Freiburg, 1908, p. 39ff.
6 See Christopher P. Kelley, 'Canterbury's first Ikon, *Sobornost*, circa 1978.
7 For a detailed study of the background history of this particular mosaic, see Walter Oakeshott, *The Mosaics of Rome*, London, Thames & Hudson, 1967, p. 70.
8 See André Grabar, *Les Ampoules de Terre Sainte*, Paris, 1958.
9 See W. Wroth, *Imperial Byzantine Coins in the British Museum*, London, 1908, pl. LIII, no. 7. Since Constantine VII appears alone on this coin it has been dated to the short period between 27 January and 6 April, AD 945, just after he had imprisoned the two younger sons of Romanus Lecapenus, and before he had made his own son, Romanus II, co-emperor. According to the French scholar A. Blanchet, this Christ image, and that on Constantine VII's and Romanus II's subsequent coinage, was specifically influenced by the arrival of the 'holy face' of Edessa in Constantinople the previous year. See A. Blanchet, 'L'influence artistique de Constantine Porphyrogenete', *Mélanges Gregoire – Annales de l'Institut de Philologie et d'Histoire Orientales et Slaves*, IC, 1949, pp. 97–104.
10 A. Whanger, 'Polarized Image Overlay Technique: A New

Image Comparison Method and its Applications', *Applied Optics*, 24, no. 16, 15 March 1985, pp. 766–72.

11 For the definitive study of this particular coin-type, see James D. Breckenridge, *The Numismatic Iconography of Justinian II (685–695, 705–711 A.D.)*, Numismatic Notes & Monographs no. 144, New York, The American Numismatic Society, 1959.

12 See Cabrol & Leclercq, *Dictionnaire d'Archéologie chrétienne et de liturgie,* op. cit., Paris, Libraire Letouzey, vol. 14, pp. 1414–15.

13 Vignon, op. cit., p. 150.


# CHAPTER FOURTEEN


1 Willard F. Libby, *Radiocarbon dating*, Chicago University Press, 1952.

2 For useful background, see M. G. L. Baillie, *Tree-Ring Dating and Archaeology*, London, Croom Helm, 1982.

3 William Meacham, 'On Carbon Dating the Turin shroud', *Shroud Spectrum International*, 19, June 1986, pp. 15–25.

4 I. Wilson, *The Turin Shroud*, Harmondsworth, Penguin, p. 264.

5 Christos G. Doumas, *Thera, Pompeii of the ancient Aegean*, London, Thames & Hudson, 1983, p. 139.

6 *Current Archaeology* August 1986.

7 Sheridan Bowman, *Radiocarbon dating*, London, British Museum Publications, 1990, p. 52.

8 Rosalie David, *Mysteries of the Mummies: The story of the Manchester University investigation*, London, Cassell, 1978.

9 S. S. E. Bowman, J. C. Ambers & M. N. Leese, 'Re-evaluation of British Museum radiocarbon dates issued between 1980 and 1984', *Radiocarbon*, vol. 32, no. 1, 1990, pp. 59–79. The Manchester Mummy appears in Table 3 on p. 79.

10 Andy Coghlan, 'Unexpected errors affect dating techniques', *New Scientist*, 30 September 1989, p. 26.

11 Dr Robert Hedges, Director, Radiocarbon Accelerator Unit, University of Oxford, letter to *New Scientist*, 14 October 1989, p. 69.

12 Coghlan, 'Unexpected errors . . .', op. cit.

13 Bowman, op. cit., p. 56.

14 John Tyrer, *British Society for the Turin Shroud Newsletter*, 20 October 1988, p. 11.
15 Professor E. T. Hall, letter to *Textile Horizons*, January 1990.
16 Richard Burleigh *et al.*, 'An Inter-comparison of some AMS and Small Gas Counter Laboratories', *Radiocarbon* 28, 1976, pp. 571–7. The Zurich laboratory is not specifically named in this paper, but has been privately acknowledged as the source of the error.
17 Bryan Kelly, letter to *New Scientist*, 22 September 1988.
18 Dr Eugenia Nitowski/Sister Damian of the Cross: privately circulated communication.

## CHAPTER FIFTEEN

1 Jean Glover, 'The Conservation of Medieval and Later Shrouds from Burials in North-West England', paper presented at York Conference, 'Textiles for the Archaeological Conservator', 28 April 1988. In press. Jean Glover is Senior Textile Conservation Officer for the North-West Museum and Art Gallery Service, Blackburn, Lancs.
2 *The Rohan Book of Hours, Bibliothèque Nationale, Paris (MS Latin 9471)*, intro. Millard Meiss, London, Thames & Hudson, 1973, pls. 71 & 73.
3 Ian Dickinson, 'Preliminary Details of New Evidence for the Authenticity of the Shroud: Measurement by the Cubit', *Shroud News* [Australia] April 1990, pp. 4–8.
4 'Il motivo fondamentale è constuito dal fatto che lo stato del Velo pare in condizioni precarie, tali da sconsigliare una apertura della teca per un esame.' Letter of Archbishop Noè to the author, 30 January 1990.
5 For interesting background insights on Archbishop Noè, see Gordon Thomas & Max Morgan-Witts, *Pontiff*, New York, Doubleday, 1983. Noè appears to have lost his post as papal master of ceremonies through differences with Pope John Paul II, e.g. Thomas & Morgan-Witts, p. 338: 'When the pope appears in public Noè positions the microphone one way and John Paul invariably changes it: during a procession the master of ceremonies will attempt to stride almost beside the pope, who will curtly motion him away; at a reception, Noè hovers at the pontiff's elbow and is studiously ignored.'

6 From personal correspondence with Isabel Piczek, March/-April 1990.
7 See chapter 3, note 15.
8 Giorgio Tessore, 'Cognoscere la Sindone – La Figura di Cristo e la Sindone nell'Iconografia', *Collegamento Pro Sindone*, March/April 1988, p. 29, fig. A.

# BIBLIOGRAPHY

ANONYMOUS, Portraits of Christ', *Quarterly Review*, London, Autumn 1867, pp. 490–509

AYRTON, MICHAEL, & MOORE, HENRY, *Giovanni Pisano, Sculptor*, London, Thames & Hudson, 1969

BARBIER DE MONTAULT, Abbé X., 'Iconographie du Chemin de la Croix', *Annales Archéologiques, vol. 23, 1863*

BAYLISS, SIR WYKE, *Rex Regum, A Painter's Study of the Likeness of Christ from the Time of the Apostles to the Present Day*, London, SPCK, 1905

BELTING, HANS, *The Image and its Public in the Middle Ages, Form & Function in Early Paintings of the Passion*, trans. Mark Bartusis & Raymond Meyer, New Rochelle, New York, Aristide D. Caratzas, 1990

BERKOVITS, ILONA, *Illuminated Manuscripts in Hungary, XI–XVI Centuries*, trans. Zsuzsanna Horn, revised Alick West, Shannon, Irish University Press, 1969

BERTELLI, CARLO, 'Storia e Vicende dell'Imagine Edessena', *Paragone* no. 217, Florence, Arte, 1968, pp. 3–33

BLANCHET, A., 'L'influence artistique de Constantine Porphyrogenete', *Mélanges Gregoire – Annales de l'Institut de Philologie et d'Histoire Orientales et Slaves*, Paris, vol. 90, 1949, pp. 97–104

BOASE, T. S. R., *Boniface VIII*, London, Constable, 1933

BOWMAN, SHERIDAN, *Radiocarbon Dating*, London, British Museum, 1990

BOZZO, COLETTE DUFOUR, *Il 'Sacro Volto' di Genova*, Rome, Istituto Nazionale d'Archeologia e Storia dell'Arte, 1974

BRECKENRIDGE, JAMES D., *The Numismatic Iconography of Justinian II (685–95, 705–11 AD)*, Numismatic Notes & Monographs no. 144, New York, The American Numismatic Society, 1959

BRENTANO, ROBERT, *Rome before Avignon, A Social History of Thirteenth-Century Rome*, London, Longmans, 1974

BRUCE, J.D., *The Evolution of Arthurian Romance from the Beginnings down to the year 1300*, vol. I, Baltimore, Johns Hopkins Press, 1923

BULST, WERNER & PFEIFFER, HEINRICH, *Das Turiner Grabtuch und das Christusbild, vol I: Das Grabtuch Forschungsberichte und Untersuchungen*, Frankfurt am Main, Knecht, 1987

JOHN BURCHARD, *The Diary of John Burchard of Strasburg*, trans. Rt. Revd Arnold Harris Mathew, vol. I, 1483–92 London, Francis Griffiths, 1910

BURIAN, JIRI & ANTONIN HARTMANN, *Prague Castle*, London, Hamlyn, 1975

BURLEIGH, RICHARD *et. al.*, 'An Intercomparison of some AMS and Small Gas Counter Laboratories', *Radiocarbon*, vol. 28, 1976, pp. 571–7

CARRASCO, BALTASAR, *La Santa Faz, Breve reseña historica de la Faz Divina que se venera en el real Monasterio de la Veronica de Alicante*, Orihuela, 1943

CECCHELLI, C., entry 'Acheropita' in *Enciclopedia Italiana*, Rome, 1949 edition, vol. I, pp. 311–12

CHAMBERLAIN, E. R., *The Sack of Rome*, London, B. T. Batsford, 1979

CHAMPION, P., *François Villon, son vie et son temps*, vol. I, Paris, 1913

CHASTEL, A., 'La Véronique', *Revue de l'Art*, vol. 40, June 1978, pp. 71–82

CHASTEL, A., *The Sack of Rome, 1527*, 26. vol. of A. W. Mellon lectures in the Fine Arts, Princeton University Press, 1983

CHRISTIE, A. G. L., *English Medieval Embroidery*, Oxford, Clarendon Press, 1938

CRAFER, T. W., 'Macarius Magnes – A Neglected Apologist', *Journal of Theological Studies*, vol. VIII, 1906–7, pp. 401–23; 546–71; also English translation of the *Apocritus* by Crafer

COLLIS, MAURICE, *Marco Polo*, London, Faber & Faber, 1951

COOPER, LINDA, 'The Old French *Life of Saint Alexis* and the Shroud of Turin', *Modern Philology*, University of Chicago Press, vol. 84, no. 1, pp. 1–17

COX, EUGENE L., *The Green Count of Savoy, Amadeus VI and Transalpine Savoy in the Fourteenth Century*, Princeton, Princeton University Press, 1967

CRASTER, H. H. E. & THORNTON, M. E., (eds.), *The Chronicle of St. Mary's Abbey, York*, Durham, Surtees Society, 1934

CRISPINO, DOROTHY, 'The Report of the Poor Clare nuns, Chambéry, 1534', *Shroud Spectrum International*, no. 2, March 1982, pp. 19–27

——'The Pilgrim badge of Lirey', *Shroud Spectrum International*, no. 25, December 1987, pp. 13–18

CURRER-BRIGGS, NOEL, *The Shroud and the Grail, A Modern Quest for the True Grail*, London, Weidenfeld & Nicolson, 1987

CUST, LIONEL & VON DOBSCHÜTZ, ERNST, 'Notes on Pictures in the Royal Collections, article III, The Likeness of Christ', *Burlington Magazine*, September 1904, pp. 517–28

DAMON, P.E., *et al.*, 'Radiocarbon dating of the Shroud of Turin', *Nature*, v.337, no. 6208, 16 February 1989, pp. 611–15

DANTE ALIGHIERI, *The Divine Comedy,* trans. & with commentary by John D. Sinclair, London, Bodley Head, 1958

DAVID, ROSALIE (ed.), *Mysteries of the Mummies. The story of the Manchester University investigation*, London, Cassell, 1978

DAVIES, M., *Early Netherlandish Schools,* National Gallery Catalogues, London, 2nd. ed., 1965

DAVIES, M., *Rogier van der Weyden*, London, Phaedon, 1972

DE CLARI, ROBERT, *The Conquest of Constantinople*, trans. E. H. McNeal, New York, Columbia University Press, 1936

DE WINTER, PATRICK, M., *La Bibliothèque de Philippe le Hardi, Duc de Bourgogne 1364–1404*, Paris, CRNS, 1985

DEMBOWSKI, PETER F., 'Sindon in the Old French Chronicle of Robert de Clari', *Shroud Spectrum International*. no. 2, March 1982, pp. 12–18

DOBSCHÜTZ, ERNST VON, *Christusbilder, Untersuchungen zur Christlichen Legende*, Leipzig, J. C. Hinrichs, 1899

DOBSON, REV. CYRIL C., 'The Likeness of Christ – Early Portraits – Two Unpublished Copies', *The Times*, 24 December 1932

DU BOURGET, PIERRE, *Early Christian Painting*, London, Weidenfeld & Nicolson, 1965

EASTLAKE, SIR CHARLES LOCKE, *Methods and Materials of Painting of the Great Schools and Masters*, London, Longman, Brown, Green & Longman, 1847, reprinted Dover, 1960

EUSEBIUS, *The History of the Church from Christ to Constantine*, trans. G. A. Williamson. Harmondsworth, Penguin, 1965

FABIANI, PADRE JOSEPH, *Disertacion Historico-Dogmatica sobre la Sagrada Reliquia de la Ssma. Faz de Nostro Señor Jesu-Christo venerada en la Cuidad de Alicante*, 1763, facsimile edition, Publicaciones de la Caja de Ahorros Provincial de la Excme. Diputacion de Alicante, 1974

FAGIOLO, M. & MADONNA, M. L., *Roma 1300–1875, L'arte degli anni santi*, Catalogo Mostra Roma, Palazzo Venezia 20–12–84–5.4.85, Milano, 1984

FORGEAIS, A., *Collection de plombs historiés trouvés dans la Seine*, Paris, 1862–66

FOSSATI, LUIGI, SDB., *La Santa Sindone, Nuova Luce su Antichi Documenti*, Turin, 1961

FOSSATI, LUIGI, 'Copies of the Shroud', three part article in *Shroud Spectrum International*, nos. 12 and 13, September & December 1984

FRANCIA, ENIO, *1506–1606, Storia della Construzza del Nuovo San Pietro*, Rome De Luca Editore, 1977

FRUGONI, ARSENIO, 'Il Giubeleo di Bonifacio VIII', *Bulletino dell'Istituto storico italiano*, LXXII, 1950, pp. 1–121.

GIRALDUS CAMBRENSIS, Autobiography of Giraldus Cambrensis, ed. H. E. Butler, London, Cape, 1937

GOULD. KAREN, *The Psalter & Hours of Yolande de Soissons*, Cambridge, Mass., The Medieval Academy of America, 1978

GRABAR, ANDRÉ, 'La Sainte Face de Laon', *Seminarium Kondakovianum*, Prague, 1935

——*Les Ampoules de Terre Sainte*, Paris, 1958

——*Byzantium from the Death of Theodosius to the Rise of Islam*, London, Thames & Hudson, 1966

——'Une hymne Syriaque sur l'Architecture de la Cathédrale

d'Edesse', *L'art de la fin de l'antiquité et du moyen âge*, College de France Fondation Schlumberger pour des études Byzantines, 1968

GREEN, MAURUS, 'Veronica and her Veil: The Growth of a Christian Legend', *The Tablet*, 31 December 1966

GREGOROVIUS, FERDINAND, *The History of the City of Rome in the Middle Ages*, trans. Mrs G. W. Hamilton, 13 vols., London, George Bell, 1894–1900

GRIMALDI, JACOPO, *Opusculum de Sacrosancto Veronicae Sudario Salvatoris Nostri Iesu Christi*, Rome, 1620

GRIMALDI, G., *Descrizione della basilica di S. Pietro in Vaticano, Codice Barberini latino 2733*, Vatican City, 1972

GRISAR, HARTMANN, *Die römische Kapelle Sancta Sanctorum*, Freiburg, 1908

HALES, E. E., Revolution and the Papacy, London, Eyre & Spottiswoode, 1960

HEAPHY, THOMAS, 'An Examination into the Antiquity of the Likeness of Our Blessed Lord', *Art-Journal*, series of articles commencing 1 January 1861
——*The Likeness of Christ, being an enquiry in to the verisimilitude of the received likeness of Our Blessed Lord*, ed. Wyke Bayliss, London, David Bogue, 1880

HEISENBERG, AUGUST, (ed.), *Nikolaos Mesarites, die Palastrevolution des Johannes Komnenos, Würzburg*, Koenigl. Universitaetsdruckerei von H. Stuertz, 1907

HIND, A. M., *An Introduction to a History of Woodcut*, London, Constable, 1935

HUDLESTON, DOM ROGER (ed.), *Revelations of Divine Love shewed to a devout ankress by name Julian of Norwich*, London, Burns Oates, 2nd ed., 1952

JACKSON, JOHN P., 'The Radiocarbon Date and How the Image was Formed on the Shroud', *Shroud Spectrum International*, nos. 28/29, September/December 1988, pp. 2–12

JACOB DA VORAGINE, *The Golden Legend*, trans. ed. G. Ryan & H. Ripperberger, London, 1941

JAMES, M. R., 'The Drawings of Matthew Paris', *Walpole Society*, XIV, 1926
——*The Apocryphal New Testament*, Oxford, Clarendon Press, 1953

JENNINGS, PETER (ed.), *Face to Face with the Turin Shroud*, Oxford, Mowbray, 1978

223

JOHNSTONE, PAULINE, *Byzantine Tradition in Church Embroidery*, London, Alec Tiranti, 1967

JONES, PETER MURRAY, *Medieval Medical Miniatures*, London, The British Library in association with the Wellcome Institute for the History of Medicine, 1984

KING, D., *Opus Anglicanum: English Medieval Embroidery*, Great Britain, Arts Council: London, Victoria & Albert Museum, 1963

KITTS, EUSTACE J., *Pope John XXIII and Master John Hus of Bohemia*, London, Constable, 1910

KUNSTHISTORISCHES MUSEUM, VIENNA (catalogue), *Flämische Malerei von Jan van Eyck bis Pieter Bruegel D. Ä., Kunsthistorisches Museum, Vienna*, 1981

LANCIANI, RODOLFO, *Pagan and Christian Rome*, London, Macmillan, 1892

LA FAVIA, LOUIS M., *The Man of Sorrows, Its Origin and Development in Trecento Painting*, Rome, Edizioni 'Sanguis' 1980

LEES-MILNE, JAMES, *Saint Peter's, The Story of Saint Peter's Basilica in Rome*, London, Hamish Hamilton, 1967

LEITHE-JASPER, MANFRED & DISTELBERGER, RUDOLF, *Kunsthistorisches Museum Wien I. Schatzkammer und Sammlung für Plastik und Kunstgewerbe*, München-London, 1982

LÉONARD, EMILE J., *Histoire de Jeanne Ire, reine de Naples, contesse de Provence, 1348–82*, Monaco, 1932

LEPICIER, ALEXIS, *Indulgences, their origin, nature & development*, London, Burns, Oates, 1928

LEWIS, SUZANNE, *The Art of Matthew Paris and the Chronica Majora*, Scolar/Corpus Christi College, Cambridge, 1987

LIBBY, WILLARD F., *Radiocarbon Dating*, Chicago, Chicago University Press, 1952

MACADAM, ALTA, *Blue Guide to Rome and Environs*, London & New York, Black & Norton, 1985

McCRONE. WALTER C., 'Light Microscopical Study of the Turin "shroud" ', I & II, *The Microscope*, vol. 28, no. 3/4. 1980; III, vol. 29, no. 1, 1981

MÂLE, EMILE, *Religious Art in France*, trans. from the French, Princeton, Princeton University Press, 1986

MANN. HORACE K., *The Lives of the Popes in the Early Middle Ages*, London, Kegan Paul, 1935

MARROW, JAMES H., *Passion Iconography in N. European Art of the Late Middle Ages & Early Renaissance*, Brussels, 1979

MEACHAM, WILLIAM, 'On Carbon Dating and the Turin shroud', *Shroud Spectrum International*, 19, June 1986, pp. 15–25

MEEK, H. A. *Guarino Guarini and his Architecture*, New Haven & London, Yale University Press, 1988

MEISS, MILLARD, *Painting in Florence and Siena after the Black Death*, Princeton, Princeton University Press, 1951

——*French Painting in the Time of Jean de Berry*, London, Phaidon, 2 vols. 1967

——(intro.), *The Rohan Book of Hours, Bibliothèque Nationale, Paris (MS Latin 471)*, London, Thames & Hudson, 1973

MEISS, MILLARD & ELIZABETH H. BEATSON, (eds), *La Vie de Nostre Benoit Sauveur Ihesuscrist & La Saincte vie de Nostre Dame*, New York, New York University Press, 1977

MENEN, AUBREY, 'St Peter's', *National Geographic*, vol. 140, no. 6, December 1971

METROPOLITAN MUSEUM OF ART, NEW YORK, *The Vatican Collections, The Papacy and Art*, New York, Harry N. Abrams, 1983

MOLLAT, GUILLAUME, *The Popes at Avignon*, London, Nelson, 1963

MORGAN, REX, *The Holy Shroud and the Earliest Paintings of Christ*, Manly (Australia), Runciman Press, 1986

MÜNTZ, E., 'Recherches sur l'oeuvre archéologique de J. Grimaldi', *Bibliothèque des Écoles françaises d'Athènes et de Rome*, Paris, 1877

——'Une broderie inédite executée pour le Pape Jean VII', *Revue de l'art chrétien, 1900, pp. 18–21*

——*Rome au temps de Jules II et de Léon X*, Paris, 1911

MURRAY, STEPHEN, *Building Troyes Cathedral, The Late Gothic Campaigns*, Bloomington, Indiana University Press, 1987

NATIONAL GALLERY OF ART, WASHINGTON, *Fifteenth-Century Woodcuts and Metalcuts from the National Gallery of Art*, Washington DC, nd

NICHOLS, F. M. (ed) *The Marvels of Rome, or a Picture of the Golden City*, London, Ellis & Elvey, 1889

NICKELL, J., *Inquest on the Shroud of Turin*, Buffalo, New York, Prometheus Books, 1983

NORDHAGEN, P.J., 'Mosaics of John VII', *Acta Instituti Romani Norvegiae*, X, vol. 2, 1965, pp. 121–66

OAKESHOTT, WALTER, *The Mosaics of Rome*, London, Thames & Hudson, 1967

OLIGER, LIVARIO, 'B. Margherita Colonnna', *Lateranum*, new series, 1 (2), 1935

PACHT, OTTO, 'The Avignon Diptych and its Eastern Ancestry', *De Artibus Opuscula in honour of E. Panofsky*, New York, New York University 1961, pp. 402–17

PARKS, GEORGE B., *The English Traveller to Italy*, vol. I, *The Middle Ages*, Palo Alto, California 1954

PARTNER, PETER, *Renaissance Rome*, Berkeley, California, University of California, 1976

PASTOR, LUDWIG VON, *The History of the Popes from the Close of the Middle Ages*, London, Kegan Paul, 1906–53

PEARSON, K., *Die Fronika, Ein Beitrag sur Geschichte des Christusbildes im Mettelalter*, Strasburg, 1887

PERDRIZET, P., 'De la Véronique et de sainte Véronique', *Seminarium Kondakovianum*, Prague, vol. V, 1932, pp. 1–15

PERRET, M., 'Essai sur l'histoire du S.Suaire du XIVe au XVIe siècle', *Memoires de l'Académie des Sciences, Belles Lettres et Arts de Savoie*, vol. IV, 1960, pp. 49–121

PHILLIPS, G., *The Doctrine of Addai the Apostle*, London, 1876

PIAGET, ARTHUR, 'Le livre Messire Geoffroi de Charni', *Romania*, 1897, T.XXVI, pp. 394–411

POLO, MARCO, *Travels*, modern translation by Teresa Waugh, New York, Facts on File Publications, 1984

RANDALL, LILLIAN M., *Images in the Margins of Gothic manuscripts*, California, University of California Press, 1966

RIANT, COMTE DE, *Exuviae Sacrae Constantinopolitanae II*, Geneva, Société de l'Orient Latin, 1878

RICE, DAVID TALBOT, *The Art of the Byzantine Era*, London, Thames & Hudson, 1963

RICHARDS, JEFFREY, *The Popes and the Papacy in the Middle Ages*, London, Routledge, 1979

RICHARDSON, H. G., 'Gervase of Tilbury', *History*, vol. 46, 1961, pp. 102–114

ROBERTS, ALEXANDER & DONALDSON, JAMES, *The*

*Ante-Nicene Fathers*, Grand Rapids, Michigan, Wm B. Eerdmans, vol. VIII, 1951

RUNCIMAN, STEVEN, 'Some Remarks on the Image of Edessa', *Cambridge Historical Journal*, 3, 1931, pp. 238–52

RUSHFORTH, GORDON McNEIL, 'The Church of S.Maria Antiqua', *The British School at Rome*, vol. I, 1902

SANUTO, M., *Diarii,* Biblioteca Marciana, Venice, MSS Ital C1 VII

SCAVONE, DANIEL, 'The Shroud of Turin in Constantinople: The Documentary Evidence', *Daidalikon, Studies in Memory of Raymond V. Schroder SJ*, ed. Robert F. Sutton Jr, Wauconda, Illinois, Bolchazy-Carducci 1990

SCHAEFFER, CLAUDE (int.), *The Hours of Etienne Chevalier, Jean Fouquet, Musée Condé, Chantilly*, London, Thames & Hudson, 1972

SCHILLER, GERTRUD, *Iconography of Christian Art*, vol, 2 trans. Janet Seligman, London, Lund Humphries, 1972

SCHRADE, H., 'Beiträge zur Erklärung des Schmerzensmannbildes', in *Deutschkundliches, Friedrich Panzer zum 60. Geburstag, Beiträge zur neueren Literaturgeschichte*, Heidelburg, 1930, p. 164ff

SEGAL, J. B., *Edessa 'The Blessed City'*, Oxford, Clarendon Press, 1970

SMART, ALISTAIR, *The Dawn of Italian Painting, 1250–1400*, London, Phaidon, 1978

SMITH, JOHN HOLLAND, *The Great Schism*, London, Hamish Hamilton, 1970

SNOW-SMITH, JOANNE, *The Salvator Mundi of Leonardo da Vinci*, Seattle, Henry Art Gallery, University of Washington, 1982

SOX, DAVID, *The Shroud Unmasked*, Basingstoke, Lamp Press, 1988

SPENCER, B., 'Medieval pilgrim badges', *Rotterdam Papers: a Contribution to Medieval Archaeology*, ed. I. G. N. Renaud, 1968, pp. 137–53

STRAITON, MICHAEL, 'The Man of the Shroud; a thirteenth-century crucifixion action-replay', *Catholic Medical Quarterly*, XL no. 3, 243, August 1989, pp. 135–43

STYLIANOU, ANDREAS & JUDITH A., *The Painted Churches of Cyprus, Treasures of Byzantine Art*, London, Trigraph, for the A. G. Leventis Foundation, 1985

TESSORE, GIORGIO, 'Cognoscere la Sindone – La Figura di Cristo e la Sindone nell'Iconografia', *Collegamento Pro Sindone*, Rome, March/April 1988, pp.26–36

THOMAS, GORDON & MORGAN-WITTS, MAX, *Pontiff*, New York, Doubleday, 1983

THOMPSON, HENRY YATES (pref. with intro. by S. C. Cockerell), *The Book of Hours of Yolande de Flanders*, London, Chiswick Press, 1905

THURSTON, HERBERT, *The Holy Year of Jubilee, an Account of the History and Ceremonial of the Roman Jubilee*, London, Sands & Co. 1900

——'The Holy Shroud and the Verdict of History', *The Month*, CI, 1903, pp, 17–29

TOESCA, ILARIA, 'La cornice dell'imagine Edessena di S.Silvestro in Capite a Rome', *Paragone*, 1968, pp. 33–37

TORRIGIO, F. M., *Le Sacre Grotte*, 2nd. ed., Rome, 1639

TUCHMAN, BARBARA, *A Distant Mirror, the Calamitous Fourteenth-Century*, New York, Knopf, 1978

VAN DIJK, S. J. P. & HAZELDEN WALKER, J., *The Origins of the Modern Roman Liturgy*, Maryland and London, Westminster, 1960

VASARI, GIORGIO, *The Lives of the Artists*, Harmondsworth, Penguin, 1965

VIGNON, PAUL, *Le Saint Suaire de Turin devant la science, l'archéologie, l'histoire, l'iconographie, la logique*, Paris, Masson, 1939

WALLIS BUDGE, Sir E. A., *The Monks of Kublai Khan, Emperor of China, or The History of the Life and Travels of Rabban Sawma, envoy and plenipotentiary of the Mongol Khans to the kings of Europe and Markos who as Mar Yahbh-allaha III became Patriarch of the Nestorian church in Asia*, London, The Religious Tract Society, 1928

WALSH, JOHN, *The Shroud*, London, W. H. Allen, 1964

WEITZMANN, KURT, 'The Mandylion and Constantine Porphyrogennetos', *Cahiers archéologiques*, XI 1960, pp. 164–84

——'The Origin of the Threnos', *De Artibus Opuscula XL, Essays in Honour of Erwin Panofsky*, ed. Millard Meiss, New York, New York University Press, 1961

WEITZMANN, KURT, *et al.*, *The Icon*, London, Bracken Books, 1982

WHANGER, ALAN & MARY, 'Polarized image overlay technique: a new image comparison method and its applications', *Applied Optics*, no. 24, March 15, 1985, pp. 766–72

WILPERT, J., *Die römischen Mosaiken und Malereien der kirchlichen Bauten vom IV bis XIII Jahrhundert*, Freiburg im Breisgua, 1916

WILSON, IAN, *The Shroud of Turin*, New York, Doubleday, 1978

——*The Mysterious Shroud*, New York, Doubleday, 1986

WITTKOWER, RUDOLF, *Gian Lorenzo Bernini, The sculptor of the Roman Baroque*, London, Phaidon, 1955

WOOD, DIANA, *Clement VI, The Pontificate and Ideas of an Avignon Pope*, Cambridge University Press, 1989

ZANINOTTO, GINO, 'Il Codice Vat.Gr.511, FF 143–150v: Una Conferma dell 'Identita' tra l'immagine Edessena e la Sindone di Torino?', *Collegamento Pro Sindone*, March/April 1988, pp. 14–25

ZUGIBE, FRED, *The Cross and the Shroud*, New York, Angelus, 1982

# PHOTOGRAPHIC CREDITS

Biblioteca Apostolica Vaticana, pls. 6–7; 22
Bibliothèque Royale, Brussels, pl. 20 (above)
Biblioteca Nazionale, Florence, pls. 23 (above right); 26–7; text figs 10; 12–16; 18–19
Bozzo, Colette Dufour, pl. 15 (above)
British Library, pls. 16 (above); 17 (below left)
British Museum, col. pl. II (right); pls. 10; 12 (below left); 13 (left); 14 (right); 15 (left); 32 (below)
British Society for the Turin Shroud, pls. 1 (above and left); 2 (right); 31d
Calouste Gulbenkian Foundation, Lisbon, pl. 17 (left)
Cliché des Musées Nationaux, Paris, pls. 3 (above); 5 (left); 9 (left)
Comerical Papisa, Alicante, col. pl. IVb
Courtauld Institute, pl. 16 (below)
Fitzwilliam Museum, Cambridge, pl. 19 (left)
Fossati, Don. L., SDB, pls. 13 (above); 14 (above); 20 (below right); 21 (above and right); 31b
Fratelli Dutto, pl. 11 (above)
Hann, George R, pl. 28 (above)
Kunsthistorisches Museum, Vienna, col. pl. VII
Lauros Giraudon, col. pl. VI (right)
Magnum, col. pl. I (above)
Manchester Museum, pl. 32 (above)
Musée du Petit Palais, Avignon, pl. 3 (left)

Museum of the Serbian Orthodox Church, Belgrade, pl. 28 (below right)
National Gallery, London, pl. 18
National Gallery of Art, Washington, Samuel H. Kress Collection, pl. 19 (above)
National Portrait Gallery, London, pl. 12 (above)
National Széchenyi Library, Budapest, pl. 29 (above)
Oxford Research Laboratory, pl. 2. (below bottom)
Pierpont Morgan Library, New York, pl. 17 (above)
Pfeiffer, Heinrich, col. pl. VIII (below); pl. 11 (left)
Rolfe, David, col. pl. V
Saint Catherine's Monastery, Sinai, pl. 30 (below right)
Scala, col. pls. VI (below); VIII (above); pl. 9 (above)
Society Don Bosco, col. pl. I (left)
Staatliche Museen, Berlin, pl. 28 (below left)
Studio Me, Ce, Rome, col. pl. III; pl. 12 (below right)
Stylianou, Judith, pl. 25 g & h
University of Arizona (Dept of Geosciences), pl. 2 (below top)
Vacchi, Dante, col. pl. IVc
Victoria & Albert Museum, London, pl. 29 (left)
Wellcome Institute for the History of Medicine, London, pl. 4. (below)


Photographs not credited are either by the author himself or from his personal collection.

# INDEX

Page numbers in **bold** indicate text figures

233

234

235

S·lorenzo fora di muri

S·Croce In Herusalem

S·MARIA MAGIORE